Integral Christianity: The Spii

"... an absolutely superb application of Integral Theory in all its dimensions to Christianity itself, resulting in a truly Integral Christianity.... highly recommended for not only individuals of any major religion, but also for agnostics and atheists looking to make sense of ultimate issues and absolute realities. The answers to many of your questions can be found here!"

—Ken Wilber, *The Integral Vision*

"A lot of us were introduced to a take-it-or-leave-it approach to Christian faith: it was a tight, stiff, one-size-fits-all system that offered little room to grow. Many of us are now discovering that there's another approach ... an expansive, adaptive approach that sees growth and development as inherent to faithfulness, for both individuals and traditions. In *Integral Christianity*, Paul Smith offers a helpful, readable, and inviting portal into this alternate approach."

—Brian McLaren, named one of *Time* magazine's "25 Most Influential Evangelicals in America," international advocate of emerging Christianity, and author of *A New Kind of Christianity*.

****

"Clarifying, honest, courageous, and genuinely helpful, making the Gospel shine with a new brilliance and beauty! All sincere believers and seekers should welcome this book."

—[Fr.] Richard Rohr, Franciscan priest, founder of the Center for Action and Contemplation and author of *Things Hidden: Scripture as Spirituality* and *Everything Belongs: The Gift of Contemplative Prayer*.

****

"... if you are like me, and appreciate well reasoned and passionate arguments on cutting edge mystical spirituality that needs consideration, you will say 'thank you' to Paul Smith, even if you don't agree with him."

—Tony Campolo, PhD, professor emeritus, Eastern University, evangelical social activist and author of *Following Jesus without Embarrassing God*.

****

"A wonderful guide for Christians seeking a personal and world-transforming spirituality."

—Jack Nelson-Pallmeyer, University of St. Thomas and author of
Jesus Against Christianity: Reclaiming the Missing Jesus.

****

"... this is the first attempt to systematically apply Wilber's integral paradigm to Christian faith and practice. It works not only because he understands Wilber very well, but because he knows Christianity like the back of his hand. It's doubly credible because he writes not from the standpoint of an academic theologian, but as a committed Christian pastor who has tested every one of these principles in actual parish ministry and demonstrated the viability of integral church. And it's triply credible because of the joy and luminosity of his being as it shines through on every page of this text. He indeed models the hope that he lays out here."

—Rev. Dr. Cynthia Bourgeault, Episcopal priest, PhD
and author of *The Wisdom Jesus.*

****

"An impressive blend of thorough scholarship and prophetic call to reformation. The integral church clearly delineated here recovers mystical spirituality often missing in modern and post-modern churches.

—Rev. Dr. Jann Aldredge-Clanton, Baptist minister
and author of *Inclusive Hymns for Liberating Christians.*

****

"A fine book on integral Christianity. It speaks directly to Christians as well as other religious persons everywhere. Highly recommended."

—Allan Combs. Professor, California Institute of Integral Studies,
neuropsychologist, systems theorist, Club of Budapest member,
author of *The Radiance of Being* and *Consciousness Explained Better.*

****

"An impassioned book that helps chart a future course of development for the Christian church, showing how the integral philosophy of evolution can illuminate our quest to find God."

—Steve McIntosh, author of *Integral Consciousness and the Future of Evolution.*

****

Integral Christianity
The Spirit's Call to Evolve

Integral Christianity
The Spirit's Call to Evolve

Paul R. Smith

PARAGON HOUSE
St. Paul, Minnesota

Published in the United States by
Paragon House

www.ParagonHouse.com

First Edition 2011
First Paperback Edition 2012

Library of Congress Cataloging-in-Publication Data

Smith, Paul R., 1937-
   Integral Christianity : the Spirit's call to evolve / by Paul R. Smith.
      p. cm.
   Includes bibliographical references (p.   ) and index.
   ISBN 978-1-55778-800-9 (pbk. : alk. paper) 1. Christianity. 2. Church.
I. Title.
   BR124.S55 2010
   230.01--dc22
                              2010033234

The paper used in this publication meets the minimum requirements of American National Standard for Information Sciences—Permanence of Paper for Printed Library Materials, ANSI standard Z39.48-1992.

Manufactured in the United States of America
10 9 8 7 6 5 4 3 2

For current information about all releases from Paragon House, visit
the website at http://www.paragonhouse.com

Chambered Nautilus Cover Image

The cover image displays the growing chambered nautilus's successive and ever-expanding dwelling places. It recalls Oliver Wendell Holmes's beautiful poem "The Chambered Nautilus." The theme of this book is exquisitely rendered in the magnificent call of the last stanza's "Build thee more stately mansions, O my soul." Here are the last three stanzas:

> Year after year beheld the silent toil
> That spread his lustrous coil;
> Still, as the spiral grew,
> He left the past year's dwelling for the new,
> Stole with soft step its shining archway through,
> Built up its idle door,
> Stretched in his last-found home, and knew the old no more.
>
> Thanks for the heavenly message brought by thee,
> Child of the wandering sea,
> Cast from her lap, forlorn!
> From thy dead lips a clearer note is born
> Than ever Triton blew from wreathed horn;
> While on mine ear it rings,
> Through the deep caves of thought I hear a voice that sings:—
>
> Build thee more stately mansions, O my soul,
> As the swift seasons roll!
> Leave thy low-vaulted past!
> Let each new temple, nobler than the last,
> Shut thee from heaven with a dome more vast,
> Till thou at length art free,
> Leaving thine outgrown shell by life's unresting sea!
>
> —Oliver Wendell Holmes (1809-1894)

Credits and Permissions

Dedication

This book is dedicated to two of the congregations of Broadway Church in Kansas City, Missouri. First, to the first congregation of 18 Swedish immigrants who founded Broadway Church in 1872 as the First Swedish Baptist Church of Kansas City. They didn't seem to fit in the other established churches because the Swedes were different. So they began a new church where they could feel at home and welcome others.

Second, to the current congregation of both long-timers and new folks. The stay-with-it loyalists have been at Broadway between 35 and 75 years. They are Kurt and Carolyn Anderson, Donna Blackwell, Christy Bowen, Ken and Marilyn Bowen, Ken and Marcia Fleischman, Evelyn Golston, Sheryl Stewart, David Hunker, Jim and Betty McKeown, Lida Moffett, and Charles and Carol Ramirez. They have stayed through all the changes during my 48 years of pastoring at Broadway, continuing to love and support the church. The new folks bring us joy and freshness as only they can. All, like the original founders in 1872, want a church to welcome those who don't seem to fit in other churches.

Contents

Part I

Stages

PART II
STATES

PART III
STANDPOINTS

PART IV
SHADOW

PART V
STEPS

Foreword by Jim Marion

Integral Christianity: The Spirit's Call to Evolve is an important book and a profound one, but it is also a work written with great modesty and simplicity. Rev. Smith begins by testifying, "I love God. I love Jesus. I love the church. This book is about my three loves." Indeed, the book is primarily a gift of love, the abundant fruit of the author's 50 years of dedicated Christian pastoral service to the people of God.

Integral Christianity, however, is not merely a book of Christian inspiration. Though simply written, it is a work of serious scholarship, and though written in everyday language, it is a work in which the revelation of the Holy Spirit shines through for our times.

As we all know, the Christian church, the primary spiritual engine of western civilization for 2,000 years, is now in deep crisis. It is in precipitous decline in Europe and shows the beginnings of a similar decline in America. More and more Christians can no longer believe in the literal truth of many Christian myths or mysteries such as the virgin birth of Jesus or his bodily resurrection from the dead. More and more Christians can no longer worship a God who lives apart from us in the sky and who required the gruesome sacrifice of his son as appeasement for human sinfulness. More and more Christians find themselves rejecting traditional Christian ethics with respect to sex-related and other issues. And, in light of current cosmology, more and more Christians can no longer understand Jesus as a god who descended from the sky and, after appeasing his Father for our sins, ascended again, bodily, into the sky. The Christian mysteries and many traditional Christian values, which we inherited from earlier centuries and worldviews long gone, are no longer believable to millions of Christians.

Rev. Smith deals with these issues with great skill and wisdom, not by offering the type of clever theological arguments that we often get from academic theologians, nor by dogmatically insisting, as many church leaders do, that we dare not depart from the understandings of the past no matter how culturally conditioned and outdated such old understandings may be. Instead, Rev. Smith approaches these issues using the teachings of Jesus himself. He explains, in depth, the teachings of Jesus, their deep spiritual meanings, and their relevance for us today.

It is a peculiar fact of history that the teachings of Jesus, as in this book, are receiving more attention now than they have ever received in the history of the church. St. Paul, the earliest writer of the New Testament, scarcely ever refers to the life of Jesus and never cites anything Jesus ever said or taught. The Christian Creed, a product of the fourth century church, says nothing whatsoever about the teachings of Jesus. Historically, Christianity has been a religion about Jesus rather than about what Jesus actually taught. Some of Jesus' major teachings, such as The Gospel of Thomas, perhaps the earliest Gospel, were even lost altogether until very recent years. Rev. Smith remedies these defects in a profoundly informative way and shows that what Jesus taught has great relevance for Christianity's chances to survive and flourish in the twenty-first century.

Integral Christianity, however, does more than explain the deep mystical teachings of Jesus. It is a work that explores the inner Christian spiritual path in both a developmental and thoroughly comprehensive (or integral) way. Drawing upon the work of American Ken Wilber, who is probably the greatest living philosopher-theologian-mystic, and whose books embrace the best of contemporary psychology, philosophy, theology, and science, *Integral Christianity* sets forth the developmental framework by which Christians grow inwardly in their understanding of Jesus and his teachings. It does this in a more complete and integral way than any other Christian book so far written. In doing so, it builds upon my own efforts in *Putting on the Mind of Christ* and *Death of the Mythic God* in many important and insightful ways.

Integral Christianity: The Spirit's Call to Evolve sets forth the evolutionary stages of human spiritual development. It also explains the three states of human spiritual development as well as the three standpoints through which humans experience the reality of God. It addresses whether all humans participate in divinity as Jesus did. It examines the importance for our spiritual growth of integrating our inner dark sides (our "shadows") and sets forth the specific steps

we each need to take to live a fulfilled Christian life. It addresses all
these topics not only from the standpoint of the individual Christian
but also from the collective standpoint of Christian church communities of all types.

It is not possible in this short foreword to explore all of the wonderful and exciting insights contained in *Integral Christianity*. Rev.
Smith demonstrates a profound understanding of the Scriptures and
of how Jesus' teachings can revitalize both our own spiritual lives and
those of the churches. I urge every reader to drink deeply of the wisdom contained in this magnificent book, the product of a lifetime of
love, service, and prayer in imitation of Jesus, the light of the world.

(Jim Marion is a contemporary Christian mystic and author of *Putting on the
Mind of Christ* and *The Death of the Mythic God*.)

Introduction

I love God. I love Jesus. I love the church. This is a book about my three loves.

God is the meaning of life and the great Lover of my soul and of all souls. God is all about life and life is all about God.

I am a follower of Jesus Christ. Jesus is my prototype of the fullest relationship to God possible in this life. He fully realized and manifested his oneness with God and calls us to do the same.

The church is people just like you and me. We are the clumsy, brilliant, messy, loving, ego-centered, glorious, awful, liberating, oppressive, interesting, boring, caring, and nervous people who go to church. That makes the church like Noah's Ark. The only reason you can stand the mess inside is that it's better than drowning on the outside. The next time you are in church, look around. Everyone there has just finished facing a struggle, is in the middle of one, or is just about to meet one! In all of our glory and dribbling fear, the church still manages to give us traveling companions in the great adventure of exploring the spiritual landscape. God love us.

A lover's quarrel with the church

However, I have had a life-long lover's quarrel with the church. This has motivated me, for over 50 years, to seek a "new and improved" church. I had my first try at it as an 18-year-old youth leader in an inner-city church in the early 1950s. I had inherited the job of running a small, four-day, once-a-year, Christian camp experience for inner-city kids. It had been a very "religious" camp with morning calisthenics, Bible studies, many boring talks, and even more boring rules. When I became the camp director, I decided that it was time to have a "new and improved" camp. In place of all the "religious" activities, we began the day with the campers going off by themselves around the beautiful valley with music playing out over the hills and just being quiet for 20 minutes. We called it "Lonesome Time." We had small groups in the afternoon that we called "Prayer Labs." We focused on sharing what was happening in our lives and praying for each other, one at a time, then and there, in creative ways. We did a campfire in the evening, mostly with quiet singing and simply sitting, staring at the fire. The rest of the time we played and had fun. I was amazed to find it was so much more powerful than the year before when we were more "religious." Within five years it had become the city-wide youth camp, with a series of two week-long camps for high schoolers and three different weekend camps for college-age youth. Thousands of young people were radically changed by that experience and we often kept up with each other during the year at "afterglow" meetings.

That entire "new and improved" camp experience shaped my thinking about what transformed lives and what didn't. I saw that it was possible to make a difference in a religious organization if we made changes that deepened our connection to God and to one another. I have taken the same approach in my first and only pastorate for these last 48 years.

A new lens

We all wear glasses, even if they are invisible, and even if we've never been to an optometrist. Our glasses are our worldview. Wise people know about their glasses and when it's time to get a new prescription. Our worldview glasses let us see what our worldview will allow. They also make it difficult to see what our worldview will not allow.

The lens through which I now look at Christianity had not taken shape and did not have a name 50 years ago. However, I was heading toward it all the time. I was the one in my Southern Baptist seminary 50 years ago who made a case for the availability today of the direct experiences of God that saturated the life of Jesus and the early church. That was a hard sell with my professors and classmates, who seemed to allow for conversion experiences only.

Some years ago, I found a name for what I was attempting to do in the Christian path—integral philosophy. With that name came, for me, the dense, difficult, and daring writings of Ken Wilber. He is the most widely translated academic writer in America. He is also the most famous contemporary philosopher and mystic you have never heard of. He focused the lens for me even more and I came into greater clarity in fascinating new ways.

What if there is a Christian path that more closely follows Jesus than many of us have seen in the past? What if it is actually possible to hear the continuing voice of the Spirit as Jesus promised?[1]

This book is about a newer, clearer lens from the Spirit through which we can see Jesus. It is, in one sense, looking through the lens of Jesus at integral philosophy, and then looking back through the lens of the integral viewpoint at Jesus.

I speak of both Christianity and the church together, for I do not believe one exists without the other. The Christian life is always communal and corporate, and ultimately cosmic. We were never intended to make this journey alone. The further we evolve, the more inclusive our vision. At the highest stage it includes everyone and everything—the Cosmic Christ. So while the title is "Integral Christianity," the subject is both Christianity and churches.

This book does not present anything particularly new about integral philosophy. I hope that those already knowledgeable about integral theory and practice might read this book and see Jesus, Christianity, and the church in a radically different way. I love being "evangelical;" that is, sharing the good news I find in Jesus Christ with others. Primarily, in this book, I am witnessing a new model of Christianity and the church.

Integral?

I use the terms "integral Christianity" and "integral church" in this book, but I am not entirely satisfied with them. According to Wilber,

> The word "integral" means comprehensive, inclusive, non-marginalizing, embracing. Integral approaches to any field attempt to be exactly that—to include as many perspectives, styles, and methodologies as possible within a coherent view of the topic. In a certain sense, integral approaches are "meta-paradigms," or ways to draw together an already existing number of separate paradigms into a network of inter-related, mutually enriching perspectives.[2]

The kind of Christianity and church I am describing may emerge using other labels that are not visible at this time. It could be called post-postmodern, transcendent, mystical, or other names by which the integral stage and beyond is sometimes named.

However, "integral" is currently the label used most widely by those who study and think about these things in the larger world of philosophy.

Beyond integral

There are also various names for what appears to be beyond integral such as transrational, self-transcendence, illumined mind, transpersonal, nondual, and unity. For that, I simply call it "integral and beyond," or "postintegral."

Much of what I deal with under the label "mystical" is technically the postintegral stage. The term "mystical" has a tradition and some sense of common recognition. Mystics are people who experience God. I want to see and experience God as Jesus did. That's the soul of this book.

CHAPTER 1

A Spiritual Positioning System
Where we have been, where we are going, and how to get there

Our ancestors had to go to extreme measures to navigate around their world. They learned to read the stars. They drew notoriously incorrect maps and kept track of landmarks to help them find their way to new lands or to just get back home. Things are much easier today. For less than $100 you can get a pocket-sized gadget that will tell you exactly where you are on Earth at any moment and how to get to where you want to go. As long as you have a Global Positioning System (GPS) receiver and a clear view of the sky, you'll never be lost again. The GPS is actually a constellation of 27 Earth-orbiting satellites (24 in operation and three extras in case one fails). A GPS receiver's job is to locate four or more of these satellites, figure out the distance to each, and use this information to deduce its own location. It can also show you how to get where you want to go.

A Life Positioning System

As amazing as the Global Positioning System is, what is even more helpful in navigating life is a Life Positioning System. Like the GPS with its 27 satellites, now for the first time in human history we have available a comprehensive positioning system for life, including the spiritual dimension. In the last 30 years global knowledge and the wisdom of the major civilizations of the world from the ancient past to modern times have been accessible to us for study and reflection. These many studies of cultures from all over the world have revealed common developmental patterns. Integral philosophy has taken everything we know about human potential from around the world and put it into a comprehensive global map about spiritual, psychological, and social growth. This is the most advanced Life Positioning System available today. It can show you where you have been, where you are, where you might want to go, and how to get there!

Integral philosopher Ken Wilber, in over 25 books, has created the first composite understanding that includes the best elements from all of these studies. It incorporates the greatest number of orienting generalizations from the greatest number of fields in human inquiry. This has resulted in a kind of map that can help us understand consciousness in far-reaching and ever-expanding ways. Wilber leaves us to fill in the details in any particular area we are investigating, even as integral philosophy itself goes beyond any one aspect of life and can help us navigate through a number of spheres of life.

Most pointedly for this book about Christianity and churches, Wilber is also making a new place for authentic spirituality in the modern world today. He can do this because he is a spiritual intellectual, making spiritual growth a centerpiece in his developmental map. Although an American who practices Buddhism, his thinking understands, includes, and affirms Christianity as well as the other great religious traditions of the world.

Integral for dummies

Wilber's vast reading and general grasp of so many streams of thought make his map of consciousness amazingly encompassing. This also results in the widespread report that reading Wilber can be a challenge for lots of people, including me. I have studied and lived with each of his books and books about his books, and I have listened to him and others many times in the last ten years. Each time I read or listen, I get a little more of the picture. I am still not an integral scholar and, in fact, I consider myself something of an integral dummy. However, in order for this book about integral church to make sense, I want to present the particular aspects of integral theory that have been most helpful in my life, church, and spiritual practice. Perhaps being an integral dummy will help me keep it simple while hoping to be reasonably faithful to the contemporary currents of integralism.

If you want more depth (and complexity) about an integral worldview, I recommend *The Integral Vision*, which is a good brief introduction, and *Integral Spirituality*, both by Ken Wilber. The Integral Institute website (http://integralinstitute.org) is a vast source of information. Wilber's massive and dense *Sex, Ecology, Spirituality* is extraordinary. For the first and foremost articulation of an integral approach in a Christian framework, I recommend Jim Marion's *Putting on the Mind of Christ* and *The Death of the Mythic God*. Steve McIntosh's book, *Integral Consciousness*, is an excellent overall presentation and refinement of the integral perspective.

In this book I have taken the generalizations of integral philosophy as articulated primarily by Ken Wilber and reflected on the details of how this might look for churches in the Christian tradition today. I want to show where various kinds of churches may be found on the map today, where some might want to explore, and how to get there. I will focus on what I call the Spiritual Positioning System that I have found in integral philosophy.

Five satellites in the Spiritual Positioning System

Five basic elements of integralism have given me a most amazing lens through which to understand and practice my Christian tradition. Each one of these five elements functions like the individual satellites of the Global Positioning System. By using several of them you can accurately locate yourself spiritually. These five elements can also show us how to get to where we want to go. I believe thoughtful Christians everywhere would benefit from understanding and using this spiritual map.

The five basic components of this Spiritual Positioning System (SPS) I have found to be most illuminating are stages, states, standpoints, shadow, and steps: (1) *stages* of spiritual development; (2) deeper *states* of spiritual awareness and experience; (3) the three basic *standpoints* or perspectives in relating to God; (4) *shadow* work and other psychological healing; and (5) *steps* to transformation using various practices.

The awareness of an individual or church *stage* provides a general location on the spiritual map in terms of latitude, up and down, north and south. The access to ever-widening *states* provides a location in terms of longitude, east and west. The ability to integrate the three basic *standpoints* in relation to God, to gain psychological *shadow* healing, and to engage in transformative *steps* or practices provides a more detailed location. Put all five of these elements together and you have not only the most sophisticated way available today to find your location on the spiritual map, but also a way to get to where you want to go.

Stages of spiritual development

Why are there so many different kinds of churches? The answer is because there are so many different kinds of people who are at different places in life. Different kinds of people at different stages gravitate to and create different kinds of churches. There is a church for just about every stage of consciousness.

It is striking to me that, in the first three chapters the book of Revelation, the Spirit said something different to each of seven churches. This is a recognition that not all churches are alike, and the creative impulse of the Spirit comes to us where we are, not where we should be. Could it be that the Spirit recognizes churches deal with uniquely diverse situations and therefore distinctively different challenges? However, it is more than just varied situations.

The most profound reason churches and their versions of Christianity are at different places is that spirituality—our under-standing and experience of God—develops in a series of unfolding levels. This is, to some, a new approach about our lives and churches. Looking at life in an evolutionary way opens up tremendous possi-bilities. Conventional Christianity has room for growth but is often preoccupied with position rather than progress. It often only seems to ask, "Are we Christians or are we not?" However, the integral approach focuses on developing our lives in the ever more loving ways that universally appear as identifiable stages. The idea of development or evolution of spiritual understanding and experience is quite different from the traditional idea of "the faith once delivered to the saints." It recognizes that the Spirit continues to move us along as Jesus predicted.[1]

A "stage" of development may also be called an altitude, a level, mode of consciousness, worldview, perspective, lens, viewpoint, or place on the unfolding spiral of life. It may be called a "wave" in order to get away from any rigidity in the metaphor. Another term for "stage" is a "station" in life. This suggests that we all develop in our own ways as we come to a new station in life and stay there for a while. We may even spend much of our adult life at one particular station. Every person has a right to be at any stage, because all stations in life are expressions of the Spirit's work in taking us along one step at a time.

What is "spiritual"?

The word "spiritual" in "spiritual development" can mean several things, and I usually mean all of the following dimensions:

(1) Peak religious experiences or nonordinary states of consciousness: "I had an incredible experience while I was praying this week."

(2) A very high level of development in such areas as values, abilities, intellectual understanding, emotions, and self-transcendence: "As a musician I felt as if in that concert the music was playing me. I was just the channel for it. It was a real spiritual high."

(3) Advanced development in the specific area of spirituality: "She is a so spiritual and meditates so much that I would call her a Christian mystic."

(4) An attitude such as compassion, trust, humility in serving, or inner peace: "They are such a spiritual family; you always feel welcomed and loved."

Some stages are obvious

We can all look back at our lives and see how we have grown and developed over the years. We started life as an infant, with its total dependence on others. Then came the stage of childhood with its exciting discoveries and explorations. We all remember what becoming a teenager felt like—what a trip! Developmental psychologists have found that as adults we can continue to move through unfolding stages. They have extensively studied these stations in life that we may encounter. These levels apply not only to individuals in all cultures but also to the cultures themselves. Our ancient Stone Age ancestors were at one station of development and we are at another. A tribal culture in New Guinea even today will be at one level of awareness and the modern, industrialized society at another. There have been many descriptions and numberings of these different altitudes, from three levels to a dozen or more.

A simple three-part stage is egocentric to ethnocentric to worldcentric—from "me" to "us" to "all of us." Every individual begins as a completely egocentric infant. As we develop, we become aware of others who are close to us, and we begin to think in terms of family. This ethnocentric stage broadens to include others who share some things in common with us such as nation, race, school, church denomination, or political group. If one continues to grow, one begins to think beyond the smaller groupings and see the larger global village, all of humankind, and the earth as an ecosystem—all worldcentric viewpoints. The world's problem is not global warming, terrorism, hunger, or disease. The world's problem is that we don't have enough people at the worldcentric level to solve our worldcentric problems.

Abraham Maslow outlined a well-known, five-stage, natural, unfolding hierarchy of development with needs ranging from physical, safety, and belonging, to the higher needs for self-esteem and self-actualization.

I will be using the six stages or stations in life outlined by Steve McIntosh in his book *Integral Consciousness*. They are tribal, warrior, traditional, modern, postmodern, and integral.[2] I also label them fantasy, fighting, fitting in, flourishing, fulfilling, and frontier. It may be obvious by now that I can only remember lists if they all start with the same letter.

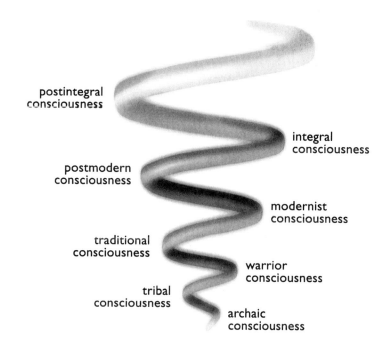

postintegral
consciousness

integral
consciousness

postmodern
consciousness

modernist
consciousness

traditional
consciousness

warrior
consciousness

tribal
consciousness

archaic
consciousness

The Spiral of Development in consciousness and culture
© 2009 Steve McIntosh, used by permission.

The purpose of church

In my understanding, the goal of integral church is to create a community where the members can accelerate their growth in (1) *stages* of understanding God, (2) *states* of consciousness in experiencing God, (3) *standpoints* in relating to God as Jesus did, (4) *shadow* work and other forms of inner healing, and (5) *steps* of practicing that lead to transformation.

It seems apparent that there is a natural progression in spiritual values and practices. For instance, we could identify the previously mentioned simple three-stage development pattern from egocentric to ethnocentric to worldcentric. Most would agree that to move from me to us, to all of us is progress in the sense of moving to more love and understanding for more people. Ego-centered persons are concerned only about themselves. When they become ethnocentric, extending their care to family or a larger group, they are able to be concerned not just about themselves but also about how others in their family or group think and feel. The worldcentric person has moved from just considering their group, family, church, religion, or nation, to also thinking in some sense about the whole world.

Moving from "some people" to "all people" is a movement toward Jesus' model of compassion. Sociologists who study these things in many cultures have not only seen this general development in spiritual and moral values, but have identified even more levels of development, 10 or 15 sometimes. I have taken a more modest approach and, following Steve McIntosh's categories, focused on six major levels of faith on the spiral of life that seem identifiable and important—tribal, warrior, traditional, modern, postmodern, and integral (post-postmodern) and beyond.

All six of these different layers of development are represented in churches today. Most churches tend to have one stage of consciousness as a dominant center with some members at preceding levels and others at following ones. Churches and belief systems are complicated and do not lend themselves to just a few words of description. However, by using some oversimplified general descriptions we can begin to think in terms of our GPS idea in the spiritual realm. This can provide a helpful framework to see where we personally are now, where we have been, and where we may choose to go in the future. Our SPS can also help us understand, respect, and appreciate all kinds of churches and how they are similar and different.

No judging allowed

Thinking people often have a resistance to anything that appears to resemble rankings. We rightly do not want to judge others. Nor do we like to say that one person or church is superior or inferior to another. This is particularly true of those at the postmodern stage. However, we are not ranking people or churches here. We are discerning the differences in worldviews or ways of approaching the spiritual life. Jesus asked us to have this kind of awareness when he said, "by their fruits you shall know them."[3] It is important not only to know "them" but to know ourselves. Jesus taught us that the way to "know," or have discerning awareness, is to look at what is produced from a particular point of view. We are not called to be people inspectors. But we are called to be produce inspectors.

Dustin DiPerna says it well:

> It is not our intention for the stages of religious orientation to be used to pigeonhole an individual to a particular altitude. Nor should lower altitudes be looked down upon, in any sort of condescending fashion. As Wilber emphasizes, it is the right of every individual to stop at any level of development he chooses. Outlining each rung on the ladder can help individuals become as healthy as possible at whatever stage they might currently rest. It is not our job to point out where other individuals fall short. Perhaps, if presented with an outline like the one above, individuals, on their own accord, will work at consciously developing through the stages. Most importantly, these distinctions are made in order to provide space and clarity so that a clearer picture of our world can be perceived. All levels serve as crucial elements to the health of the whole system. Infections forced upon lower levels only hurt the higher stages that use them as a foundation. A proper sketch of religious orientation allows us to make clear and accurate assessments of people and situations. Understanding that the stepping stones in each tradition are, at least in part, constructed by human psychological development, provides a platform on which we can all build and relate. If we hope to have a more compassionate and inclusive world, then these stages of religious orientation must be made known to all of the world's religious traditions.[4]

What about "beliefs"?

Theology is loving God with our minds. Therefore, beliefs are important at every level of faith. The tendency of those who are "spiritual but not religious" is to claim they are tossing out all religious dogmas, doctrines, and definitions. I understand the antagonism directed at oppressive and rigid belief systems because I have had my share of that resentment. We may not even be able to become more compassionate without first becoming more angry—angry enough to reject parts of previous belief systems that no longer appear truthful or loving to us.

However, moving to more expansive and compassionate beliefs is quite different than rejecting all "beliefs." We cannot get away from belief systems. The idea that "all religious beliefs are bad" is in itself a belief. The transformation that comes from following Jesus means, among other things, changing your beliefs. "Be transformed by the renewing of your minds."[5] It is a change in what one believes, not a rejection of believing. Let's be honest—some beliefs are less Christ-like and some are more Christ-like. Good beliefs give us open space for great spiritual experiences to propel us into higher stages of awareness.

I will oversimplify

What follows are pointed generalizations, even caricatures, of various belief systems. I offer them because I don't know of any other way to communicate a brief picture of various sets of beliefs. Our belief systems are much more nuanced than I describe here. We Christians who hold these beliefs are also much more complicated than our beliefs. I admit that I am oversimplifying beliefs, but hopefully I am not stereotyping people.

Jesus was a master of the pointed generalization with his pithy sayings. He said, "It's harder for a rich person to get into the Kingdom of Heaven than for a camel to go through the eye of a needle."[6] I know rich people who inhabit the Kingdom more fully than I do, so we could argue that Jesus should have given us a more nuanced statement rather than stereotyping all rich people. But, on the other hand, most of us know exactly what he was talking about. He could have given us a long, in-depth, expansive treatise on riches, but he chose not to for the sake of making his point. He used an oversimplified generalization to zap us into a new way of seeing things. A good point is always a sharp "point" so that it gets through our thick skins. I hope you will take the following descriptions in this light.

In order to be relevant, I have named churches and denominations you may value, identified beliefs and theologians you may treasure, and pointed at religious practices you may observe because they are meaningful to you. When we come to wherever you may find yourself in the spiritual line of development, you may have much to criticize in my description of that place. Most of us do not like photographs of ourselves because they never seem to resemble how we see ourselves. I will not do you justice either. So take what fits and discard the rest in any picture I attempt to paint of you.

Six stages in eight common areas of belief

I believe this is the most advanced Spiritual Positioning System available today. In addition to identifying where we are, it can help us understand and respect where others are so that the world can be a more compassionate and wiser place.

In the following chapters I will describe the six levels of church by using eight common areas of belief among Christians: (1) the Bible, (2) God, (3) Jesus, (4) prayer, (5) sin and salvation, (6) heaven and hell, (7) the Kingdom of Heaven,[7] and (8) the mystical. I will also discuss the strengths and limitations of each level.

PART I

STAGES

Stages are the broad levels of development we see in history and in every human life. We have learned to identify such historical periods as the Stone Age, the Enlightenment, and the Industrial Revolution in terms of human cultural development. Personally, we regularly speak of stages that we call infancy, childhood, adolescence, young adulthood, middle age, senior living, and old age. These are developmental classifications that center on age. Researchers have identified various stages of cultural and personal evolution in our lives. In this section I will be using six broad categories that seem identifiable and important both historically and in an individual's personal life development. They might be called levels of faith in the context of this book about the Christian spiritual path. They are tribal, warrior, traditional, modern, postmodern, and integral. They are each Spirit's call to "Build thee more stately mansions, O my soul."

CHAPTER 2

Tribal Church
Fantasy and Family

Little Carol came into the kitchen where her mother was making dinner. Her birthday was coming up and she thought this was a good time to tell her mother what she wanted. "Mom, I want a bike for my birthday." Now, little Carol had been getting into trouble at school and at home. Carol's mother asked her if she thought she deserved to get a bike for her birthday. Little Carol, of course, thought she did. Carol's mother, being a Christian woman, wanted her to reflect on her behavior over the last year. So she asked Carol to write a letter to God and say why she deserved a bike for her birthday. Little Carol stomped up the steps to her room and sat down to write God a letter. LETTER #1 went: "Dear God: I have been a very good girl this year, and I would like a bike for my birthday. I want a red one. Your friend, Carol."

Carol knew this wasn't true. She had not been a very good girl this year, so she tore up the letter and started over with LETTER #2: "Dear God: This is your friend Carol. I have been a pretty good girl this year, and I would like a red bike for my birthday. Thank you, Carol."

Carol knew this wasn't true either. She tore up the letter and started again with a little more bargaining in LETTER #3: "Dear God: I know I haven't been a good girl this year. I am very sorry. I will be a good girl if you just send me a red bike for my birthday. Thank you, Carol."

Carol knew, even if it was true, this letter was not going to get her a bike. By now, she was very upset. She went downstairs and told her mother she wanted to go to church. Carol's mother thought her plan had worked because Carol looked very sad. "Just be home in time for dinner," her mother said. Carol walked down the street to the church and up to the altar. She looked around to see if anyone was there. She picked up the small statue of the Virgin Mary, slipped it under her jacket, and ran out of the church, down the street, into her house, and up to her room. She shut the door and sat down and wrote LETTER #4 to God:

> I GOT YOUR MAMA. IF YOU WANT TO SEE HER AGAIN, SEND THE BIKE.
>
> Signed, YOU KNOW WHO

Bargaining with God represents a tribal stage consciousness that is still with us today and not just with kids. Little Carol's mother was also teaching Carol how to bargain with a tribal God who grants favors to the good kids and withholds favors from the bad kids, even punishing them.

Tribal Consciousness

The tribal era began some 50,000 years ago, and all of us have come from the tribal cultures of our past. Fear-based fantasy was a major factor in these early tribes. The world was filled with gods, demons, ghosts, and other beings that might be vengeful and attack you. Tribal members needed to bargain with and cajole these beings in order to protect themselves and get what they wanted.

Today's superstitions are holdovers from tribal thinking, little pieces of fear-based fantasy. Folklorists say that the most widespread superstition in our culture today is the idea of misfortune occurring on Friday the 13th. Avoiding walking under a ladder can be common sense or it can carry some of the superstitious foreboding of its origin: In the ancient world, a ladder leaning against a wall formed a triangle with the ground. This was considered a sacred symbol of life and anyone who walked through this sacred triangle would be punished.

The very meaning of the term from which we get our word superstition, *supersisto*, means "to stand in terror of the deity." When was the last time you—just in case—passed on a chain letter that came with a promise of blessing or warning of bad luck if you failed to pass it on?[1]

All of us as children from about ages one to seven pass through this stage. The world can be controlled by magic rituals. "Step on a crack and break your mother's back" and "Cross my heart and hope to die" are both ancient magic rituals. Indigenous tribes in some parts of the world today still live at this mode of consciousness. "Don't let an outsider take your picture because he will capture your spirit."

This is the childhood home of the magical worldview as young children see the world through a lens of imagination. Impulsiveness and fantasy are unrestrained by logic in a world where anything is possible. The tribal consciousness is found today not only in superstitions but also astrology column advice and comic book and television heroes like Superman and Buffy the Vampire Slayer. Tribal level adults feel secure within their group or family clan where parents and leaders are god-like, providing everything needed in an ego-centered existence. Therefore, tribal consciousness is also seen in those who over-identify with their race, nationality, politics, religion, or other ethnocentric group.

Each station along the way in our development has healthy aspects as well as unhealthy ones. The unhealthy parts are best transcended, while the healthy parts make a lasting contribution to the further development of the individual or culture.

Historically, tribal is the very stable stage found at the beginning of the Old Testament, which included the Israelite and Canaanite tribal cultures, among others. This stability and loyalty of kinship and clan ties is one of the enduring aspects of the tribal level which can be included in future stages along with the experience of enchantment, imagination, and being touched by something bigger than ourselves. Ceremonies, symbols, and special rites can inspire us, reminding us of spiritual matters. Deeply connecting with nature and sensing a situation intuitively rather than by intellectual analysis are also elements of the tribal level that we can build upon.

An estimated 5–10 percent of the world's adult population lives at this altitude. Many more of us have parts of us that are at this mode of consciousness.

Tribal Church

In western industrialized societies there are only a few kinds of ultraconservative churches whose dominant center is tribal. Tribal spirituality is filled with fearful fantasies and focused on the closed and closely-knit group with its magical beliefs.

The Bible

In the tribal church, the Bible is held in great reverence and studied closely, since it is seen as God's Word to us and without error. These Christians band together in their group in order to be true to their particular understanding of the Bible, which is the only right one. The Bible itself may appear to be treated as a book of magic because it, as a book, possesses supernatural qualities. You swear on it. You give it place of honor. You never place another book on top of it. You can find guidance by letting it fall open and whatever page it opens to contains the answer to your particular problem. There is a verse for every situation and some verses are repeated like an incantation to provide protection and to send what you need down from heaven. The Bible can, of course, be treated with respect, and processing down the church aisle with Bible held aloft can be a mark of esteem and beautiful pageantry. However, at the tribal level, it may look like holding aloft a powerful charm that possesses magical powers for everyone to behold with proper awe.

Today's fear-filled religious beliefs in popular Christianity come from the tribal stage of the Israelites as recorded in the Bible throughout the Old Testament and into the New Testament. Major elements of this have become enshrined in beliefs about God sending disasters and other punishments in this life and eternal torment in hell in the next.

Every thinking Christian at the modern level and beyond must wrestle with what parts of the Bible resemble tribal level magical stories that seem more like fanciful legends than historical facts. Did God really create the world in seven literal days? Did Methuselah really live 969 years? Did the priests' staffs really turn into snakes? Did the sun really stand still? Did God really wipe out everyone but Noah and his family in a flood? Did God really order the Israelites to kill all those people? Was Jesus really born of a virgin? Did he really multiply the loaves and fishes? Did he really heal people? Did he rise from the dead, and if so, in what way?

God

Ninety percent of Americans believe in God. But this "God" is seen in different ways in the various worldviews. In the tribal church, God is seen as an awe-inspiring, often capricious, superhero who lives up there in the sky. God is responsible for everything and is to be feared and appeased at all costs. Like the mythical gods of Rome and Greece, God intervenes at times in our life with miracles and punishments. God is often addressed as "Heavenly Father" and always spoken about in exclusively male language.

Like early tribal cultures, the tribal element of church life is based in fear. The idea of fearing God would not be considered a negative judgment in the tribal church, but would be taught as genuine wisdom. "The fear of the Lord is the beginning of wisdom."[2] God is a holy, supernatural being who is completely separate from us. The major concern of the spiritual life at this stage is reward and punishment from God. Righteous actions are rewarded now and unrighteous behavior is punished with sickness, calamities, and, ultimately, eternal hell if one has not repented and trusted in Christ for the forgiveness of their sins.

Jesus

The words "Jesus" and "Christ" at the tribal level are like the first and last names for the same person. Jesus is uniquely God come down from heaven and resembles the local gods of an African tribe, a magician-like wonder worker who has come from the spirit world to save their group from harm. Jesus gave himself as a sacrificial offering to appease God's wrath so when believers die they will not suffer God's wrath in eternal hell but can be with Christ in heaven. Jesus Christ is the divine son of God, with more emphasis on *divine* than the *human*. Jesus answers prayers, sometimes performs miracles when requested, and works wonders among believers.

Prayer

Prayer is talking with God or Jesus with an emphasis on repeated confession of sins and accepting forgiveness. In prayer, we ask Jesus, a magical super being, to do things we need in this world. These sincere prayers are usually concluded with the phrase "in Jesus' name." At the modern level the phrase "in Jesus' name" can be a meaningful reminder to pray in the character and spirit of Jesus. At the tribal level, this phrase may appear to be a magical incantation that assures maximum impact of the prayer.

At times, praying appears to be a good luck superstition—such as praying before a golf shot or a school exam for divine extra help. The little boy was asked why he had prayed, "Oh Lord, please make St. Louis the capital of Missouri." His response was, "Because that's what I put on the test."

Good luck charms and lucky signs and symbols are prayerfully used to calm fears. Saying "God bless you" when someone sneezes can be just a nice thought or it may carry some of its beginnings as a religious superstition. In ancient times, people thought their breath was also their soul. A sneeze was the same as expelling life from one's body, leaving a vacuum in the head through which evil spirits could enter. The phrase "God bless you" then came about to shield sneezers from any ill effects.

The tribal level tends to believe that God directly controls the weather from up in heaven above the clouds. If there is a hurricane, it is because God sent it. If the sun comes out, it is because God caused it to happen that very minute. A prayer sent toward the Big Weather Maker in the Sky may magically make a change in the weather toward your preference, rain or sunshine. Insurance companies still call it "an act of God" when a disaster like a hurricane or tornado causes destruction. At the tribal consciousness, one may be more likely to pray for a parking space than for grace to handle however far away one must park.

While writing this chapter, I received a letter from a church offering to send me a golden "prosperity" cross if I would request it. I was to place a checkmark on the enclosed card next to the things that I wanted. Among the items listed were a new car, more money, children, health, and a new home. The letter was filled with Bible verses and concluded with this warning: "If you are not going to send this on to five others, you will have a run of bad luck. If you share it with five others, you will be blessed by God." This is a strongly magical level of belief.

Sin and Salvation

Sin is doing things that are against God's commandments. Sin is whatever is not pleasing to God, who can be pleased or displeased, depending on the situation. Salvation is being rescued from certain eternal punishment in a literal hell. We are saved from hell by believing that Jesus died in our place for our sins, taking the punishment from God that we deserve on himself instead and therefore satisfying God's wrath.

Heaven and Hell

Hell is a place of demons, literal fire, eternal punishment, separation from God and the clan of Christians. It is to be feared above everything else. Heaven is a place of eternal safety with others like your church family. We are sent to one or the other on the basis of our faith in Jesus Christ or certain rituals such as baptism.

The Kingdom of Heaven

The Kingdom of Heaven is the place Christians go after death. Believing in Jesus guarantees being rescued from the devil and God's wrath. A strongly held belief at the tribal stage is that one's church or group is uniquely the depository of divine truth. Their group has the only path to heaven and salvation. Everyone else is doomed to spend eternity in hell.

The Mystical

Mystical beliefs abound at this level of consciousness but are confused with magic. Mysticism that represents actual spiritual realities transcends the rational whereas magical fantasies are pre-rational and do not represent actual spiritual realities. The magical level confuses the symbol with what it represents. Historically, tribal cultures have not yet differentiated mind from body. They confuse symbols with the reality that they symbolize. Things like trees, animals, and even objects such as statues or carvings from non-Christian religions can contain bad spirits. To those at the modern rational level, tribal church religious rituals, such as believing that baptism actually keeps a person out of hell, appear to be more filled with magic than meaning.

The elements of Communion are literally changed into Christ's body and blood. Catholics who may personally have a strong tribal/magic element in their faith will embrace the Mass in a magical way, thinking in terms of incantations and mysterious rites. Moving from Latin to English words in the Mass removed some of this magical atmosphere and was resisted greatly by some.

At the tribal stage, statues or pictures of Jesus and the saints may be treated with a sense of talisman or magical power. This is a different perception than what I feel when I look at any of my three Buddha statues or the hundreds of Jesus pictures I have collected. I do not ascribe any inherent magical power to them although I do experience them carrying an actual energy field that I perceive as peaceful and inspiring.

Tribal level "mystical" Christianity is filled with fantasy and fear. Do you know anyone with a foreboding about the number 666, a magical superstition supposedly based on the book of Revelation? Wearing an angel pin or a cross can be little reminders of positive spiritual matters—or they hold the superstitious element of a talisman, amulet, or charm that will bring good luck or protect us from harm. Looking from the modern altitude, these are fear-based fantasies, not realities.

Evil comes from demonic forces and Satan. One must guard against being corrupted by the demonic influence of other religions, including other Christians who do not agree with them. The world is filled with evil spirits attempting to lure them away from the only true faith. Demon possession is real and sometimes a person needs an exorcism or ritual incantation for the demons to leave.

The Christian with elements of this level may genuinely experience the Spirit of God and have a vital relationship with Jesus. They may actually be more open to spiritual experience in altered states than those in the traditional and modern stages because they have not yet discounted inspired states. These experiences will be interpreted to reinforce the prerational magical beliefs of the community. "I have felt the presence of God and so what I believe about God must be right." Sometimes these believers may experience "demon possession" or a trance-like state when with a charismatic leader. Churches that practice snake handling find the ritual may be accompanied by the "power of God" coming down upon them leading them to believe they have immunity from harm. They typically experience total calmness with no fear of the snakes or drinking poison.

A church at this stage is necessarily very centered on itself since the beliefs and practices of the church are perceived as a survival issue. This may be seen in the hold that a leader has on the members' lives. The leaders and members of these groups have sometimes been seen as socially isolating members and practicing heavy indoctrination, physical abuse, child abuse, murder, militia-type preparation, and even mass suicide.

Limitations and Strengths

It is eventually limiting to mistake superstition for spirituality. All fear-based spirituality today comes from the remnants of the ancient consciousness of thousands of years ago. The worry that an angry God will punish you was rejected by Jesus. One does not need to toss out the authentic mystical consciousness of the tribal stage in order to transcend its fearful elements.

Magical thinking increases with feelings of vulnerability and powerlessness and decreases as we begin to own our own spiritual power. Christians with this worldview may be filled with a sense of personal powerlessness, with the leadership owning all the power. Also, believing that the world of truly spiritual people is limited to those who think exactly as you do presents a very small world in today's global village.

From an integral perspective, any culture, group, church, or individual has every right to be at this level and deserves our understanding and respect. This level, as with any level, only becomes problematic when it uses force or manipulation to impose its beliefs and values upon others. Any part of us that personally remains in the fantasies and magical thinking of the tribal stage also deserves our understanding, respect, and nurture. It is not necessary to be judgmental about these parts of us, even those that we may eventually decide to change. Every stage is valuable in itself. Age 12 is not better than age five—it is just a different place in life. We value age five because it is important in itself and necessary to reach age 12. The same is true with each evolving level of growth in consciousness. Sometimes we find ourselves becoming angry about the stage we are in. That can be a signal that it is time in our life to make a change. The anger can give us the energy to move on to the next level. However, we eventually need to get over our anger and honor every stage we have passed through. We can then reconcile ourselves to the truth that each of the past stations in our life has contributed to our moving to the next stage and where we are now.

The strength of tribal church is its family and group loyalty

The people here can experience the value of belonging and appropriate levels of leadership. This is an enduring value. At whatever level a church is, it is important to function as a tribe in some ways. A small church is like a tribe in itself. Larger churches have "tribes" in them that may be called Sunday School classes, small groups, or mission groups. If we are to develop spiritually, it is imperative to have a network or small group of friends on the same journey.

When Jesus wanted to change the world, the first thing he did was to gather a few others around him in a new spiritual tribe. He affirmed this new spiritual family, saying that it took precedence over one's birth family.[3] The first tribe of Jesus' people consisted of a dozen or so men who were prominently named in the New Testament accounts as the "twelve apostles" together with a small group of women who didn't get as much formal recognition but, interestingly, paid the bills.[4]

Later on, the house churches of the New Testament served as clans in the rapidly spreading Christianity of the first two hundred years. The apostle Paul and other leaders always operated in teams. Connecting to a network of others seeking God consciousness is crucial to our spiritual growth.

CHAPTER 3

Warrior Church
Fighting and Fervor

Warrior consciousness is not an abstract theoretical construct. It is a reality today. As I was writing this chapter, we observed the seventh anniversary of the 9/11 terrorist attacks. It was warrior consciousness that conceived, planned, and launched those attacks. We must expose terrorism for what it is and protect ourselves against it. But in doing so we must operate from a much higher level than the terrorists. This involves much more than a military response. The military cannot by itself protect us from terrorism. It ultimately must involve political, social, and, above all, spiritual solutions that invite the world to grow beyond warrior consciousness.

Warrior Consciousness

The warrior stage of culture began to develop about 10,000 years ago when the tribal level grew in wealth and power, and conflicts erupted between neighboring tribes. Might makes right at the warrior stage. The warrior world is about who is the most powerful. Aggression, impulsive behavior, pleasure, and violence rule. We fight to be in control. Exploitation reigns. The world is like a jungle where the tough win and the weak lose.

At this station in life, beliefs and understandings are less magical and more literal. There is an absolute authority that is outside of me such as a parent, a teacher, a boss, a minister, or a God who makes the rules that I follow without question. "My teacher says . . ." "The

Bible says . . . " "The government says . . . " The world is black and white, good or evil, with no need to reflect on the nuances in between.

Live for the moment and act impulsively. Don't worry about what may happen because of your actions. Fight aggressively without any guilt. After all, you are the center of the world.

People here act without consideration for others. Right and wrong are felt more by impulse than reason. Fear of wrathful deities (or a single vengeful God) often keeps people at this stage in line.

Historically, the spiritual leaders of these times were the shamans. They had altered-state experiences where they saw nature spirits and gods of rain, fire, wind, and other natural phenomena. They perceived powerful spirit beings directing much of life. They experienced psychic intuition and a sense of union with nature.

Contemporary representatives of this mode of consciousness are the terrible twos, grade school/early high school bullying and teasing, rebellious youth, street gangs, wild rock stars, prisons, frontier mentality, comic book superheroes, sword and sorcery stories, warrior tribes such as in Afghanistan, athletic teams, aggressive unethical corporations, and the rise of terrorism around the world.

The enduring elements of this worldview, which we can build upon, are the healthy use of power to restrain violence, individual initiative, and taking appropriate action to liberate the oppressed of the world. An estimated 20 percent of the world population is at the warrior stage.

Warrior Church

It was warrior consciousness that killed Jesus. That was the mentality of the leaders of Jesus' religion who plotted to have him killed. Those religious leaders then invited the collaboration of the warrior society of Rome that carried out the execution. Therefore, it is reasonable to say that the warrior "church" of Jesus' day crucified him.

Historically, the warrior church can be seen in holy wars, the Crusades, and the Inquisition. The warrior mentality is the desire to dominate the world. It is the crusade mentality of "convert or destroy." Today the warrior level church is commonly referred to as a fundamentalist church. While the word "fundamentalism" can be used in a pejorative sense, I do not use it that way here. I use it as these groups themselves do in proudly calling themselves Fundamentalists. Fundamentalism is a significant religious movement in Christianity that came into prominence with a series of 94 essays which were published between 1910 and 1915 with 3 million copies distributed to English-speaking Protestants around the world. The term "fundamentalist" refers to the five fundamentals which are foundational in these churches:

(1) The Bible contains the literal words of God without error.

(2) The virgin birth and the deity of Jesus.

(3) The doctrine of substitutionary atonement.

(4) The bodily resurrection of Jesus.

(5) The authenticity of Christ's miracles (or, alternatively, his pre-millennial second coming).

In addition to these doctrines, the word "fundamentalism" also refers to a mindset which warns others who do not agree with them of the danger of their wrong beliefs. Many Christians believe some or all of these five "fundamentals." However, warrior Christians are angry about it all, especially at those Christians who do not share their beliefs. I vividly remember the first time, 25 years ago, when a visitor spoke to me at the door after church service. She said, sternly, "Pastor, you are leading these people straight to hell, and you are going there for sure." Her comment stirred up some of my terminal niceness and I wanted to assure her I was a really nice guy. Beyond that, I felt strangely sad. She didn't see what I saw, and I was sorry. I felt liberated while she was angry, both of us affected in different ways by our worldviews.

The Bible

As stated in the "five fundamentals" the Bible is without error and everything written there is taken as historically and scientifically accurate. The Bible contains everything God wants us to know about the spiritual life. The translation most often preferred is the King James version of 1611. Contemporary versions may be frowned upon or openly rejected.

At this level, the Bible is often used as a weapon. The remark "They beat me over the head with the Bible" reflects this sentiment. Warrior/egocentric-type churches tend to find justification for their violent "righteous" actions in the Bible. They usually favor the death penalty because the God of the Bible killed the wicked. They warn about judgment to come for anyone who does not agree with them. Warrior churches are especially attracted to the apocalyptic books of Daniel and Revelation where the wrath of God figures prominently.

Playing an important role in their beliefs are certain biblical passages such as, "Never avenge yourselves but leave room for the wrath of God, for it is written, 'Vengeance is mine, I will repay, says the Lord.'"[1] For the warrior church, this is a glorious promise that those who do not agree with them will eventually get the punishment they deserve from God.

These churches are greatly concerned with doctrinal purity and resist any effort to cooperate with other Christian groups who do not hold to their same beliefs. Recently, a teacher in fundamentalist school was fired for participating in a prayer service with Christians of a different denomination. It would be even more unthinkable to meet to worship, pray, or enjoy fellowship with others such as Muslims or Hindus except for purpose of evangelism.

God

God lives up in heaven but comes down to earth as an avenging warrior mixed with elements of justice and compassion. There is strong biblical justification for this view with over four hundred passages in the Bible that speak of the wrath of God. If one adds up the actual named figures of how many people God is reported to have killed in the Old Testament, it will range well over 300,000, not including entire cities, communities, and, in one instance, the entire population of the Earth except for Noah and his family. To those who take the Bible literally, these powerful biblical images provide a firm foundation for the wrathful God of the warrior stage.

These famous Texas billboards, all signed with the name "God," are greatly loved by the warrior church:

"Don't make me come there."

"You think it's hot here?"

"Have you read my #1 best seller? There will be a test."

"Keep using my name in vain and I'll make rush hour even longer."

God is addressed exclusively in male terms such as Heavenly Father and Lord God Almighty. Like the previous level, the spiritual life is fear-based and this is considered a good thing, as in, "The fear of the Lord is pure, enduring forever."[2] This is one of the 27 biblical references to "the fear of the Lord," including Paul's statement, "Therefore, knowing the fear of the Lord, we try to persuade others. . ."[3]

Jesus

Jesus is the mighty agent of the wrath of God in the book of Revelation.[4] He makes war against sin, death, and the devil and conquers them. Jesus is the strong conqueror who one day shall return with flaming swords and angels "inflicting vengeance on those who do not know God and on those who do not obey the gospel of our Lord Jesus."[5]

A personal relationship with Jesus within a fundamentalist belief system tends to be more legal than caring and more dependent on rule keeping than on relating.

Characteristic of the ethnocentric level, Jesus is seen as the only way to access God, and Christianity is the only true religion. Those who do not know Jesus are doomed. Hellfire and damnation sermons are common and well received. They advocate the "Christianizing" of America to save the country from divine punishment as they understand Sodom and Gomorrah were punished by God.

Prayer

Warrior prayer may contain spiritual curses upon enemies, conversations with the avenging God about battle stuff, asking God to help them convert or destroy all other groups. Prayer may also be fighting evil in the form of sickness and doing battle with the illness by rebuking the devil or the sickness itself.

Warrior church services emphasize the church triumphant and their hymns are filled with images of God winning over all his enemies. God is worshipped as the male King and Ruler over the world who dispenses justice to the wicked. Sermons deal with biblical passages about the Second Coming, the Rapture (when true believers will be caught up into heaven, leaving the wicked behind to suffer), and predictions of doom that warn of the Last Days.

The *New York Times* reported an example of a warrior-stage church in Washington, D.C.[6] Students, taxicab drivers, homemakers, and entrepreneurs, all Christians, mostly from French-speaking Africa, attend a midnight service four nights a week doing "spiritual warfare." They sing, pray fervently, and kick and shadowbox with what they contend is the real force behind life's problems: the witches and devils whose curses they believe have ground down their families, towns, entire nations in Africa, and that have pursued them to a new country, making it hard to find work, be healthy, and survive. The pastor said, "Some situations you need to address at night, because in the ministry of spiritual warfare, demons, the spirits bewitching people, choose this time to work."

This church believes that the battle between God and Satan shapes all world events. The congregants believe that, because their ancestors were not Christians, they were cursed, Africa is cursed, and the sins of their fathers are now visited upon all the children. The revulsion toward one's ancestors represents the shift from the tribal/warrior stages to the beginning of a more traditional stage. What is fascinating, though, is they are using warrior prayer tactics to move themselves out of the warrior stage.

Sin and Salvation

Sin is offending God by going against his rules, often ones about sexual "purity." Like the tribal level, salvation from our sins comes from violent atonement theory: Jesus came to die for our sins to appease the wrath of God. On the cross, Jesus took the terrible punishment that God's justice demands for our sins. Only by believing in Jesus can we escape the wrath of God. The resurrection of Jesus from the dead proclaimed God's victory in the great cosmic battle between God and Satan.

Heaven and Hell

Heaven is the place one goes at death if they have been saved from the wrath of the warrior God by believing in Jesus. It is where the victorious in battle come to rest. Hell is the place where God gets the ultimate revenge against evil people. The wicked finally get what they deserve—eternal suffering.

The Kingdom of Heaven

The Kingdom of Heaven is another way of talking about heaven. It is where God's will is done perfectly. In order to bring the Kingdom of Heaven down to earth as much as possible, these "Christian warriors" wage war against sin, immorality, abortion, the theory of evolution, other religions, and, in general, all who differ from their beliefs. They fight against homosexuality and one group has been known to picket churches (including my church a number of times) and funerals with signs that say "God hates gays." God is male and only men should be in charge at home and at church. They may view the Crusades and the Inquisition as models of faithful action. Politically, they tend to advocate deadly force against international enemies and the annihilation of any nation they perceive as a threat.

The Mystical

The warrior church, like the tribal church, confuses authentic mystical awareness with the magical level of religious fantasy. Demons are real and can possess a person. Exorcism is a battle with Satan where the demons are authoritatively commanded to leave a person's physical body.

Rituals like baptism and communion are weapons at the warrior ethnocentric level. They are used as a way to control what members believe and practice. You might not be able to receive baptism or take communion unless you adhere to certain policies and even political viewpoints such as supporting the criminalization of abortion. This can be quite distressing for those who believe baptism and/or communion have to do with your eternal destiny after death.

Limitations and Strengths

The limitation of the warrior church is its fighting mentality. This leads to always being at war with something or someone, and believing that only you and your group have the truth. This in turn can manifest various forms of discrimination, oppression, and even warfare.

Fear is also present as a carryover from the tribal stage. Karen Armstrong says, "Every single fundamentalist movement that I have studied in Judaism, Christianity, and Islam is rooted in profound fear."[7]

The strength and dignity of this worldview is fervor—the ability to be passionate about what matters to you. Other strengths are the value of belonging, the inspiration of their heroic myths, and taking passionate action on behalf of the group. The church needs activists who will do battle in a non-violent way. All Christians can value true fervor in standing up for the oppressed and doing the right thing. Jesus was passionate about God and God's will. We can be, too.

We can appreciate the ability of the warrior church to communicate a spiritual path that is accessible to those at the tribal and warrior levels. This is especially clear with those trapped in drugs, gangs, or a criminal culture. Fundamentalists sometimes seem to be the most successful at inviting these persons into a genuine spiritual path with real conversion and commitment.

Christian fundamentalists often possess a great passion for Jesus and energy in seeking their spiritual path. Christian fundamentalists, perhaps sometimes unlike fundamentalists of other religions, have within their embrace a clear path to moving toward more compassion, inclusivity, and truth. This is embodied in Jesus himself. It is truly difficult to take Jesus' life and teaching seriously and end up embracing the less-than-Christ-like parts of today's ultraconservative Christianity.

It is legitimate for any nation, group, church, or individual to be at the warrior level. They deserve to be understood and respected. However, the warrior stage presents a great challenge to being respected because of its militancy. It is necessary for those at other levels to resist the nature of this level to want to impose its views on everyone else.

This is another value of our Spiritual Positioning System: it helps us see the conflict more precisely. The idea is to resist any group's attempt to force their views upon others through social harassment or force while upholding their right to hold these views. Any element of this perspective within us needs to be treated with care and respect while we curb our expectation that everyone should think like we do and attempt to impose our beliefs on others.

The challenge for the growing Christian is learning not to get angry about people who get angry. It is how to avoid having a warrior consciousness about warrior consciousness. The challenge is to be passionate without persecuting, protective without punishing, and vehement without violence.

As we shall explore later, postmodernism has created a permissive atmosphere that allows warrior consciousness to remain in its midst. Contrary to that permissive thinking, we must make value judgments. Jesus did. We need the more discerning view that Jesus demonstrated when he did not hesitate to judge the religious leaders of his own religion when he saw them being destructive. Even as all levels have a right to exist, we also have a responsibility to recognize that some levels are healthier, more loving, and more developed than others. We can cultivate, support, and encourage the more Christ-like levels while respecting those persons and groups who do not share our values.

CHAPTER 4

Traditional Church
Faithful and Fitting In

Traditional Consciousness

The traditional worldview emerged about 5,000 years ago as people longed for law and order in the chaotic, "evil" world of the warrior. External rules and guilt produced a more controlled society. This conformist station in life dominated society until the time of the Renaissance and the Enlightenment. The traditional stage is still the primary mode of awareness for the followers of all the major religions of the world today, including Christianity.

In the traditional altitude, the individual's ultimate concern begins to move away from egocentric self-gratification and toward the meaning found in role and identity. Now, instead of "might makes right," it is my group that makes it right. The individual is willing to control current impulses for later fulfillment in a way that recognizes the good of structure and order.

The world is controlled by a God that punishes evil and rewards righteousness. There is only one right way to that God. Those at this stage tend not to question their traditional mode of thinking. It must be true if it is in the Bible or their group says that it is true. Individuals can now think logically but do not do much logical thinking about whether their own beliefs are reasonable or not. Their beliefs are not arrived at by reason and therefore are not susceptible to change by arguments using reason. As one jokester put it, the difference between an angry terrorist and a traditional fundamentalist is that you can reason with a terrorist. The truth is they both are coming from a nonrational mindset.

Individuals at this level appear moralistic, conventional, and tend to give up their individuality in order to conform. There is a great desire to fit in with the group as seen especially in children and young teens. Rigid thinking dominates since my God is right, my country is right, and my people are right no matter what others say. The right values are what an outside authority such as church, the Bible, country, or political group, considers to be right.

Historically, this station in life found its peak in the Middle Ages and continued in Puritan America. The traditional level today is seen in non-violent fundamentalism, Boy and Girl Scouts, the religious right, extreme patriotism, and in most church leadership and structures. An estimated 40–55 percent of the world's population is at the altitude of traditional consciousness. This means that the great majority, 65–80 percent, of people in the world are at the pre-modern stages of traditional, warrior, or tribal.

Traditional Church

The trouble in describing traditional church is that it just seems like we are talking about most churches as they are today. When you say, "I go to such and such church," most people hear you say that you go to a traditional church because that's the only kind they know about. However, as we have seen, traditional church is different from tribal and warrior church. As we shall see, it is also different from modern, postmodern, and integral church.

The vast majority of churches in this country are at the traditional level. Traditional churches are filled with good people who fit in with one another and are faithful to their church's understanding of Christianity. This would include churches such as Roman Catholic, Eastern Orthodox, Baptist, Methodist, Lutheran, Episcopalian, and Presbyterian. Some, like the United Church of Christ, have a mixture of both traditional and modern/postmodern churches. The largest Protestant denomination, Southern Baptist, ranges from fundamentalist warrior to traditional. Black, Pentecostal, and charismatic churches are very much a part of the traditional stage. Evangelicals tend to have a similar theology to that of the previous warrior stage, but they have stopped being angry about those who do not share their views. Charismatically-oriented churches, coming from the charismatic movement of the 1960s, were the product of the flow of typical Pentecostal experiences into non-Pentecostal churches. Sometimes entirely new churches were formed, which resulted in many "independent charismatic" churches and new denominations such as the Vineyard churches, which have a traditional orthodox theology mixed with graciousness and spiritual gifts.

Some of what are called "mainline" churches—such as Lutheran, Methodist, Episcopalian, Presbyterian, Congregational, Disciples of Christ, United Church of Christ, and American Baptist churches have moved from the traditional stage to the modern stage. This can be confusing since churches with names similar to these mainline churches may be very traditional-level evangelical churches such as Southern Baptist, (the largest Protestant denomination in America with 16 million members in 42,000 churches), Lutheran Church Missouri Synod, and the Presbyterian Church in America.

The address of the traditional Christian church in the 21st century has dramatically changed. It has moved from the Northern Hemisphere to the Southern Hemisphere. The center of traditional Christianity has moved from the United States and Western Europe to Africa, Asia, Latin America, and Eastern Europe. This means that there will be an even greater cultural divide between western Christianity and the new center. Western Christianity tends to have some room for modern and postmodern consciousness. The new center in the East and South is very much at the traditional level and is adamantly opposed to any understanding of Christianity that is at a higher altitude. The Episcopal Church in the United States currently finds itself outvoted and at odds with others in the worldwide Anglican Communion on issues such as women priests and affirming all sexual orientations as gifts from God. This is because of the very traditional stage of its churches in third world countries.

The traditional altitude was the dominant level of the emerging Old Testament culture as Moses brought law and order to the

Hebrew people. Later on, the prophets of the Old Testament began calling for a breakthrough to a higher level beyond rules and rituals. Unfortunately, their voices were not heeded and the scribes and Pharisees of Jesus' day were staunch defenders of the conventional traditions, even as Jesus challenged them. The literal/traditional version of Christianity that is prevalent today is primarily a version of Christianity that was customized for Greek and Roman society in the fifth century.

What follows, as with all my church descriptions, is not a complete or nuanced description of traditional beliefs. These are just a few snapshots of familiar and common poses of the traditional church.

The Bible

Thirty-three percent of the United States population believes that the Bible is the Word of God and literally true word for word. Another 30 percent believe that the Bible is the Word of God but not literally true word for word. Twenty-eight percent believe it is not the Word of God but was written by men. Traditional evangelical and historically black churches have the highest number, around 60 percent, of their members who believe the Bible is the Word of God and literally true word for word.[1] While there is some variation about whether the Bible is true word for word, most traditional churches believe that all the stories in the Bible, including the violent and vengeful ones, reveal the truth about God.

God

At this altitude, God is a righteous judge. "He" is thought of as a divine being who is separate from creation and spoken about only in masculine terms when gender specific words are used. God lives up in heaven but has come down to us in Jesus. God is both loving and vengeful. God is thought of in 2nd-person terms only; that is, as a separate being with whom one can connect personally and intimately. The traditional church is often in conflict with 3rd-person perspective of God revealed in science around the theory of evolution. The conventional church vehemently denies any 1st-person perspective of the Inner Face of God which understands that human beings are divine. (See Chapters 12 and 13.)

Like the previous two stages, God controls many things, or even everything, such as the weather. "The tornado swept through our area killing five people. But God spared us." That's a comforting thought to everyone except the families of the five people who were killed. At the next level, the modern one, natural phenomenon is better left to nature, not to a super being sitting in a heaven above directing various catastrophes.

Jesus

The traditional level seeks a personal relationship with God and a drive for true companionship with Jesus. It understands Jesus Christ as the incarnation of God in human form who is revealed only in the Bible. Jesus is seen as a miracle worker and the only son of God who came to die in our place on the cross for our sins. Jesus and Christ appear, to most, to be two different names for the same person. At the traditional level there is a rich variety of metaphors in understanding Jesus. He is the Savior, Lord, Master, Counselor, Lamb of God, Rock, Lily of the Valley, Rose of Sharon, Teacher, and Emmanuel—God with us. Jesus is both fully divine and fully human. The Nicene Creed and Apostle's Creed are staples of traditional beliefs about Jesus.

Prayer

The spiritual shamans of the earlier magic stage with its many gods and spirits gave way to the mystics who began to sense that underneath everything was a Oneness or Supreme Being. This led to the idea of only one God, monotheism, and eventually even higher stages of spiritual awareness. Then came the move from magical thinking to mythical, or traditional thinking. Magical thinking is believing that if we can find the right words and rituals, then we can control the harmful spirits. Mythical thinking is believing that if we can find the right God and ask him in the right way, then we can control the world around us to keep from being harmed.

This leads to two primary kinds of prayer at the traditional level. One is seeking divine intervention in human affairs by asking God up there to do things for us down here. Prayer for healing is asking a God, who is a separate and "super" being out there, to intervene in the physical world. The other form of prayer is communing with God in worship and thanksgiving. Therefore, God is both distant and personal.

In worship services, some traditional-stage churches may exclude those not of their group from the Lord's Supper. Roman Catholic churches routinely exclude non-Catholics from Holy Communion.

Sin and Salvation

Sin is primarily offending God by disobedience. Sin may also be thought of as harming others. Sin must be dealt with in practice, but first it must be dealt with in salvation. For the traditional church, the most important teaching of the Bible is that Jesus died for our sins. This is the basic meaning of the Mass or Holy Communion. We are saved by embracing Jesus' death on the cross for our sins. When asked "saved from what?" the answer is usually, "our sins " or "hell." However, the underlying understanding is that we are actually saved from God. The death of Jesus satisfies God's wrath. In traditional Christianity, Jesus protects us from God. This is the continuation of the Old Testament image of God as both loving and angry. God the Father has the role of the vengeful God whose "justice" requires a penalty for sin and God the Son, Jesus, has the role of the compassionate aspect of God who takes the penalty upon himself. It is a bad cop, good cop scenario all the way.

For the traditional church, Jesus' teaching about the Kingdom of Heaven tends to be replaced with Paul's teaching about salvation.

The official creeds, seminaries, and teachers of the traditional level hold a primarily ethnocentric perspective in that only Christians can find God or be saved. Traditional Christianity at the institutional level definitely has an exclusivity clause in it. However, it is interesting that well over half of the traditional Christians themselves in this country do not invoke that clause. They believe that other religions can lead to eternal life. These include 79 percent of Catholics,

57 percent of evangelicals, and 83 percent of mainline Christians. The mainline figure is the largest because it would include modern and postmodern churches. Evangelicals are called by that name because they believe it is very important to evangelize others into the Christian faith. But that appears to be changing as now over half of evangelicals themselves, regardless of their official creeds or leaders, believe that other religions can lead to eternal life.[2]

Heaven and Hell

Seventy-four percent of Americans believe in heaven. Heaven is usually understood as a place of bliss where those who have gained eternal life dwell with God forever. Belief in hell is cooling off. Fifty-nine per cent of Americans believe in hell, down from the 71 percent six years earlier.[3] Hell is primarily understood as a place of eternal torment for those who are not Christians.[4] A less official but probably more popular understanding is that good people go to heaven and bad people go to hell. A small group of traditional Christians believe those in hell are annihilated rather than punished unendingly.

The Kingdom of Heaven

The Kingdom of Heaven is seen as the reign of God present in Jesus and a future reality. It is the vision of God for righteousness, peace, justice, and oneness in Christ. As I pointed out previously, the traditional church tends to focus more on Paul's idea of salvation than on Jesus' understanding of the Kingdom of Heaven. The apostle Paul's teaching, in the traditional interpretation, is popularly understood to center on being saved from our sins and eternity in hell by repenting and believing in Jesus. This understanding of Paul's idea of salvation overshadows Jesus' view of the Kingdom of Heaven in traditional Christianity.

The Mystical

The traditional church thinks highly of mystics as long as they are dead. The longer they have been dead the better. Perhaps the only really safe ones are in the Bible where they can be seen as unique.

In my traditional seminary I was taught that "mysticism" begins with mist, centers on I, and ends in schism. That sounded scary. That was because it was meant to sound that way. It seemed to me, back then, that exceptions to this must be Pentecostal and charismatic churches that gather together and experience elevated states of awareness of God's presence. However, non-charismatics frown upon communal mysticism because of what they see as prerational elements, emotionalism, and because their beginning modern sensibilities reject it altogether.

Traditional conservative churches tend to, perhaps inadvertently, focus on outward conformity with rules and expectations rather than aim at an inner transformation of consciousness. The individual with traditional religious orientation values the approval of the group and feels guilty for breaking the rules.

This can produce a coercive atmosphere rather than a contemplative or inviting one where one goes into their own inner space and experiences God. Altered state experiences are discouraged in traditional Christianity except for conversion experiences among evangelicals and certain spiritual experiences during worship and ministry among Pentecostal and charismatic groups.

Strengths

The traditional church is a faithful church. It is true and faithful to its understanding of the gospel. The healthy and enduring elements of the traditional stage include honoring traditions, the stability of the law and order mindset, respect for authority, and loyalty. People at this level do what is expected of them to help the world function in established ways. They have a strong sense of faith and religious foundation that anchors them through the storms of life.

The traditional level of church deserves our respect and gratitude. Most of us on the Christian path today got there via this stage. Those who live at the tribal, warrior, and traditional levels can often only respond to the gospel when it is presented by a traditional level church. We need traditional churches that will minister to those firmly rooted in the traditional consciousness and invite people to move up from the tribal and warrior stages. Good examples of religious leaders at this level are Billy Graham and Pope John Paul II. I am grateful for the traditional-level church. This is where I grew up, learned about the Bible, and found meaningful worship and fellowship. It was an indispensable and nurturing launching pad for me in my ongoing spiritual evolution.

Recently, my ten-year-old granddaughter wanted a rip stick, which is like a skateboard but with only one wheel in front and one in back. I live near a store that sells them and we purchased one. My granddaughter and I returned there often as she talked with the young man who was the store manager and an expert in "rip sticking." They would both take their rip sticks out on the sidewalk in front of the store where they would both rip stick for a while, expertly weaving in and out around the sidewalk. In the process, I struck up a friendship with this young man. He was a recent convert to Christ in a conservative Christian church which was carefully watching over him and inviting him to Bible study and prayer. I was aware of how grateful I was for that traditional church, which is quite different from my church. They were able to connect with this young man about a spiritual path in a helpful way that I probably could not. Although I am quite an evangelist for my understanding of Christianity, I found myself not the least interested in challenging this young man's new-found traditional beliefs and practices. Rather, I encouraged him and praised him for starting to follow Jesus according to his church's understanding.

On the other hand, many of us who have left the traditional stage have had to deal with our anger at the oppressive elements there. Our anger, at the time, gave us energy to move on. Eventually, we need to also move on from our anger at the traditional church and see it as a valuable and often necessary step in our spiritual evolution.

Many of us whose center of gravity is modern, postmodern, or integral, still have aspects of our own perspective at the traditional level. In a healthy spiritual path, these components of a faith journey should be honored and nurtured until they no longer seem relevant for us. *It's a wise person who knows what time it is in their life.* Is it time to stabilize and strengthen where you are—or time to change? Either option can be a healthy choice. Only you know what time it is for you.

Limitations

While the strength of the traditional church is stability, that can also be its greatest limitation. The desire to keep things the way they are in order to be comfortable in the familiar can hinder spiritual growth. Spiritual breakthroughs and deepening can be a wild ride at times. Of course, we need to be civilized and accommodate ourselves in various social situations. But to overly value fitting in negates Jesus' strong words about *not* fitting it.

We can see this at work in how Jesus treated the family of his day. No society ever valued the "traditional" family more than the Jewish people of Jesus' day. It was incredibly strong and stable. It was structured according to the religious code of the Old Testament. It was how you survived physically, economically, and spiritually. *However, every time Jesus talked about the Jewish family, he attacked it!*

He said parents and children would rise up against each other because of him.[5] When his birth family showed up looking for him, he pointed out to the crowd that his real family members were those who did God's will.[6] He told the man who was being a good traditional son when he dutifully wanted to stay with his family until his father died, "Let the dead bury the dead. You come and follow me."[7] He taught,

> Don't think I've come to make life cozy. I've come to cut—make a sharp knife-cut between son and father, daughter and mother, bride and mother-in-law—cut through these cozy domestic arrangements and free you for God. Well-meaning family members can be your worst enemies. If you prefer father or mother over me, you don't deserve me. If you prefer son or daughter over me, you don't deserve me.[8]

Why did Jesus attack the family of his day so passionately? He did so because he knew that the strong family ties of his Jewish religion would keep family members clinging to their traditional religious ideas and practices rather than drinking the new wine of the Spirit. He knew that the strongly patriarchal family would resist treating women as equals to men and church history testifies to that very thing. Jesus subverted *all* systems that kept people from hearing what the Spirit was saying in new ways. That is why he attacked the family and religious systems of his day.

This remains true today, whether it is one's birth family, church family, ethnic family, religious denomination, social circle, close friends, political party, or another group. Jesus warns us not to cling to our group in any way that will keep us from evolving spirituality. Anything that competes with the call of the Spirit to new wineskins is a disaster, no matter how virtuous it may seem.

I call it the "crawdad syndrome." Watch a bucketful of crawdads. When one crawdad starts to crawl up the wall and out of the bucket, the others hang on to it and pull it back down. The group's power to pull us back into it is very strong. Here lies the difficulty that the traditional church has in making significant changes. The very strength and stability of the traditional church can keep it from hearing the "I have more to teach you" of the Spirit's call.

The pressure to conform in the traditional church leads to its other weaknesses such as intolerance of those who are different and prejudice toward those who do not fit into the "traditional" mold. The traditional church is familiar, warm, safe, reassuring, and comforting—as long as you look traditional. The question we all consciously or unconsciously ask of any person or group is, "Will I be safe here?" Will I be safe in a traditional church if I am a woman with pastoring and leadership gifts, a gay person, or a theologically unorthodox person? These are challenging issues for the traditional church because even talking about them can be destabilizing.

Resistance to making necessary and healthy changes appears when the desire to "fit in" is stronger than the desire to follow the Spirit. Jesus refused to let stand anything that would keep people from hearing the Spirit's call to keep learning and growing.

The oldest thing you can say about God is that God is always doing something new. Doing something new can be extremely difficult for traditional church.

The traditional church, beginning with the New Testament church, allowed slavery to flourish for two thousand years. It was not until the modern consciousness took over governments and began to slightly influence the church that all industrialized countries have now outlawed slavery.

Women's equality and freedom still suffer in the traditional church and, once again, it is the modern culture which has forged the way—not the church. The most sexist hour of the American week is not on Monday morning in the office but on Sunday morning in many churches. The majority of the churches of the world still will not allow women to be ministers, pastors, or priests.

The most segregated and homophobic hour in the American week is also not on Monday morning in the workplace but on Sunday morning in many churches. Look at how long it took the traditional church to hear the Spirit's call about slavery. How long will it take the traditional church to hear the Spirit's call about women and gays?

However, all stages, including integral, have their limitations. Pointing out limitations in the traditional church does not lessen its inherent value in the ever developing spiritual path. We esteem and honor the traditional church as it has sheltered and fed multitudes of serious Christians for centuries upon centuries. It is the nurturing place for most of the Christians in the world today. It has given us profound theologians, great saints, and pioneering mystics. It has provided a launching pad for all the following stages. It has been and continues to be a stately mansion, even as we evolve more stately mansions.

CHAPTER 5

Modern Church
Flourishing and Flailing

Modern Consciousness

The pastor was at the door greeting people as they left the church service. One woman said, as she left, "You really made me think today, Pastor. Don't ever do that again!"

That's a fine summary of the clash between the traditional stage and the modern stage, which began five hundred years ago in the West, during the periods known as the Renaissance and the Reformation, and flowered two hundred years ago in the Enlightenment. It developed as traditional answers stopped making sense and dogmatic systems and unthinking religion were called into account. Individuals began to question and examine all of their existing beliefs. It was a time of conflict, disappointment, and anger as some found that their beliefs did not stand up under scrutiny. This is the world of the inquiring self. This stage is individualistic, rational, and achievement-oriented.

For individuals in industrialized countries, the rational worldview begins to emerge in late high school, college, or adulthood. I can remember talking at the dinner table at home, at age 16, when my mother said, "Where are you getting all these ideas? What is this crazy stuff you are thinking about?" I was entering the questioning, thinking stage and it was sounding unfamiliar to her. The belief that "truth is not delivered; it is discovered" sparked amazing scientific discoveries and the Industrial Revolution. Ninety percent of the scientists who have ever lived are living today. Democracy flourishes in this stage and the United States Constitution, Bill of Rights, and many of the laws written to protect individual freedom all flow from this worldview.

Individuals begin to realize they have a right to have their own opinions regardless of what the Bible, religion, or their group says. Some become agnostics and atheists at this level. This can represent a movement forward in their spiritual growth.

For the first time, large groups of people began to think in worldcentric terms. Tolerance and compassion for others around the world became a high order value. The modern rational stage can be seen in the rise of democracy, banishing slavery, scientific endeavors, dramatically increasing life spans, Wall Street, emerging middle classes around the world, market capitalism, and liberal self-interest. The dominant consciousness of most institutions of the civilized world is at the modern level—except for the world's religious institutions.

The unhealthy aspects of the modern station in life are materialism, greed, reduction of values and meaning in life, and discounting the inner subjective realm of the spiritual path by believing that the only way to know anything is by scientific exploration.

The valuable elements include vast medical and scientific breakthroughs, healthy competition, and opening up new avenues of spiritual exploration. As spirituality was separated from its magical and literal elements, deeper stage and state explorations of the mystical realms of spirit could eventually open up in postmodernism.

An estimated 15–30 percent of the world population is at the modern station of life.

Modern Church

Before the Renaissance, the Reformation, and the Enlightenment, the Catholic Church dominated every aspect of church life. Then scientific discoveries began to push at the infallibility of the Church. Reason challenged the very basis of the Church itself. Artists pressed at what was permitted. Human freedom came to be valued over religious dogma. Eventually the separation of church and state marked the final blow to the power of the Catholic Church to determine all things. As modern Christian scholars began to apply a more reason-based approach to interpreting the Bible, they began to believe that much of Christianity was immersed in mythical-level stories and viewpoints. They worked to make Christianity more understandable to the modern rational mind. The results of the Renaissance, the Reformation, and the Enlightenment finally made their way into church life about a hundred years ago. The modern church was birthed in the liberal social justice movement and the influence of the New Thought Movement such as Church of Religious Science, Church of Divine Science, and Unity Church.

The modern church is represented by mainstream Protestant liberalism. These are the classic liberal churches which are usually found in mainline denominations such as Episcopalian, Presbyterian, Methodist, Christian (Disciples of Christ), Congregational, and preeminently in the United Church of Christ. The Unitarian Universalist Church is solidly in the modern stage. However, even though they are still referred to as a "church," they are not included in our discussion because they no longer identify themselves as a Christian church but as a "liberal religious tradition."

The modern culture has seen the decline of religion. That decline represents a movement away from traditional religion and a search for something that makes more sense. Since the Spirit is behind all evolutionary development, we may see this decline as a result of the Spirit's work.

People growing spiritually into the rational stage begin to reject prerational traditional religion. Often they are angry about it all. One result of the modern stage is the so-called "New Atheists." Their ranks include Richard Dawkins, Sam Harris, and Christopher Hitchens, who maintain that not only is religious belief wrong, but terribly wrong. They take aim at the traditional church's idea of God and toss it out as nonrational. They point out that all the major institutions of the civilized world are at the rational level, except for one. The one institution in the world that is still primarily at the mythical level is Christianity. Very rational people in the rational world of the business world during the week go to church on Sunday morning and immediately move into a prerational worldview. The New Atheists have discarded this traditional "god" as nonrational.

It is good to recognize that doubt not only is a part of life, it can be a most creative place along the way. The Gospel of Thomas speaks to this when Jesus says, "Those who seek should not stop seeking until they find. When they find, they will be disturbed."[1] That disturbance can be very upsetting and worrisome. Yet, it is most often, a natural expression of spiritual evolution. One friend of mine said to me, "You know I don't believe in prayer. But would you pray about this, just in case." She was okay about her doubts, and at this point was beginning to have enough doubt about her doubts, that she could make such a request. I have been one of her cheerleaders in telling her it is not only okay but also quite important to be wherever you are.

And when the time is right, it is okay to move along. Jesus concludes his previous statement from the Gospel of Thomas with, "When they are disturbed, they will marvel, and will reign over all. And after they have reigned, they will rest." My friend has yet to marvel, but I know at some point, in this life or the next, she will marvel and rest.

Episcopal Bishop Spong represents classic modern level Christian thinking. He wants to dislodge the deeply embedded traditional/mythic/prerational viewpoint of traditional Christianity. Here are the topics he calls the Christians of the world to debate:

(1) Theism, as a way of defining God, is dead. So most theological God-talk is today meaningless. A new way to speak of God must be found.

(2) Since God can no longer be conceived in theistic terms, it becomes nonsensical to seek to understand Jesus as the incarnation of the theistic deity. So the Christology of the ages is bankrupt.

(3) The biblical story of the perfect and finished creation from which human beings fell into sin is pre-Darwinian mythology and post-Darwinian nonsense.

(4)　The virgin birth, understood as literal biology, makes Christ's divinity, as traditionally understood, impossible.

(5)　The miracle stories of the New Testament can no longer be interpreted in a post-Newtonian world as supernatural events performed by an incarnate deity.

(6)　The view of the cross as the sacrifice for the sins of the world is a barbarian idea based on primitive concepts of God and must be dismissed.

(7)　Resurrection is an action of God. Jesus was raised into the meaning of God. It, therefore, cannot be a physical resuscitation occurring inside human history.

(8)　The story of the Ascension assumed a three-tiered universe and is, therefore, not capable of being translated into the concepts of a post-Copernican space age.

(9)　There is no external, objective, revealed standard writ in scripture or on tablets of stone that will govern our ethical behavior for all time.

(10)　Prayer cannot be a request made to a theistic deity to act in human history in a particular way.

(11)　The hope for life after death must be separated forever from the behavior-control mentality of reward and punishment. The Church must abandon, therefore, its reliance on guilt as a motivator of behavior.

(12)　All human beings bear God's image and must be respected for what each person is. Therefore, no external description of one's being, whether based on race, ethnicity, gender, or sexual orientation, can properly be used as the basis for either rejection or discrimination.[2]

The Bible

The modern church has made friends with science and is still searching for how to make friends with the Bible. The Bible is often viewed suspiciously as a relic from the past. It may be basically discarded or radically reinterpreted. Thomas Jefferson simply cut out the "irrational" parts of the Bible to produce a truly "holey" Bible. Today's modern rational Christianity may look like the Jesus Seminar, which searched for the authentic words of Jesus in the four gospels in the New Testament and the Gospel of Thomas. They wanted to discover the real Jesus viewed "through the lens of historical reason and research rather than through the perspective of theology and traditional creedal formulations." They ended up with 18 percent of the 1,500 sayings traditionally ascribed to Jesus qualifying as probably or possibly said by Jesus.[3] They concluded the majority of the sayings attributed to Jesus "have been embellished or created by his followers, or borrowed from common lore."[4] Their research methods and conclusions are hotly debated by other modern scholars who opt for a much less drastic picture.[5]

The modern stage asks, "Why does the traditional church cling to a literally and factually interpreted Bible? On the surface, "The Bible says it. I believe it. That settles it." appears simply to be a religious belief. But underneath the language of belief is a whole constellation of things that make the traditional perspective what it is. This includes that what is right, good, and true is what one has grown up with or been converted to. The modern level understands that it is this *stage of consciousness,* not the Bible, that makes the traditional Christian cling to a literal interpretation of the Bible. For example, one can show that it is not reasonable to believe these two things are both true: (1) God is like the God of the Old Testament in terms of being vengeful, wrathful, and getting even with the wicked and (2) God is also like the *Abba* of Jesus, totally compassionate and merciful to all, including the wicked and ungrateful. Showing that a traditional stage belief in a God who is both loving and vengeful is not consistent with what Jesus taught and does not make much of an impression on the traditional consciousness. Looking for reasonable consistency with what Jesus taught is a rational modern stage understanding, not a traditional one. *We cannot see what our world-view will not allow.*

One cannot use reason to argue someone out of a position they did not arrive at by reason. This is why using reason to change a person's beliefs who is deeply embedded in the traditional religious level does not work. Their belief system was not arrived at primarily by reason and, therefore, reason may not touch it unless they are searching or in enough angst or pain to be open to the rational stage of spirituality. I believe that a major work of the Spirit for the last two thousand years has been to nudge the world into the rational stage. Most modern institutions have moved into the rational altitude with the challenging exception being the church.

God

Many of us who were nurtured in the traditional church relate to God in what I will call, in Chapter 12, the 2nd-person perspective of God—the Intimate Face of God. We sense that God is close to us, like another person such as Jesus or another "spiritual being." That is a powerful and authentic way to connect with God. Jesus said that if we saw him, we saw God. However, Jesus also said that God was greater than he was.[6] How are we to think about this "greater" God? This is the God that is beyond the personal or any personification. (I call this the Infinite Face of God in Chapter 12.) If we continue to think of this transpersonal God as a big supernatural being out there, we haven't yet come to the God that is greater than Jesus.

The supernatural theistic God is the God that is rejected at the modern rational level. That God is not big enough, or in Jesus' terms "great" enough, for either Jesus or the modern mind. This "small" God is one that is completely separate from creation, an all-powerful divine being in a heaven somewhere up there. Both the ancient and modern mind saw another vision of God that might be best be seen as "panentheistic." God is in everything and everything is in God. This is the God which Jesus said was greater than he was. This is the One about whom the apostle Paul said, "in whom we live, and move, and have our being."[7] Panentheism comes to the surface in the modern church and to its fullest expression in the postmodern church.

The worship service of the church at the modern level may still use some traditional forms and terms about God, but usually the leadership has decisively rejected God as a distinct supernatural being. The God of Spong reigns.

The God of the modern mind, in integral terms, is viewed primarily from a 3rd-person perspective. The idea of God can be studied and reflected upon, but a distinct supernatural God which one can personally relate to is not needed in the laws of universe. God is understood as something like "the Sacred" or "the Ground of All Being" or "Divine Creativity." Relating to God in 2nd-person practice often appears to resemble the traditional level too much to be taken very seriously by the modern viewpoint. A 1st-person perspective of seeing human beings as divine like Jesus may also be seen as unreasonable because even Jesus is usually not seen as divine. (See Chapter 12 for a fuller discussion of the three basic standpoints of 1st-, 2nd-, and 3rd-person.)

Jesus

The focus on Jesus as an historical human being takes the forefront when looking through the modern lens. Jesus is viewed as an extraordinary human being and an exceptional teacher of wisdom and love. There are serious questions about how much we can actually know about him in any accurate way. Reason tells those in the modern church that you can't seem to have church or Christianity without Jesus, but at the same time, the modern church is never quite sure what to do with him.

Prayer

Prayer is problematic at the modern level because prayer is traditionally thought of in 2nd-person terms of addressing God as a separate being, and that idea has been soundly rejected. Prayer may be understood as meditation, contemplation, or reflection. When I asked Bishop Spong about his prayer life, that is the answer I received.[8]

Questions about healing prayer often lead to a cessation of prayer for healing or a mixture of faith and doubt when praying. "Is this just magical or wishful thinking?"

At the modern rational stage, worship rituals may move from magic to meaning. Instead of doing something to you, baptism can become a wonderful symbol of blessing and welcome into the church. Instead of magically changing into Jesus' actual body and blood, Communion becomes the beautiful symbol of union with Christ and communion with others who are on that same journey.

Sin and Salvation

The word "sin," if used at all, means doing harm to others or ourselves. The idea of sin in the New Testament is understood as more of a legal term in Paul who was primarily concerned with putting Jews and Gentiles on equal footing. Both groups were "sinners" who needed Christ. Later on, Augustinian ideas of sin came into dominance, wrapped up in the introspective conscience of the West. Martin Luther is the prime example of becoming overly burdened with the weight of personal sin.[9] The modern idea of sin is focused strongly on social injustice and oppression.

By the time one reaches the modern level one has soundly rejected all of the five fundamentals of the warrior stage. Modern churches usually consider all people to be "saved" if we need saving at all, or at least destined for heaven, if there really is a "heaven."

Heaven and Hell

One cannot be sure if there is a heaven or if life continues after death. Death may just be a dissolution of molecules, but that's okay. There is no hell except for the one we create by our own lack of love and injustice to others.

The Kingdom of Heaven

The Kingdom of Heaven as a present dimension is now taken seriously. If we remove all the "spiritual" and "mystical" content from Jesus' life and teaching, what is left is his challenge to love, especially the vulnerable and oppressed. The Kingdom of Heaven is focused on social justice and liberation from oppression in this world, not necessarily the next. Liberation theology is very much a modern mindset.

The Mystical

If the traditional level believes that the only good mystic is a dead mystic, then the modern level believes that all mystics are hallucinating. Mysticism is usually considered irrational, and it is discarded. Mystics from other times and cultures were simply delusional. What is real is only what can be measured and observed in the physical world.

Limitations

The limitations of the modern church include a tendency to buy into our cultural materialism and self-centeredness. In making friends with science, the modern church has also at times become guilty of scientism. Scientism declares that the only way to know anything is through science. That statement is one of faith and not science since it cannot be verified scientifically. Scientism claims that if science can't prove it, then it doesn't exist. That's bad science.

This leads to the discounting of expanded states of consciousness which provide other authentic ways of knowing reality. A worldview that can't go deep into our souls or reach high into the infinite is limited. I use the term "flailing" for the modern church's limitations here because it is trying to be church with only one door open—a rational one. They are genuinely seeking the spiritual path, but the door of higher state experience is closed.

The modern church preaches social action because they are certain that Jesus went about doing good. Both Jesus and the modern church do that with passion and grace. But they are not as passionate about Jesus' connection to God, who or whatever God may be. They are often not very sure about Jesus' prayer life. Once you remove the vertical dimension of spirituality, only the horizontal is left. If you deny inner spiritual realities, all that's left of Christianity is doing good. "God" can then appear to be spelled with two "o's."

Strengths

I also see the modern church as "flourishing." The blossoming strengths of this kind of church include incorporating the value of science and reason along with faith. There is a strong interest in the historical Jesus and scientific method to help understand the Bible. Jesus has been newly discovered as a social revolutionary who sought liberation for the oppressed. The modern-level church advocates thinking for oneself. Other religions are seen as legitimate attempts to find spiritual meaning. People are seen first as human beings, regardless of race, color, class, creed, or sexual orientation. Human rights are crucial. This is the beginning of a worldcentric level.

At the modern level, individuals may become agnostic or atheist. This can be a healthy expression of spiritual evolution at this stage. I am not suggesting that all Christians who are going to move beyond the traditional stage must at some point become atheists. That is what can happen when they can't find anyone who is rational and still follows Jesus. I made my way through the modern rational stage while embracing the postrational mystical levels at the same time. It was an exhilarating adventure that did not require me to stop experiencing God while I revamped my understanding of God.

Each stage takes into account the value of the previous stage and then adds to it. Nothing of value is lost. Something new is added that increases the new stage's usefulness by adding expanded perspective, a more integrative consciousness, and greater capacity to love.

Wilber says, "As Hegel first put it, and as developmentalists have echoed ever since, each stage is adequate and valuable, but each deeper or higher stage is more adequate and, in that sense only, more valuable (which always means more holistic, or capable of a wider response).[10]

The modern level has flourished and magnificently benefited all of humankind, including the church.

CHAPTER 6

Postmodern Church
Fulfilling and Flat

Postmodern Consciousness

The postmodern station began roughly 150 years ago and became most noticeable in this country during the 1960s. Postmodernism is a general, much-debated term that is applied to many fields such as literature, art, philosophy, architecture, fiction, and cultural and literary criticism. It is a reaction to the modern idea that objective science can explain reality. Postmodernism understands that reality is not just something objective but that our minds also play a part in constructing what we think of as reality. It is skeptical of any universal claims or ultimate principles that claim to be true for everything. It makes the rather universal truth claim that there are no universal truth claims!

Coming into prominence with the Enlightenment, modern consciousness focused on questioning the foundations of past knowledge. Postmodern viewpoints question whether we can really know much of anything at all. The modernist bumper sticker advises, "Question Authority." The postmodern bumper sticker says, "Question Reality."

Modernism says there is absolute truth. Postmodernism says we construct our own truth. Modernism says that what is important are observable facts and logic. Postmodernism says that what is important are feelings and experience. Modernism limits itself to scientific exploration while postmodernism encourages spiritual exploration. Modernism says there are absolute values while postmodernism says that it's all relative.

Traditional consciousness allows for us to "Love your neighbor, hate your enemy," especially if your enemy is attacking you, or even just different from you. The modern level tells us to "Love your neighbor, tolerate your enemy." Postmodernism goes on to "Love your neighbor and love your enemy." In Jesus' terms, this is progress.

Postmodernism is the world of the sensitive self, the pluralistic worldview, and believing that there are many ways of looking at reality. It has given birth to the green earth movement, feminism, civil rights, and gay rights. Those at this altitude can see things from many perspectives and embrace a more inclusive compassion that thinks, feels, and acts globally. It moves beyond the mere tolerance of the modern level to embracing and honoring other religious traditions.

Some actively seek out other spiritual paths for their own enrichment. One begins to see commonalities among the religions of the world, not just differences. All ways are seen as equally valid. Because of this, there is a tendency to despise any kind of hierarchy that says anything is better than something else. Religious hierarchies are seen as especially oppressive. In the name of equality, all hierarchies tend to be rejected, including natural hierarchies.

Natural hierarchy is seeing that there is a natural development such as from atoms to molecules, cells to plants, or animals to humans. A natural hierarchy would be one that sees the traditional stage as better able to love others than the warrior stage. However, postmodernism often rejects the premise of integralism that there really are identifiable stages of development, considering it elitism.

The postmodern altitude, rather than seeing everything in black and white terms, is more comfortable with shades of gray and even paradox. We don't have to blow out anyone else's light in order for ours to shine. We can all shine together without judgment.

If we can see reality only through our interpretations, then interpretations are everything. Rather than claiming absolute truth, we are to celebrate the world of always-changing relationships among people and between people and the world.

Postmodern philosophy says that absolute truth cannot be discovered at all, neither through reason nor tradition. There is no objective meaning, only subjective meaning, the meaning one brings to anything. History is seen as merely various fictional interpretations. The postmodern worldview was cleverly summed up in an editorial cartoon that showed a boy sitting on Santa's lap. Santa is saying to him, "And have you been a good boy this year?" The boy replies, "It depends on what good means." In back of him a girl is thinking, "Sixty-five percent of my peers say I'm good." Another girl in the line says, "That's a private matter between me and my family." The last boy says, "It's time to move on to the real issue: what I want."[1]

Postmodernists say such things as, "There are no facts, only interpretations," "Nobody tells me what to do," "Your truth is as good as my truth," "I have no limits," and the foundation of them all—"We create our own reality." Sometimes there is a deep agony over the way things seem. Postmodernists see so much diversity that they can't see any unity. Postmodernists value community, consensus, and diversity. The rights of minorities are upheld so that a majority does not crush the minority.

Looking through the postmodern lens, one sees that there is more to life than thinking clearly and being rational. It again embraces the mystical and numinous, which was lost in the modern rational stage. Enchantment has returned. Networks and connections are often developed between others who share a similar interest in spirituality. Talks, workshops, and seminars on various aspects of human potential and spirituality are popular. Meditation, prayer, and the inner life are explored with new fascination.

However, in its rush to embrace mystery, it does not always distinguish mystical from magical. One is an authentic connection to what is real, the other is a fantasy. This new appreciation of the mystical sometimes moves into the fantastical. The New Age reigns!

The traditional level sees authority and God as something external. Individuals at the postmodern station in life tend to think more about God in terms of Spirit being everywhere and in everyone. Moving away from the Bible, churches, and religious leaders as authorities, there is a move to see one's own experience as authoritative for one's own life.

Postmodernity is seen in ecological awareness, political correctness, diversity movements, universal human rights, multiculturalism, humanistic psychology, liberation theology, and the human potential movement.

In its unhealthy form, postmodern worldviews can lead to extreme relativism where all beliefs are seen as relative and equally true, and all discernment is abandoned in the name of pluralism. Narcissism and meaninglessness abound, as well as the double standard contempt for those who do not hold postmodern views.

Healthy elements of postmodern altitude which have enduring desirability are embracing diversity, feminism, civil rights, spirituality, creativity, sensitivity, exploring the inner self, cherishing the earth, community, world compassion, and sharing the world's resources,

The postmodern stage is also called culturally creative, pluralistic, relativistic, individualistic, reflective, and "green" in other approaches. An estimated 5–10 percent of the world's population is here.

Postmodern Church

Postmodern religious thought was originally a reaction against mainstream Protestant liberalism. The cold idea of a religion that just "thinks" finally gave way to opening the door to dimensions that were warmer than reason alone. Reason was not discarded, but it no longer reigned as the only way to "know." Rationalism alone does not work anymore in the postmodern church.

While the modern level is filled with scientific exploration, the postmodern one is filled with spiritual exploration. Science said that seeing is believing. Postmodernism comes along and says that believing is seeing. There is a move from facts and logic to feelings and personal experience. This move is not always navigated well and some postmodern religion under the rubric of "New Age" includes elements of prerational magic along with postrational mysticism. There is a move from only the God of the Bible to considering the God (or non-deity) of other religious paths.

Postmodern churches are represented by the most progressive of the churches of the United Church of Christ and other mainline denominations. Also included are Unity, Religious Science, and other New Thought churches that still self-identify as Christian.

Speaking of the earlier (traditional) paradigm, and the emerging (postmodern) one, Marcus Borg says, "The division is so great that it virtually produces two different religions, both using the same Bible and the same language."[2] Here are a few snapshots of some of the common poses of postmodern churches.

The Bible

Postmodern churches sometimes tend to think of themselves as beyond the Bible. They are not against Jesus, but to take Jesus seriously means you have to dig into at least the canonical gospels, which gets you back into that awful Bible again. When they do look at the Bible, they find universal postmodern liberation themes. Jesus really does indeed look like a feminist in his day, and he spoke out for all the religiously, politically, and socially oppressed.

Marcus Borg is an outstanding model of the postmodern theologian who does take the Bible seriously. Concerning the Bible, Borg says, "Over the past century an older way of reading the Bible has ceased to be persuasive for millions of people, and thus one of the most imperative needs in our time is a way of reading the Bible anew."[3]

He describes the traditional stage understanding of the Bible as literalistic, doctrinal, moralistic, patriarchal, exclusive, and after-life oriented.[4] He sees the Bible as a combination of history and non-literal linguist art which he calls metaphor. In the postmodern stage one can see that the biblical stories can be true without having to be literally and factually true. Borg says, "The emerging paradigm's central features are a response to the enlightenment." Borg describes it as "a way of seeing the Bible (and the Christian tradition as a whole): historical, metaphorical, and sacramental. And a way of seeing the Christian life: relational and transformational."[5]

God

While agreeing, in general, with Spong's modern-stage theology, Borg warms things up spiritually in postmodern fashion by focusing on a relationship with God that is transforming.

Concerning God, Borg says, "God is not a supernatural being separate from the universe; rather God (the sacred Spirit) is a non-material layer or level or dimension of reality all around us. God is more than the universe, yet the universe is in God. Thus, in a spatial sense, God is not 'somewhere else' but 'right here.'"[6]

Borg holds three central convictions about God: (1) God is real; (2) the Christian life is about entering into a relationship with God as known in Jesus Christ; (3) that relationship can—and will—change your life.[7]

Panentheism reigns in the postmodern church as a way of understanding God. It is succinctly described in Acts 17:28 where Paul in Athens quotes from a local poet who says, "In him we live and move and have our being." This indicates that such an idea of God existed in the first-century Christian church.[8]

Theism is the view of God that sees God as separate from creation. Pantheism is the belief that God is everything and every part of creation. Panentheism offers a third way of viewing God with an emphasis on the middle syllable "en." God is in everything and everything is in God. God is in creation but is also greater than creation. I believe panentheism is the most advanced way of thinking about the Infinite Face of God that is compatible with both postmodernism and integralism.

Jesus

Jesus may or may not be central to the postmodern church. New Thought churches wrestle with this and some settle it by not talking about Jesus much at all or only along with Buddha and Krishna. Jesus may be seen as divisive and excluding those who are not followers of Jesus, and this does not fit the sometimes radical pluralism of this level. At the extreme postmodern level talking about Jesus can be almost taboo. I know of several Unity churches that have decided not to talk about Jesus because this appeared to exclude Buddhists and others from the spiritual path.

Christians looking through the postmodern lens are less likely to believe that the baby Jesus was God come down from heaven in bodily form and more likely to believe that Jesus grew up to be a wonderful person who realized and manifested his own divinity in a breakthrough way.

For those who remain open to Jesus, there can be an understanding that Jesus and Christ are two different descriptors. Jesus refers to the historical person who taught and lived in first-century Galilee. Jesus revealed an awareness of God that might be called the "Christ consciousness." The word "Christ" then becomes a description of "Spirit anointing" that not only Jesus had, but is available to, or already present, in everyone. Jesus is not only a great teacher and human being, but there is something about the Spirit that comes through him in an extraordinary way.

At this point, if one still considers a relationship with Jesus a vital part of the spiritual life, Jesus will be seen as incredibly loving and inclusive of everyone.

For the postmodern church, justice issues come alive in both the Old and New Testament. The Jesus of the postmodern church is a liberator. The prophets are valued and Jesus' parables are seen in the context of subverting the oppressive social/political structures of the day.[9]

Borg understands Jesus as a Jewish mystic, healer, wisdom teacher, social prophet, and movement initiator.[10] He reveals a warm, important Jesus who is full of life, saying:

> The Bible paints a picture of Jesus by making extraordinary claims about him. He is one with God and shares in the power of authority of God. He is the revelation of God. He is also the revelation of "the way," not only in John but also in the synoptics. He is the bread of life who satisfies the deepest hunger of human beings and the light shining in the darkness who brings enlightenment. He lifts us out of death into life. He is the World and Wisdom of God embodied in a human life. He is the disclosure of what a life full of God—a life filled with the Spirit—looks like. This is who Jesus is for us as Christians. Some modern Christians have been uncomfortable with these claims because they seem to partake of Christian triumphalism. But for Christians these claims should not be watered down. For us as Christians,

Jesus is not less than this—he is all of this. And we can say, "This is who Jesus is for us" without also saying, "and God is known only in Jesus." [11]

Prayer

Prayer for the postmodernist takes many different forms from ancient to contemporary. Go ahead and pray any way you like because everything is okay. Healing prayer becomes a recognition that every person has the capacity to send healing energy to another. Energy healing can be practiced and the results scientifically verified.

Sin and Salvation

Sin, if the word is used at all, at the personal level, is not living up to our own potential. At the systemic level it is the domination systems which oppress others. Human folly is described by Eckhart Tolle this way: "If the history of humanity were the clinical case history of a single human being, the diagnosis would have to be: chronic paranoid delusions, a pathological propensity to commit murder, and acts of extreme violence and cruelty."[12]

The postmodern church has moved away from the idea that only they have the truth. While God may be defined by Jesus, God is not confined to Jesus. At the modern level, other religions are tolerated. At the postmodern they are warmly embraced. Not only are they welcomed, but all spiritual paths lead equally to God, however that spiritual goal or God is defined. Everyone is correct within the worldview they inhabit. In extreme postmodern thought, terrorists are just operating within their worldview which is not to be devalued. This creates no small degree of angst and consternation among postmodernists.

Even the Roman Catholic Church has recently evolved. Jesuit priest William Johnston explains how it happened:

> Then came the Second Vatican Council (1962-1965). Overnight the Catholic Church which had been a Western institution exporting its wares to the East became a world

community. Asian and African bishops and theologians assembled in Rome and, with their European and American confreres, acknowledged that the Spirit of God is at work in all peoples and in all religions. Since then, most theologians recognize non-Christian religions as "valid ways."[13]

The postmodern Christian understands that everyone is already included in God's love. No one will be left behind.

Heaven and Hell

Heaven may be renamed nirvana, enlightenment, or internal peace. It is an inner experience. Death is a mystery and there is much speculation, especially from New Age writers, about what life after death is like. The idea of resurrection may be replaced by some concept of reincarnation. Our essence, our Authentic Self, is eternal and never dies but continues to emerge from ego constraints in new forms.

The word "hell" would not be used in a postmodern church, but the idea might be framed in terms of alienation. It is psychic estrangement from God and/or others.

The Kingdom of Heaven

In the postmodern church, as with the modern church, doing God's will here on Earth is the preferred goal of life rather than being saved from our sins. The Kingdom of Heaven is where God's will is done in the here and now as it is in Heaven. We may not need saving individually, but we do need to save the world and release the Kingdom of God into all of creation.

The Mystical

In the modern stage, even the most elevated mystical experiences of Jesus and others are seen as merely mythical. However, postmodernism thrives on spiritual experiences and embraces the mystical. Borg considers Jesus a spirit person. (However, in a conversation with Borg, I found he was quite suspect of personal spiritual experiences that sounded like owning one's own divinity.)[14]

There is such a pluralistic worldview in postmodernism that an anti-intellectual bias emerges which refuses to distinguish between competing truths. Hierarchies, natural or otherwise, are such an abomination to this level that they refuse to see that some truth may be "higher" or "more true" than others. Therefore, Jesus' teaching is just one among all the many other viewpoints, all of which have equal standing and are equally true. All sacred writings contain the truth, even if they are contradictory or prerational. Postmodernists do not always distinguish between prerational magical and postrational mystical. Everything is okay in postmodern theology. If traditional consciousness is black and white, then postmodern is gray, only gray, and unendingly gray.

Since the prerational magical stage and the postrational mystical stage are both nonrational they sometimes seem to be confused at the postmodern stage. The magical can be elevated to the mystical stage as when early tribal societies are romantically seen as paragons of advanced stages of spiritual growth.

Limitations

All stages have limitations. If they did not, then there would be no need for further evolution. Then whatever the current stage is would be fully the Kingdom of Heaven. So it is helpful to see the limitations of each stage so we can know where the possibilities are or our own growth and that there is more to come.

The primary weakness of the postmodern church is resistance to any kind of hierarchy. Jesus certainly resisted dominator hierarchies. However, he affirmed the natural hierarches that evolution brings to all areas of life. Molecules are more complex and able to function at a higher level than atoms. Humans are more complex and able to function at a higher level than monkeys. When Jesus said that "you have heard, but I say to you," he was pointing out a natural hierarchy in the spiritual realm. The new was fuller and more loving than the old.

Resisting natural hierarchies can lead to extreme relativism and a refusal to make value judgments. We feel guilty if we openly say this is better than that. Or this viewpoint is more advanced. The postmodern view can leave one very uncomfortable making those distinctions, because they appear to be judgmental. Postmodern religion is not the modern view that doesn't believe anything. Rather, postmodernism can believe in everything. That kind of religion can be three hundred miles wide and three inches deep.

Jesus never criticized any other religion. He was a good postmodern in that respect. On the other hand, he was devastatingly pointed in his criticism of his own religion. That was not very postmodern at all. He made clear distinctions between what he considered the best in his religion and the worst.

I call the postmodern church "flat" because nothing rises higher than anything else. There sometimes seems to be an uncritical acceptance of all values and practices. Yet, for all their inclusiveness, they are often angry at the tribal, warrior, traditional, and modern church.

The postmodern church also seems at times to embrace the narcissism in the message of "prosperity." The gospel of prosperity can easily turn into spirituality in the service of the ego.

Strengths

The vast strengths of the postmodern church include the embrace of the marginalized, diversity, personal growth, advocacy of justice issues, eco-friendliness, and altered states of consciousness. This makes it quite fulfilling in many important areas. It is also the beautiful and glorious launching place for the next stage, integral church.

However, before I can describe integral church, I need to deal with three other topics first—a different way of looking at the Bible, deeper *states* of consciousness, and the three basic *standpoints* in relating to God. Then I will describe my vision of integral church in Chapter 15, followed by chapters on *shadow* healing work and *steps* of transforming practice.

CHAPTER 7

Reading the Bible in a Jesus-Friendly Way

The Bible Is an Indispensable Resource

In an integral understanding, the Bible is a fascinating account of the evolutionary progress of the spiritual path. It is an indispensable resource for the integral church. Seen in a developmental perspective, the Hebrew Bible, which we Christians usually call the Old Testament, moves from magic and myth to meaning. What, to some, may seem like a mishmash of ancient stories, an angry god, and outdated rules, becomes a history of the development of spiritual awareness filled with sparkling gems of wisdom and insight for each evolving level.

When we understand the Bible in terms of stages of spiritual development we then have a way to appreciate and value the Bible in all of its aspects. The levels of faith which the Bible traces are all still with us today around the world and even in our own western culture. If we can understand the people in these stages thousands of years ago, we can better understand those at these levels today.

Two extreme positions

There are two extreme positions about the Bible today. One sees the Bible as a book that is without error, or at least not wrong about anything important. It was dictated or inspired by God in every word. The Bible contains the answer for every spiritual problem today. The other extreme views the Bible as a collection of old myths and fairy tales without much use today. This view tosses the Bible out as uninteresting and irrelevant.

For the Bible to be an essential resource for Integral Christianity and church it must be seen in terms of the evolving stages of spiritual development from the ancient Jewish people on out into the larger world of yesterday and today. Both traditional/conservative and modern/progressive Christians might consider a new position—one that integrates the partial truths that are in all previous viewpoints and transcends the less-than-Christ-like parts.

The New Testament Gospels are indispensable because they contain most of what we currently know of Jesus' life and teaching. The Gospel of Thomas is another rich resource that was written about the same time. Parts of it were most likely written even earlier than the canonical gospels and probably contain the most original sayings of Jesus. The Old Testament is crucial because it contains the context for Jesus' life and teaching. The rest of the New Testament is important because it is the interpretation of Jesus' life and teaching that came to dominance in the three centuries after Jesus. The Gospel of Thomas is of singular importance because of its early dating and its revelation of an early, seemingly, integral Jesus.

Integral understanding weaves together all the parts of the Bible into an understandable account that does not dilute or distort the teachings of Jesus. In addition, an integral Bible will point us away from previous lower stages of development and release us to more evolved levels of spiritual growth.

Progressive revelation?

A traditional approach to biblical scholarship often attempts to handle what I am saying here under the name of "progressive revelation." This is the idea that the New Testament was built on the Old Testament as a progressive revelation of new truth which supports, expands, and stands upon former revelations of God's truth. It is like brick-laying where every new brick is placed on the foundation of the previous ones.

However, there are four important differences between the idea of progressive revelation and the integral understanding of ongoing spiritual evolution. First, progressive revelation does not mean that anything revealed about God in the Old Testament is actually contradicted by what Jesus taught. Rather the Old Testament is just seen as incomplete. *In progressive revelation one never removes a previously laid brick.* But an evolutionary approach offers a sharper contrast at times between a previous stage and a later one. While each stage builds on the previous one by including parts of it, it also transcends or rejects parts of the previous one in sometimes decisive ways. The God of the Old Testament kills his enemies. The God of Jesus loves his enemies.

Secondly, progressive revelation is seen to stop with the closing of the final selection of books for the New Testament. There is no more revelation after that. An integral understanding of spiritual evolution is that it continues today and forever.

Thirdly, traditionalists do not apply the principle of varying levels of revelation to the New Testament itself. They see every word of the New Testament now as straight from God, never to be improved upon or evaluated as to its level of truth. A statement by Jesus in the gospels carries the same weight as a statement by Paul in one of his letters. They trade "Jesus is Lord" for "the Bible is Lord."

Finally, the traditional concept of progressive revelation would reject any revelatory value in other Christian writings or other religious traditions. An integral approach welcomes not only the highly evolved spiritual truths from Christian saints and mystics down through the centuries but also the most elevated truths from the other world religions.

This may be shocking

Next, I will be using what may seem, to some, to be harsh language to describe parts of the Bible. This is to point out more sharply the differences between "progressive revelation" and the integral understanding of transcending and including in the ongoing stages of spiritual evolution. My purpose is not to make fun of those who believe differently than I do about these parts, or to fuel the anger of those who are already upset by the traditional view of the Bible. My purpose is to shock those who are ready for it into considering Jesus' message in a new way. I want to invite the traditionalist who takes the Bible more seriously than Jesus to rethink that position and opt for Jesus. I want to invite the modernist and postmodernist who identify Jesus only with the traditional level to take another look. In my understanding, an integral Jesus is the foundation of the integral church.

The Evolving Path of the Old Testament

The Warrior Stage

The first book of the Bible, Genesis, paints a picture of people moving from the tribal stage of development to the warrior stage. This is followed by the beginning of the traditional stage with the laws of Moses. We see elements of all three levels. As the history of the Jewish people begins, much of life was beyond understanding, and people believed they were at the mercy of numerous gods and spirits which controlled everything in their world. These gods and spirits of magic and superstition had to be bribed and cajoled into not hurting them and, if possible, helping them. Religion was concerned with making sacrifices, sometimes of humans, to appease the angry gods. People bonded together into tribes for protection both against the warrior-like threat of the magical world of the gods and of other tribes. Fear dominated the tribal and warrior consciousness.

As Genesis begins, the most powerful and violent warrior of all is God. According to the biblical writers in their early accounts of humankind, God decided upon a massive flood in his war to wipe out the wicked and to start over with populating the earth. Genesis reports that one of the reasons God sent this devastation was that "the earth was filled with violence."[1] When the warrior God does not like violence, he violently kills everyone! (As the bumper sticker so eloquently states, "Why do we kill people who kill people to teach them that killing people is wrong?")

As the account goes, the divinely caused flood killed all the people of the world except for Noah and his family. As we now retell the story in Sunday School, it usually focuses on how wonderful

God is for saving Noah and his family and promising never again to send such devastation. Those who want us to believe that this God is coming from the same perspective as the Abba of Jesus have an insurmountable problem.

Suppose a terrorist was going to destroy a major office complex with thousands of people it in. However, before the explosion he warns one family to get out first. Then he blows up the entire center, killing everyone in it. Would we marvel at the terrorist's compassion in saving one family—or be horrified at the destruction of thousands? Would we exonerate him if he promises never to do it again? Would the newspaper headlines read, "Wonderful Man With Bomb Saves Family. Vows to Never Blow Up Anyone Else Again?" That sounds absurd. But it is precisely what we have done with the God portrayed in the flood story to soften his image into something a little more compatible with Jesus. God is pictured as the gracious savior of one family who makes a promise not to be as violent again. From a higher, more loving perspective, this God appears as a monstrous killer of genocidal proportions.

However, from the perspective of those in the tribal and warrior stage, this makes perfect sense. God can only be interpreted through the lens of magic and warrior-like vengeance because that is the only lens available at the time. Only a warrior-like God could effectively communicate with a warrior-like people. *It is this very warrior God who challenges the people to move forward in their spiritual development!*

At another point early in the biblical history, according to the biblical writers, God orders Abraham to offer up his only son Isaac, whom he loves, as a burnt offering. Human religious sacrifice was common among the tribes in the area. Without arguing, Abraham takes his son to the mountaintop, binds him to an altar, and raises his knife, ready to kill him, believing this is what God has commanded. Then comes the successful conclusion as an angel intervenes at the last minute to tell Abraham that he has passed the test of devotion to God. He is now a model of true spirituality and faith for all future generations.

What if any of us saw an Abraham today on the roof of his house, raising a knife over a young boy? From our level of consciousness it is fair to say that we would call the police, wrestle him down, and expect the Department of Children and Family Services to take his son away and charge the man with child abuse. We would do all of that no matter how much the man claimed God ordered him to do this, because our modern sensibilities and system of law has emerged from the tribal and warrior systems. When many of those same modern people go to their traditional-stage churches, they often unconsciously change worlds and believe that their God is really like the deity in this story.

However, seen from a developmental perspective, the story of Abraham and his son was *a breakthrough in spiritual evolution.* At this point in human history it was a move away from human sacrifice. Later, in a brilliant step that moves forward with Abraham's discovery that he did not need to sacrifice his son to God, Moses introduces a new level of spiritual development: There is only one God and that God does not want human sacrifices. Now only animal and grain sacrifices are required to please a warrior God and keep his anger in check.

Warrior God at work

Here are more indications of the warrior stage with God identified as the avenging warrior. "On the way, at a place where they spent the night, the Lord met him (Moses) and tried to kill him."[2] One would think that if God wanted you dead, he could get it done.

Later, Moses did feats of violent magic to convince Pharaoh to let the Israelites out of Egyptian bondage. At God's direction, there were plagues of bloody water, frogs, gnats, flies, diseased cattle, boils, thunder and hail, locusts, darkness, and finally God killed all the Egyptian firstborn males. "At midnight the Lord struck down all the firstborn in the land of Egypt."[3]

These firstborn included all the ordinary Egyptians and others who had nothing to do with keeping the Israelites in slavery. The biblical writers said that God not only caused all these disasters, God was even the one who made the Pharaoh resistant to letting the people go. God "hardens his heart."[4]

This is consistent with the magical view of God described in

1 Samuel 1:14 where God sent an evil spirit to torment Saul. Isaiah also recorded that God was the author of both good and evil. "I am the Lord, and there is no other. I form light and create darkness, I make weal and create woe; I, the Lord, do all these things."[5]

Joshua also portrays God behind all things, good and bad: "For it was the Lord's doing to harden their hearts so that they would come against Israel in battle, in order that they might be utterly destroyed, and might receive no mercy, but be exterminated, just as the Lord commanded."[6]

Moses introduces the law and order stage

Next, the inspired Moses introduces the Israelites to the laws by which they were to live. This is a new level where life was to be governed by rules which would begin to move them from the warrior stage into the "law and order" stage. This is the beginning of what we are calling the "traditional" level. The laws of the Israelites are described in the detail in the next four books of the Torah: Exodus, Leviticus (mostly narrative), Numbers, and Deuteronomy.

The warrior God still hangs around

In spite of the new laws, the divine violence continued and the warrior stage was still dominant. It takes a long time for a culture to move from one stage to another. For instance, God is perceived as saying: "For I will hand over to you the inhabitants of the land and you shall drive them out before you. You must utterly destroy them. Show them no mercy."[7]

Numbers records this: "When the Israelites were in the wilderness, they found a man gathering sticks on the Sabbath day. Then the Lord said to Moses, 'The man shall be put to death; the entire congregation shall stone him outside the camp.'"[8]

Among the 150 Psalms there are many wonderful words such as those found in Psalm 23 which give us comfort and inspiration. These must be distinguished from among the over one hundred war songs in the Psalms about enemies, hate, and destruction done in God's name. Here are two of them: "Let sinners be consumed from the earth, and let the wicked be no more. Bless the Lord, O my soul. Praise the Lord!"[9] Another passage from Psalms says, "Happy shall they be who take your little ones and dash them against a rock."[10]

There are six hundred passages of explicit violence in the Old Testament and one thousand verses that describe God's own violent actions in punishing humankind. There are one hundred passages where God expressly commands his followers to kill people.

Divine violence dominates the image of God

Jack Nelson-Pallmeyer concludes that violence is easily the most prominent theme in the Bible and the dominant characteristic of God.[11] It seems that outside of all the murder and killing, the Bible is a great book!

If you acted today as God is described as acting in the Old Testament, you would be called criminally and pathologically insane and put away. I make this rather severe criticism of the Bible in order to invite Christians to be more faithful to Jesus' teaching. If Jesus' words that God is kind and merciful to the wicked are true, then these hundreds of passages about divine violence cannot also present a true picture of God for us today.

Loving the Bible

I grew up loving the Bible. I was president of my high school Bible club (in the 1950s they had such things) and rather courageously carried my Bible on top of my other books every day of those four years. I still love the Bible but only because I have come to a viewpoint that allows me to make Jesus lord of my life and thinking, as opposed to my previous understandings of God that were less than Christ-like.

An old acquaintance from my high school Bible club days e-mailed me as I was working on this book. He was interested in what had happened to his old Bible club leader. I realized he still held the same view of the Bible that I did back then, so I hesitated to disillusion him. But I still believe in "witnessing" and I wanted to invite him to another viewpoint. I suggested he look at my website (www.revpaulsmith.com) to see where I was coming from. He e-mailed me back and asked why I had "left the literal understanding" of the Bible. I replied:

> I left the literal interpretation of the Bible when I decided to follow Jesus instead of a literal Bible. Before that I had been trying to reconcile Jesus' understanding of God with the Old Testament and parts of the New. Jesus' Abba was unconditionally loving and inclusive. The angry and vengeful God of the Old Testament, and parts of the New, were simply incompatible with my understanding of Jesus. I was tired of trying to reconcile God wiping out most of the human race in the flood, and commanding others to be brutally killed with the Jesus revealed in the same Bible. I could not reconcile a God who sends most people to hell with what Jesus taught and modeled about that God. So my commitment to be faithful to Jesus won out. My spiritual understanding and growth has increased tremendously since I decided that thirty years ago.

He responded with:

> I went through the same questioning but just figured there was no way our finite minds could understand that infinite all-knowing Mind, so I feel that's what faith and trust is all about. God doesn't need to explain everything to us. As my psychology professor used to say, "Maturity is the ability to accept the ambiguities of life."

His response, although couched in the language of faith and trust, was basically that his commitment and trust in a literal Bible was greater than his trust in and commitment to Jesus Christ. I still love the Bible because now I see it in a new way.

The prophets push for further spiritual evolution

The Old Testament shows us that great leaders like Abraham and Moses were willing to listen to the Spirit's call to evolve, even if it was radically new. Even more liberating visions of new light came from those great souls called "prophets." The prophets heard the call of the Spirit for the people to evolve toward a higher spiritual path. They cried out against oppression and urged compassion. They pointed out, with dramatic feminine images, the great themes of God's great womb-like compassion[12] and her covenant with the people.

They showed God wrestling with the Israelites to bring them up to their potential to be a blessing and a light for all the nations.[13] The prophets pointed out that God had blessed Israel so they could be a blessing to all nations. The Spirit, through these awakened (for their time) men, was attempting to move the people from their ethnocentric tribal level to a worldcentric view.

They also aimed their more evolved prophetic insight at the Temple sacrificial system established previously by Moses. They declared that God desired "steadfast love and not sacrifice, the knowledge of God rather than burnt offerings."[14] Jesus was quoting Hosea when he confronted the religious leaders saying, "Go and learn what this means," "I desire mercy and not sacrifice.'"[15]

The angry, war-like God of the Old Testament was appropriate to the warrior/egocentric stage of spiritual development at the time. This was necessarily the way God was perceived. Even when perceived as an angry warrior, God was pushing "his" followers up to new levels that were breakthroughs for that time and culture.

In the midst of the story of the spiritual development of the Israelites are wonderful spiritual insights and wisdom. We are so familiar with the incredible passages of beauty of inspiration from the Old Testament that I will not list them. Would we want to do without Psalm 23 or Genesis 1 or Isaiah 52? However, my point has been that we have heard a great deal about these lofty passages, but the angry passages are either glossed over or interpreted in a way that ignores how they contradict Jesus' view of God.

Then Comes Jesus

Jesus practiced integral philosophy. I am not suggesting that he saw and articulated it the way we do. But he practiced an amazing form of it appropriate for the culture and time in which he lived. Jesus pointed to *stages* of spiritual development.

Jesus entered into the life of the Jewish people when they were well established in the law of Moses. This does not mean they lived it perfectly, but rather they saw life primarily through the perspective of the law. This was literally the law and order stage of the traditional consciousness. The religion Jesus grew up with was set in the stone of the Torah. It could not be changed. Reinterpreted, yes, but not changed.

Jesus insisted on change

Jesus taught a different model that not only allowed for change, but insisted upon it! It was an evolutionary model that introduced a new level of spiritual development. He said: "You have heard it said . . . but I say to you . . . ." Jesus recognized a previous level of understanding and now there was a new one which he was announcing: "In the old stage you heard it said, but in this new stage I say to you . . . ."

Jesus said that they had heard from ancient times that you shall not murder.[16] That was a good law. However, he moved it to an even higher stage by pointing to their inward attitude. He said they should not even live in anger.

Jesus said that you have heard it said that you should not commit adultery.[17] Then Jesus moved it up to a higher internalized level by telling them that they should not look at a woman, who was considered property, with the intent of stealing or possessing her.

Jesus announced that he was transcending the dominant theme of violence in the Old Testament when he reminded people that they had heard it said: "An eye for an eye and a tooth for a tooth."[18]

This law of "just retaliation" was itself up a level higher from the previous standard which allowed violent retaliation that could even involve killing someone who took out your eye or knocked out your teeth. Jesus moved the concept of just retaliation up to an even more enlightened stage by saying that one should not retaliate at all.[19] He clearly rejected the old law stated in the Torah and gave a new one in its place.

The most radically profound change

The most profound change from the previous stage of spiritual development is found in Jesus' words which began, "You have heard that it was said, 'You shall love your neighbor and hate your enemy.'"[20]

Where had they heard to hate your enemy? On almost every page of their Scriptures! Throughout their Jewish history God hated God's enemies and God taught the Israelites to hate their enemies.

Now listen for the radically new image of God in what Jesus taught:

> But I say to you, Love your enemies, and pray for those who persecute you, so that you may be children of your Father-Mother in heaven; for God makes the sun rise on the evil and on the good, and sends rain on the righteous and on the unrighteous. For God is kind to the ungrateful and the wicked. Be merciful, just as your Father-Mother is merciful.[21]

Jesus not only taught a radically new stage of unconditional love toward one another, he based it on a new perspective about God. He rejected the previous perception of God as violent and vengeful to the wicked which runs throughout the Old Testament. The new perspective is that God is kind and merciful to the wicked. Jesus modeled this and taught this. He stood in direct opposition to the divine violence of the Old Testament and, later on, parts of the New Testament. "Kind and merciful" was Jesus' attitude toward the "sinners" of his day. The essence of his own relationship to his Abba God was that God was compassionate—not vengeful. Jesus practiced and preached this. If God practiced what Jesus preached, then God is *not* vengeful as the Old Testament vividly and repeatedly portrays. According to the new developmental stage introduced by Jesus, God is *only* compassion, not a strange blend of both mercy *and* revenge. Many followers of Jesus have yet to come to believe that God practices what Jesus preached.

The traditional-level understanding that the Bible reveals God on every page must be relinquished if one is going to move to the next level of Jesus' modern rationality. It simply is not rational, and does not look rational to modern people to think one can hold both the perspective of Jesus that God was unconditionally loving and an opposite perspective that God is sometimes loving and sometimes vengeful.

Fulfilled, expired, and transcended

According to Jesus, some of the inspired words in the Bible were now expired. Jesus stated the developmental stage principle again this way as recorded in the most Jewish of the Gospels, Matthew: "Do not think I have come to abolish the law or the prophets: I have come not to abolish but to fulfill. For truly I tell you, until heaven and earth pass away, not one letter, not one stroke of a letter will pass from the law until all is accomplished."[22]

What is the "all" that needed to be accomplished? It is the work of the law and the prophets. The people had learned and done what they were supposed to do in the "law and order" stage. They had moved their center of gravity from warrior to the more civilized traditional conformist stage.

What did Jesus mean that he came to "fulfill"? The word "fulfill" here means, according to one scholarly resource, that Jesus "has come in order that God's Word may be completely fulfilled, in order that the full measure appointed by God Himself may be reached in Him."[23] When "God's Word" is fulfilled, or has done what it was intended to do in the traditional law and order stage, then the next thing, "the full measure," is ready to be inaugurated. This was the next stage, which Jesus came to usher in. This is integralist thinking—include the good from a previous stage and transcend what needs to be left behind.

One can say that when we were in the infancy stage, that stage was fulfilled when we did the things infants need to do and learn—a healthy weight gain, a certain degree of physical growth, emotional bonding with parents, etc. When that stage is fulfilled, successfully navigated, then we are ready for the next stage of babyhood. It is time to transcend infancy. If any of those things do not happen, that is, are not fulfilled, then we are in trouble and will have great difficulty in moving to later, more complex stages. When we were teenagers we hopefully embraced and fulfilled the angst and complexity of the adolescent stage enough so that we were ready to transcend adolescence and move on to the adult level. If we did not move through adolescence successfully, we could be stuck there and not ready for authentic adulthood. *"Fulfilling" means the task has been successfully completed and it is time to move to the next level.*

Jesus said that he "did not come to abolish the law." Jesus did not come to do away with the traditional stage. In the integral perspective, every stage has a vital function that is absolutely necessary. One does not abolish infancy or adolescence when they are fulfilled. One simply builds upon them, includes and then transcends them. They are an important part of a stage of development that must be embraced and successfully navigated before the next stage can properly emerge. This is so literally true at a psychosocial level that developmental psychologists have identified this stage Jesus was speaking of and call it a "conformist" or "law and order" stage. We must all, somewhere between the ages of seven and adolescence, pass through it if we are to become well-adjusted adults. Children who do not "fulfill" this stage end up not getting civilized. Entire cultures can be in the "law and order" stage. People in the warrior stage must move to "fulfill" the traditional/law and order stage in order to become civilized if they are to move to even higher stages.

Jesus honored the previous stage and its accomplishments while recognizing the need to move beyond it. He said, "Among those born of women no one has arisen greater than John the Baptist; yet the least in the kingdom of heaven is greater than he. From the days of John the Baptist until now the kingdom of heaven has suffered violence, and the violent take it by force."[24]

John, in his prophetic cry to repent "Old Testament style," represented the warrior stage which approached the spiritual realm in a "violent" way. Jesus affirmed that John was a great man for that stage. Then he decisively announced the new stage—*a vision of the realm of God that had no violence in it at all!* Jesus says that John's "violent" approach at this new stage meant that "the least in the kingdom of heaven is greater than he."

Jesus honored Moses and then transcended him by rejecting parts of the Mosaic tradition. Paul honored the law and then radically transcended it. He said that the "law" stage was necessary until the stage that Jesus brought. ("Therefore the law was our disciplinarian until Christ came.")[25]

The Jewish people had lived with the law stage long enough that they had embraced it. That is not to say they "did" it perfectly. We never get a stage down perfectly but we get enough to know and understand it, to see life from that perspective. It was time now for Jesus to introduce the rational and postrational mystical levels.

We cannot go around or over stages of spiritual growth. We can only go through them and "fulfill" them if we are to develop. We simply cannot move into stage five when we are at stage two because we "cannot bear it now."[26] We can only get to stage five by going through stages two, three, and four. Then we are ready for level five. We must learn each altitude until we get it or "fulfill" it in New Testament terminology, and then we are ready for the next one.

Jesus transcends the old religious systems

Jesus also transcended the all-pervasive Temple sin/sacrifice system with its priests and sacrificial offerings. He aligned himself with the prophetic stream of the Old Testament as Hosea, Amos, and Micah proclaimed that God desired "steadfast love and not sacrifice, the knowledge of God rather than burnt offerings."[27] Jesus was quoting these prophets when he confronted the religious leaders by saying, "Go and learn what this means, 'I desire mercy and not sacrifice.'"[28]

He forgave sins in the name of God which only priests in temple could do. Even more threatening for some in the traditional stage today, Jesus announced that unrepentant sinners were already forgiven![29] Imagine, if God has already forgiven us, that is more good news than our current traditional sin/repentance/salvation system can handle!

Jesus moved away from the outward observance of rigid purity rules that attempted to separate Jews from Gentiles in ways that no longer were needed. Instead he moved them to a deeper level of an internal attitude of purity of heart.

He transcended the distant God of Moses to the family image of a close personal relationship with a loving father and, most radically, to the Spirit within.

He rejected the cultural disparagement and oppressive treatment of certain groups of people such as women. He went out of his way to include those who did not share his particular religion such as the Samaritans and a Roman centurion. He welcomed the social outcasts, the prostitutes, the tax collectors, the sick, the lepers, and the poor.

Jesus moved his religion up to a new level by transcending parts of it and including other parts. This is a model for all of us in any of the historic religious traditions.

Early church leaders wrestled with the divine violence of the Old Testament

Some of the early Christian leaders were aware of the significant differences between Jesus and the religion based on the Torah and the Prophets. Marcion was one of these. He concluded the differences were so great that the God of the Old Testament was simply a different God than the one Jesus served.[30] However, an integral understanding simply sees this as two different understandings of God which come from two different levels of consciousness. It is not two different Gods, but two different perspectives on the Ultimate Mystery we call God.

Paul pointed to this cognitive part of spiritual development when he wrote, "Be transformed by the renewing of your minds."[31] God is after our transformation and Paul gives us one clue about it. The renewing of our minds leads us into the ever upwardly evolving spiral of divine awareness, of seeing things more from God's point of view and less from our ego's limited one. While we must eventually move into actually experiencing it to inhabit a new level, we can usually grasp an intellectual understanding of the next level before we move into it.

Jesus predicted further stages of understanding

Finally, Jesus pointed to the next stages of the ever-evolving spiritual life when he said:

I have many things to say to you, but you cannot bear them now. When the Spirit of truth comes, that Spirit will guide you into all the truth.[32]

In integral language, Jesus was saying there are more stages. There is more evolution to come if you will listen to the Spirit. At the very least, Jesus spoke of three stages—the past stage, the present stage, and the next stage. I believe he was suggesting there will be many more "stages" and that the Spirit will never stop teaching us. This means an endless succession of unfolding waves of ever more encompassing love and liberation.

Jesus revealed a profound understanding of developmental levels. He said that we literally cannot "bear" the next stage until we have thoroughly engaged the previous stage. We simply cannot comprehend the next stage until we have understood the previous one. Stages cannot be skipped. Someone said to me, "What can I do to get my friend over the stage he is in now?" I said, "You can't get anyone over a stage. You can only help them through it."

The Apostle Paul spoke of the gradual change involved in the spiritual path when he wrote, "All of us, with unveiled faces, seeing the glory of the Lord as though reflected in a mirror, are being transformed into the same image from one degree of glory to another.[33] This is a beautiful way of talking about what we are calling developmental stages. We are moving toward looking like Christ as we change by degrees to that very same image.

Surely the "more things" that the Spirit will teach us will be just as revolutionary and exciting as what the Spirit had to show us through the human Jesus two thousand years ago. It will be just as challenging and liberating. Will we be able to bear it? Will we be willing hearers? Will we be looking for the "more things?" Are you a part of the church that is searching for the "more things?" Integral church understands that the Spirit comes to us not from the past but from the future. The Spirit draws us into the yet-to-unfold future. I can't wait!

Jesus comes from a higher stage

Jesus' view of what we are calling developmental stages was summed up in the vast understanding behind his words from the cross, "Father, forgive them for they know not what they do."[34] Jesus could forgive those who were crucifying him because he saw where they were coming from. They were not at the place yet where they had awakened to who Jesus was and the power of the systems that crucified him. What they were doing made sense at the law and order traditional level. They simply could not see beyond that to what Jesus saw.

Notice that Jesus was free to be angry when he saw *others* being oppressed. He blasted the religious leaders who told lies in the name of God. He angrily attacked the Temple system which excluded the Gentiles from worship by carrying on the temple business in the only part of the temple they could worship in. He shouted, "My house shall be a house of prayer *for all nations*."[35]

Yet when attacked personally by those very systems that led to his crucifixion, he did not take it personally. He understood where the soldiers who nailed him to the cross were coming from. He understood where the religious leaders were coming from. He saw the big picture and, therefore, understood the place the religious, social, and political systems had in the ongoing development of his culture. What was his understanding?

It was, "Father, forgive them for they know not what they do." He expressed in these profound words his overall attitude and understanding of what we are calling the stages of development of his day. The people simply did not "know." They were unaware. They were unconscious. They were asleep. They were unenlightened. There are many ways to express this great truth that is always running in the background behind every program in the software system of our lives.

What was it they did not know? They did not know how the world looked from higher stages. *We can only know what our worldview allows us to know.*

When we understand that spiritual growth comes in waves or levels, then we realize we can only see the world from the stage we are at. The bigger, more compassionate, more inclusive, more truthful view of the next stage is not yet present in us. It can be "near." As Jesus told one person, "You are not far from the Kingdom." But until it is present within us, we will not "know." The greater perspective is not ours until we enter the land and take it.

Solving the problems of one stage requires the next stage

Einstein is reported to have said that we cannot solve a problem from the same stage which created it. The problems of a religious, social, and political system that would crucify pure goodness such as Jesus could not be solved by seeing the world from that place. The people, from the soldiers carrying out orders, to the religious and political leaders who instigated them could only see the world from their prerational, mythic level. Since Jesus saw the world from a considerably higher level, he also saw that they could not understand him. He had come to lead them into that "knowing," but they were not there yet. The integral level is the first level that looks around in the awareness of where people really are and kindly says, "They really *don't* know what they are doing. When they attack me, they don't know what they are doing, so I don't need to take it personally. When they attack others furiously, I will speak out against those attacks in order to break their hold on the oppressed. But behind it all are people who are simply viewing the world from where they are." It was from this viewpoint that Jesus recognized the liberating truth that they, indeed, did not know what they were doing.

It is true for us, too, no matter how aware, enlightened, or conscious we are. There are some things about which we "don't know what we are doing." We cannot know from our current perspective. In this book I am advocating an integral stage of understanding. Nevertheless, there is a post-integral, and a post-post-integral yet to unfold. In the coming years, looking back from those yet to unfold levels, we will then be able to see how much "we did not know" right now. Understanding this profound truth opens us to a kinder, gentler understanding of the world. This is a call to move on up to the next level. Grow up some more! Move on up to where the problems we have created can actually be solved. The world can only be changed from the inside out. This is the Spirit's call to evolve.

After Jesus, Come His Interpreters

The New Testament documents the rise—and fall—of spiritual consciousness as Jesus breaks through to an incredible new high. Jesus' interpreters sometimes grasp his message and sometimes do not. Often they reinvented it at a lower level because their consciousness was at that level. This was not all bad, because people have a need to slowly—oh so slowly—move along one stage at a time. Unless those who take the Bible seriously see that these interpreters have moved to a lower level they will move there with them and try to blend the lower level with the higher. This distorts the message of Jesus.

Here are three examples of New Testament writers reverting to the previous warrior stage of a vengeful God from the Gospel of John: "Whoever disobeys the Son will not see life, but must endure God's wrath." [36] This is the gospel writer's commentary and reflects a lower stage, inconsistent with Jesus.

From the second letter to the Thessalonians: "For it is indeed just of God to repay with affliction those who afflict you . . . inflicting vengeance on those who do not know God. These will suffer the punishment of eternal destruction."[37]

And from the book of Revelation, "I heard a loud voice from the temple telling the seven angels, 'Go and pour out on the earth the seven bowls of the wrath of God.'"[38]

These are clearly warrior level revisions of Jesus and his teaching.

All things must be discerned

As with all messages that purport to be from God, including the Bible, we must do the work of spiritual discernment. These three passages represent a lower understanding of Jesus' life and teaching as the writers of the gospels and the other books of the New Testament shaped and interpreted Jesus' message to fit their awareness and their particular viewpoint. But his original message keeps shining through for those able to see it.

PART II
STATES

States are modes of consciousness. The types of consciousness we are most familiar with are wakefulness, dreaming, and dreamless sleep. Right now in reading this, you are in a waking state of consciousness. We also are aware of altered states of consciousness such as deep prayer or quiet meditation. There are drug-induced states where one is drunk or hallucinating. We can temporarily move into an intense problem-solving state or creative artistic flow. Viewing a spectacular landscape or listening to great music can move us into a passionate and altered mode of awareness. In this section we will be examining states of consciousness that are associated with spiritual experiences.

CHAPTER 8

The Spirit Zone
Moving into the flow

The next time you are at an exciting sports event, musical performance, or movie, look around at the spectators. Wildly excited participants at rock concerts or quiet listeners at a symphony orchestra performance can both move into an awareness that is so concentrated on the music that all other awarenesses drop away.

A gripping movie may have us glued to the screen, totally immersed in the drama that is unfolding in front of us. These are ordinary examples of getting into a "zone" or "flow."[1]

At a closely played ballgame, you can observe those around you who are caught up in the excitement and focused attention of the game. The players themselves often enter what is called a "zone." They move out of their heads and into a zone where their playing is so focused and in a state of flow that they perform above their normal ability.

Researchers examined over 300 athletes' "ideal performance state" by asking the athletes to describe their "finest hour" in sport participation. The researches identified 12 different things the athletes experienced when they were in the zone: physical relaxation, mental calm, low anxiety, heightened energy, optimism, enjoyment, effortlessness, automatic functioning, alertness, mental focus, self-confidence, and control.[2] Those 12 elements are amazingly similar to what mystics and those who pray deeply down through the centuries have experienced.[3]

The Spirit zone

What I am calling the "Spirit zone" goes by many names such as non-ordinary states, elevated levels of awareness, deep meditative states, direct experiences with God, transcendent awareness, ecstatic states, the numinous, or trances.

These peak spiritual experiences happen spontaneously when we move into the flow of the Spirit. Our group discussants reported:

"I was reading a book in bed when suddenly it seemed like I was floating and a part of everything. I couldn't tell where I stopped and everything else began. I felt so peaceful and alive, like I was waking up from a long, long sleep."

"I was praying while walking in a beautiful nearby park. At one point, I realized I was not just seeing the earth as dirt and rocks, but it seemed more like a living Presence. I became aware of having never been born and never dying. I felt a part of eternal life and there was no time or space. This lasted several minutes."

"I went to bed thinking about a problem I was wrestling with. Sometime during the night I woke up with a flash of brilliant insight bursting into my head that seemed to solve the problem. I don't know where it came from but it was amazing."

"I was singing a hymn in church when I felt this uplifting joy. I suddenly felt like I could do anything I set my mind to. It was a wonderful moment."

"I was sitting at a bus stop when suddenly I felt love pouring from me into everything around me. I stopped being angry with various people, from politicians to former friends, and was now full of compassion and understanding. I saw that there were no evil people, just ignorance and hurt. I continued to feel like that even when I got on the bus and pretty much the whole day. The intensity of that feeling was gone the next day but something seemed to still linger on for several days."

Spiritual experience is widespread

Many people have these "zone" experiences in the spiritual realm. Well over 75 percent of people, according to many polls, have had some kind of mystical, spiritual, religious, or altered state experience.[4] One in every five people says that they have heard God's voice.[5] An August 2005 poll on religion and spirituality conducted by *Newsweek* magazine found that 75 percent of all individuals considering themselves religious were earnestly looking for personal contact and union with God or a Higher Power such as Buddha. This included an immediate transcendent experience, a personal relationship with Spirit, and the transformation such experiences might deliver. Andrew Weil, M.D., believes that the need to experience transcendent states is more powerful that the need for sex.[6]

Mary, Martha, and Jesus Minds

We can distinguish three states of awareness by looking at the story of Mary and Martha in Luke 10. Jesus visits a woman named Martha in her home. Mary, Martha's sister, was also there sitting at Jesus' feet as he spoke. She was entranced, experiencing Jesus' powerful presence and listening to his words. She was bathed in God's presence in and through Jesus.

In the meantime, Martha was busy being a hostess and getting things done. At one point, she complains to Jesus that Mary has left her to do all the work and Jesus should tell Mary to help out. Jesus points out to Martha that she is worried and distracted and also missing a great opportunity to connect with him and the wisdom and presence of God that he brings. "Mary," he says, "has chosen the better part, which will not be taken away from her." Jesus calls attention to a simple fact: Martha's busyness has taken her away from something wonderful. Mary had decided that nothing was going to distract her from this opportunity to connect with Jesus. Martha stayed in ordinary, everyday awareness. Mary moved into the connecting level of spiritual awareness which led her to experience a deep connection with Jesus.

Here are the three major states of consciousness all in one setting. First, Martha is going about her day in *ordinary, everyday awareness* with what may be, for her, a regular way of complaining, whining, and playing the victim.

Mary, on the other hand, is enchanted with Jesus, completely focused on him, and tuned into something that is spiritually awakening for her. She is *connected* to Jesus in an intense way. She is *connected to the spiritual reality* that flows from him.

Then, there is Jesus. He talks, moves, and interacts with the deep consciousness of his connection with his Abba God. He has an ever-present awareness that he is one with God. Everything he does flows from this inner divine attentiveness and identification. He is not only connected to spiritual reality, he *identifies with the divine light within*. He comes from a deep state of simply *being*.

Here it is in diagram form:

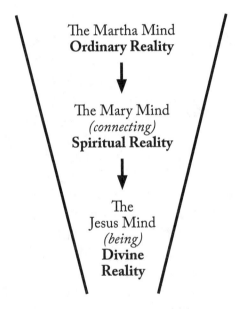

The Martha Mind
Ordinary Reality

The Mary Mind
(connecting)
Spiritual Reality

The
Jesus Mind
(being)
**Divine
Reality**

These are three different and identifiable states of consciousness which have been experienced by the mystics of many traditions around the world, down through history, and continuing today: Martha's *ordinary* awareness of everyday physical reality, Mary's *connecting* awareness with non-physical spiritual reality, and Jesus' *being* awareness of divine identification. They are called gross, subtle, and causal states by some.[7] Or, we might call them ordinary awareness, spiritual awareness, and divine awareness as illustrated in the following diagram.

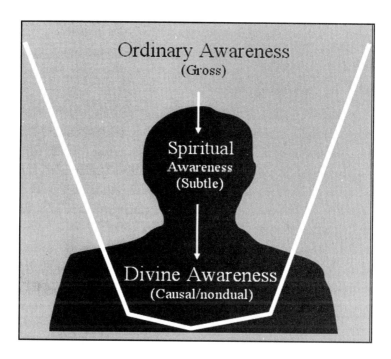

Similar to our everyday waking and sleeping cycles

Each of us moves through the most common version of these three states of awareness every day. Each day, without thinking much about it, we naturally experience wakefulness, dreaming sleep, and deep dreamless sleep. Wakefulness is our ordinary state going about our day, busy with the tasks of work and home. In our waking state, we move and think. We see, feel, smell, and hear things in the physical world. This awareness of the material universe is sometimes called a gross state.

When we fall asleep and begin dreaming, we move from the gross world of material objects to the dream world of non-physical objects, sensations, activity, and adventures. What we see, hear, and feel is "real" but in a different way than the physical world. The dreaming state in sleep has also been called a subtle state of awareness because of the appearance of material objects and "physical" sensations in a non-material and non-physical way—a more "subtle" form.

At some point as we sleep, we move into deep dreamless sleep. Here we do not experience objects, feelings, or thoughts. Yet, this deep dreamless state refreshes and revitalizes us.

Mary and the connecting state

At that moment, sitting at Jesus' feet, Mary was intensely connected with Jesus who personified spiritual reality in the physical world. He was physically present then, and is spiritually present now, and available to us in a similar way if we know how to connect with the non-physical spiritual reality that includes him, other spiritual beings, divine healing energies, and the Spirit's presence. That is why I call this the "*connecting*" state.

The followers of Jesus and spiritual seekers of many traditions throughout history have learned, when they worship, pray, or mediate, to remain awake and alert while they enter the dream-like subtle level of attentiveness.

In this awareness we may see visions on the screen of our mind, hear messages from the Spirit in our head, have joyful, peaceful feelings, and various bodily sensations such as being touched, vibration, warmth, and energy. We may experience spiritual guides, angels, new insights, transmission of healing energy, prayer languages, and other awakened faculties which are described by both the New Testament and Christians down through the centuries and today, and by mystics of all spiritual traditions.

This is the Spirit zone where attention is focused on spiritual realities which appear as forms such as images, thoughts, feelings, and sensations. The world of physical reality is perceived with our senses of sight, hearing, touch, taste, and smell at an ordinary level. The world of spiritual reality is perceived with an "interior" or "subtle" version of sight, hearing, touch, taste, and smell. When we are dreaming, it is these interior senses that pick up these sensations, not our outward physical body. These are just as real, only they are not usually available to our ordinary physical senses. When we are in what I call the "connecting zone" we are much more consciously connected to the realities of the non-physical world of Spirit.

Jesus modeled the "being" state

Jesus was also very much at home in connecting with spiritual realities as we shall explore in the next chapter. However, he lived even more deeply in the level of consciousness that made him aware of his own divinity, his oneness with God. Mary had yet to experience this. Being a good Jew, she would have never thought of herself as divine or one with God. It was all she could do to handle connecting with "outward" spiritual phenomena at this time and not her own deepest inner, divine, spiritual Self.

Jesus was present to others, taught, and healed from a level of awareness which was an even deeper and more focused state where he embraced and manifested his own divine identity. I call this the "being" state of consciousness. He was *being* his True Self, his divine self.

Being prayer is different from *connecting* prayer. In being prayer all the images, sensations, and forms leave just like in dreamless sleep, except that we are awake. All that is left is an indescribable awareness of the God's presence, the direct experience of union with God.[8] It is simply *being* in the Spirit. For the Christian, it is the experience of knowing that we are divine spiritual beings. It is identification with God, which is *beyond connecting* to God. It is knowing that your deepest self, your true "I," is divine. Jesus' "I am" statements in the gospel of John came from this exalted consciousness.

All forms are transcended in the "*being*" state. It appears to be "empty" and may be called "emptiness" in some religious traditions. But it is far from empty. It is a "nothing" state or, more clearly, a "no thing" consciousness. The absence of things or forms allows us to deeply experience unmediated pure Spirit. All that is left, when the forms and symbols leave, is the direct experience of the presence of God. Some call this a "causal state" of awareness because they consider this to be the "non-conscious" ground from which the physical and subtle planes of existence are "caused" or continuously spring. The deep end of causal is called "nondual."

Christians may call the *being* state by several different names, including the Kingdom of Heaven, the Christ consciousness, unity consciousness, awakening, no separation, or realized divinity. Jesus described it when he said, "The Father and I are one."[9] Paul described it when he said, "I live, yet not I but Christ lives within me."[10]

Mystics of all traditions have experienced these *connecting* and *being* states and tell us there is a vast treasure trove of spiritual awakening waiting for us there. It is in this kind of transcendent, numinous awareness that we have our most wonderful and direct experiences of God.

States are different from stages

States of consciousness are different from the stages of consciousness which we addressed in Chapters 2 though 7. Stages of consciousness are entered gradually over a significant period of time and may last from several years to a lifetime. *States of consciousness* are temporary and passing. They come, stay a while, and then they go as we return to normal awareness. States are temporary. That is different from a stage which is a permanent structure of our awareness. Any one state of consciousness automatically excludes all other states of awareness. If you are in a normal waking state, then you are not in a dreaming state. If you are in an inspired state of worship, you are not also in an "anxious" state worrying about how to pay your bills. This is different from stages. Any stage is an informed structure that includes all the previous stages. It has built upon them and they can be accessed. Stages are inclusive and deep states are exclusive.

Our states are interpreted by our stage

A person at any stage may move into a connecting state of spiritual awareness or a being state of divine consciousness. However, these mystical state experiences are always interpreted by the symbols of the particular stage of spiritual development in which the person or church inhabits. Let's say that a person has an overwhelming sense of Jesus' presence that lasts for several minutes. A tribal church might call it "being touched by the spirit that is called 'Jesus.'" The warrior church might see it a call to arms from the Lord. The traditional church might label it conversion, spiritual rededication, or being baptized by the Spirit. A modern church might call it a sense of the

Infinite—or perhaps indigestion or a hallucination. A postmodern church might help the person interpret the experience in the light of their own understanding. An integral church might call it an awakening or a new release into the transcendent realm of Spirit.

A church member has a vivid dream of evil people attempting to harm him. If in a tribal church, he might find himself fearful of impending doom. The warrior level would see an attack by evil. The traditional church might see it as a bad dream, or, if charismatic, might have someone with a gift of discernment or prophecy discern its meaning. The modern church would recommend therapy if the dream continues. The postmodern church might recommend a local psychic. The integral church would suggest shadow work to own the projection. (See Chapter 16.)

A woman occasionally senses an unseen presence in her house. The tribal church might worry this was an evil spirit. The warrior church would do an exorcism. The traditional church would ignore it or label it an unexplained mystery. A traditional Pentecostal or charismatic church might suggest someone with the gift of discernment to help determine if this is good or evil. The modern church might think it was just one of those weird feelings. The postmodern church might suggest talking with a highly intuitive person or psychic. The integral level church might encourage her to ask the presence to reveal itself or visit a prayer group that has people who operate at the connecting level to help discern what is happening and transmit release and healing from this negative energy.

A man has a spiritual experience of seeing a golden light which changes into a glowing being who seems to be Jesus. If the individual is a Christian at a tribal altitude he might see this as a magical Jesus who can walk on water, resurrect the dead, turn water into wine, and who has come to protect him from all harm. At the warrior level the person may see this as a powerful Jesus who intervenes in miraculous ways in one's life, punishes the wicked, and rewards the good. At the traditional worldview he might see this Jesus as the comforting one who has come to save believers from eternal hell and has given his commandments in the inspired book called the Bible. At the modern altitude, if the experience is not automatically dismissed as unreal, this person might see this Jesus as an incredible human being teaching universal love. At the postmodern level one might understand this mystical Jesus as one of many great spiritual teachers who has brought liberation into this life. At integral awareness he might see this Jesus as a personification of the Christ consciousness which is accessible to everyone through whatever spiritual tradition they follow. He might passionately embrace the manifestation of union with God modeled by Jesus while also respecting those who have found it in Krishna, Buddha, or other paths.

The point is that altered state experiences will always be interpreted according to one's stage of consciousness.

While I was writing

As I was writing this section, I had an unexpected connecting state of elevated awareness while driving my car. You have to be careful about those, and I should have pulled over. Trying to mix states of consciousness while driving can be disastrous. My experience was fostered a month before by having read Richard Tarnas's strange book *Cosmos and Psyche*. I had loved his wonderful *Passion of the Western Mind*. In *Cosmos* he explores what he sees as the mysterious connection a number of studies seem to have found between significant life and cultural changes and the planets. He does not postulate a cause and effect, merely some kind of connection. This is not the comic book astrological drivel found in the newspapers, although it still appears quite speculative. The Spirit can even use seemingly weird stuff to move us along. Regardless, I was again thinking about how we are connected with all of creation. I was driving home from the organic food market and looking at the beautiful blue sky ahead with its white fluffy clouds. I began thinking beyond them about our solar system and beyond even that to the further reaches of the cosmos. I reflected on how it all exploded into being almost 15 billion years ago from a tiny particle smaller than the head of a pin. I remembered how some scientists and philosophers today see that behind the Big Bang is a Creative Intelligence that is both a part of everything and beyond everything. Suddenly I was filled with awe and wonder. I had this cosmic sense of the unity of all things. Feeling and thinking at the same time, I remembered the nonlocal particle experiments of quantum physics. They show how affecting one of two particles that were once together instantly affects the other, no matter how far they are separated. That threw me into an even greater and overwhelming sense of the oneness of everything. I enjoyed that flow of harmonious unity as much as I could while navigating the freeway. As I arrived home, I realized I had briefly floated into what some mystics call the subtle experience of nature mysticism.

The Psalmist wrote these sublime words: "O taste and see that the Lord is good."[11] This is an invitation to taste, not just think or reflect about God or the Spirit. If we taste God in a higher state of "God awareness," we will see that God *is* good. This is not a belief—*it is an experience*, an inner knowing. Just as one can taste with the physical senses, one can also taste with the spiritual senses. The knowing that comes from the spiritual is just as valid a way of knowing that comes from the physical. Deeper spiritual states of consciousness are wonderful moments of tasting the Spirit.

We cannot usually function normally in our daily activities in these elevated states. However, intensely spiritual states of mindfulness are an intentional goal in integral church and beyond, especially in worship and prayer. It is both possible and desirable to make these elevated states permanently accessible so that, whenever we choose to, we may enter them. In the following three chapters we will explore these states in the life of Jesus, the early church as recorded in the New Testament, and our lives today.

CHAPTER 9

Jesus in the Spirit Zone
Prototype for all

Jesus was very much at home with spiritual experiences in these altered "zone" states. They were truly his home—this is where he lived. It is amazing to me that so many devoted Christians and scholars seem to have no idea of the importance of these experiences in the life of Jesus. In another sense, it is not amazing at all. They see Jesus through the "stained glass windows" of tradition and academic scholarship. His mystical experiences are attributed to his uniqueness or to elaborations in the accounts. Since it appears to them that these experiences no longer occur, they mistakenly assume they were either nonexistent, meant to pass away, or merely unimportant. They seem oblivious to the biblical accounts where Jesus passed these experiences on down to his first followers. This results in the relative absence of these non-ordinary states of consciousness in the lives of Christians today.

Within two hundreds years these spiritual states of awareness began to diminish as the church became more an organization with a prescribed set of beliefs. Being a follower of Jesus came to be defined by what you believed *about* him and not what you experienced *with* him.

Apostolic succession, in its deepest form, was originally the transmission of the awakening of the Spirit from spiritual leaders to others just as Jesus did with his followers. When the awakening experiences died out, all that was left were ceremonies that ritualized it and a set of beliefs and ecclesiastical appointments that legitimized the new leaders.

The baby Jesus

I value the attempts of scholars to differentiate what may be the actual words and accounts of Jesus in the gospels from those of later writers and editors. However, for our purpose here I will assume that many, if not most, of the words and events attributed to Jesus in the canonical gospels have their basis with him in some form.

Looking at the four gospels we find that we know little about Jesus until he began his public ministry. But we can assume he developed through the normal stages of growth, although, apparently, at an accelerated rate. The baby Jesus was not crying, cooing, babbling, and pooping, all the while looking into his mother's eyes thinking, "Ha, you think I'm a little baby, but actually I have the complete God consciousness of the most advanced saint." Jesus had to grow up just like we all do.

The young Jesus

Luke states, "Jesus increased in wisdom and in years, and in divine and human favor."[1] It appears that he was not seen as an oddball at this point. He evidently advanced in mind and heart at an increased pace as evidenced in his interaction with the religious teachers at age 12 in the temple at Jerusalem. Somewhere in his development he began to experience the awesome and distant God of Judaism in a stunningly intimate way. He began calling God by the same name that he and every other child of his community called their own father—*Abba*, meaning papa or daddy. This was a term of intimacy and respect used by both youngsters and adults in Jesus' day.[2] Jesus had a breakthrough awareness of a direct relationship to Ultimate Reality.

Baptism—mystical event

Jesus' first major recorded elevated state experience of the Spirit was at his water baptism. His baptism could have just been a symbol of commitment that involved getting really wet. Instead, it involved bodily sensations, visions, and auditory affirmations from God. Coming up from the water, Jesus "saw the heavens opening." This was looking into the spiritual world while still in the material world. Jesus had a visual and tactile experience of the Spirit that resembled a dove descending and resting on him. He heard the voice of God affirming him. Jesus' mystical experience of seeing, feeling, and hearing the world of Spirit eventually propelled him into his public ministry. But first, there were more altered state experiences.

Ego death in the wilderness

His elevated consciousness at his baptism was immediately followed by a vision quest in the wilderness for 40 days. Here Jesus wrestled with how he would use his highly evolved spiritual powers. He struggled with his own ego self, personified and projected outward as "Satan," in vivid scenarios involving his use of his heightened spiritual abilities. Jesus had an ego like any normal healthy human being. He grappled with whether to use his spiritual power in service of his ego or in service of God. This is also the contemporary challenge facing all spiritual seekers, especially in some church and New Age beliefs and practices. Many "prosperity beliefs" do not seem to end up where Jesus did, which was to deny his false self (identifying with ego) in order to honor his True Self (the Christ consciousness of complete identification with and service to God).

Seen as an extended connecting or subtle state experience, the temptation experience is a model for all of us. At times called "wrestling with the devil," "struggling with ego death," or a "dark night of the soul," it shows that such deeply spiritual states are not always pleasant, and certainly not gone through easily.

Hebrews 2:10 says that Jesus was "made perfect through suffering." The word "perfect" may be more fully translated as whole, complete, mature, or grown-up.[3] The Spirit used Jesus' struggles here and other places to help him evolve into a more "complete" person. The Spirit does the same with us.

Jesus as a telepath

Jesus said to Nathaniel upon meeting him that he was an "Israelite in whom there was no guile." Startled, Nathaniel asked him, "How do you know me?" "I saw you under the fig tree," responded Jesus. Evidently, Jesus, some distance away, was not referring to physically seeing Nathaniel. Perhaps Nathaniel was praying or wondering about this man Jesus whom everyone was talking about. Nathaniel then said something like, "You must be the Messiah to have read my thoughts." Jesus responded with, "Because I said to you, I saw you under the fig tree, do you believe? You shall see greater things than these."[4] The lower end of the connecting or subtle level is called psychic awareness by some. Sensing another's thoughts and feelings is a telepathic psychic phenomenon that is common both historically and today. Jesus indicated this psychic level apprehension was not all that great compared to what was to come.

Jesus told an unrepentant man, who had not gone through the Temple ritual of cleansing, that his sins were already forgiven. The religious leaders were "questioning in their hearts," believing that Jesus had committed the sin of blasphemy by acting like God in forgiving sins.[5] Mark records, "At once Jesus perceived in his spirit that they had questioned this within themselves." He brought this up by asking, "Why do you raise such questions in your hearts?" Jesus psychically "heard" the inner thoughts of these leaders.

In talking with the woman at the well, Jesus tells her that he knows she has had five husbands and the man she is living with now is not her husband. The woman responds with, "You must be a prophet." Jesus has accurately intuited, at a telepathic psychic level, the conditions of the women's life in order to bring about a redemptive situation.

I am always astounded at the Christian leaders who warn of the evil of psychic phenomena. Yet Jesus often operated at this level of awareness. Psychic phenomena, like all things, must be discerned as to the level of truth it contains. But to dismiss it totally is to dismiss Jesus' experiences.

Jesus as energy healer

Most scholars believe that Jesus' healing miracles have an authentic historical core. The experiences of healing down through the centuries and today also witness to this reality. The many healing events in Jesus' ministry certainly involved non-ordinary states of consciousness that seemed to flow from Jesus in almost ordinary ways. That is, Jesus experienced such a high level of spiritual awareness, that he maintained it almost all of the time. This non-ordinary consciousness was his ordinary state.

Jesus healed others from a state of consciousness that transmitted healing energy from himself to others. "And all in the crowd were trying to touch him, for power came out from him and healed them all."[6] This is a revealing incident about Jesus' healing transmissions as he noticed, in his elevated spiritual awareness, that someone had touched him and received healing. He then said, "Someone touched me for I was aware that power had gone out from me."[7]

Jean-Pierre Isbouts, professor of culture and media studies at Fielding Graduate University, comments on this passage saying, "Some form of energy had spontaneously surged from Jesus' physical presence even though he himself did not direct it." Isbouts believes that Jesus was an energy healer and that his method of healing was a transfer of electromagnetic energy from himself to another.[8]

This "power" that went out from Jesus is the word *dunamis* in the Greek New Testament from which we get our word "dynamite." It was an *energy that releases God's love, healing, and creative vitality into the world.*[9]

We conventionally think of Jesus healing others by calling on a God up there to come down and touch a person with a miracle. That is the traditional-level way that Christians pray today. But there is no record of Jesus ever praying that way. Rather, as this incident reveals, it was Spirit zone healing energy within Jesus himself that was transmitted to release healing in others. Jesus, as fully human and fully divine, had this power of God within and *as* himself. This is how he taught disciples to heal and is a model for us as we pray for others. We can move from the traditional level of calling on God out there to touch a person and instead know that the Spirit within and *as* us is where the healing energy comes from. Our ability to transmit healing energy to others as Jesus did is based on what seems to be a universal potential within each of us to develop and intensify this kind of energy.

Traditional Chinese healers and today's alternative healers doing energy work may well be transmitting healing just as Jesus did. I have personally had almost weekly sessions with a very spiritual and highly developed energy worker for the last ten years and have benefited greatly both physically and spiritually. This is integral-and-beyond-level healing prayer. It is what Jim Marion calls "translating energy either up or down."[10] In this case, it is manifesting spiritual energy in the form of physical and emotional healing.

This enlightened awareness of healing energy seems also to have been transmitted from Jesus to his disciples so they were able to bring healing to others with the same power. "Then Jesus called the twelve together and gave them power and authority over all demons and to cure diseases, and he sent them out to proclaim the dominion of God and to heal."[11]

Jesus taught his disciples to heal others as he did. Jesus did not teach his followers to ask God "up there" to heal. Instead, he taught them to heal from the spiritual energy that was within them. On what basis did he do that? He was able to do that because he knew they, too, were divine beings and could do what he did if they were able to tap into it. Therefore, the disciples were able to heal from their own divine consciousness. I doubt that they labeled it as such then, since that would have been too much of a leap. Therefore, they conceived of it as Jesus "giving them the authority" to heal. I am sure it felt very "authoritative."

Jesus said if you want to move mountains, don't ask God to do it. Instead, *tell* the mountain to move![12] Our refusal to embrace our divinity as Jesus did keeps us asking a God "out there" to do for us what we can do ourselves. This means we are operating at a lower level of faith.

This is a model for all things we might ask for "from" God. Yes, it is okay to holler for help from God. Sometimes it seems to be the only thing we can do. But a higher level of faith is to *tell* the mountain to move. But isn't this a magical level of faith? It could be if you think your ritual is going to accomplish something. However, if you understand that you, as an incarnation of divine Spirit, are doing the doing, then it is not magic. It's spiritual action. Here is how the difference between traditional and integral mystical "Jesus-style" healing prayer looks in diagram form.

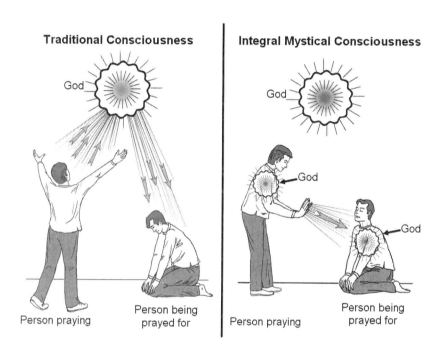

Jesus honors traditional but practices mystical

Jesus honored the traditional level of prayer of his day while he taught and practiced a much higher one, the one we are calling integral and beyond. In raising Lazarus from the dead Jesus offered a beautiful model of honoring a traditional mode of consciousness while personally operating at a higher one. "And Jesus looked upward and said, 'Father, I thank you for having heard me. I know that you always hear me, but I have said this for the sake of the crowd standing here, so that they may believe that you sent me.' When he said this, he cried with a loud voice, 'Lazarus, come out!' The dead man came out . . ."[13]

Notice that Jesus looked upward in this public prayer. Then he said that he knew that the God "up there" always heard him. Next, in a profoundly revealing declaration, he said: "I have said this for the sake of the crowds standing here, so that they may believe that you sent me." He accommodated himself to the traditional level of faith and prayer held by the crowd by announcing that he was praying to a God "up there who always hears us." Then he proceeded to do what he always did when doing healing prayer: He did not address God up there. *He did not address God at all!* Rather, he spoke from the God within as an incarnation of the Divine Spirit. He said to Lazarus, evidently to either Lazarus' dead physical body or to his lingering spirit body, "Come out!" And Lazarus, once again inhabiting his physical body, came out!

Jesus talks with his spirit guides

Jesus sets up for his disciples what I consider the central spiritual experience of Jesus' life—the "Transfiguration." He makes a one-of-a-kind statement that some of his followers were soon to see "the kingdom of God has come with power."[14] In no other situation does Jesus make the claim that what they are about to see is a power-filled picture of the realm of God manifest in the here and now. Immediately the gospel writers move to saying that "six days later"[15] Jesus was transfigured. If we want a picture of the Kingdom of God, Jesus says, here it is!

The crucifixion became the focus of the New Testament writers and the church later on as they tried to understand how their hero could have been crucified. The Apostle Paul brilliantly devised a transitional theological understanding using the Temple sacrificial system of the day with Jesus as the final sacrifice to God. However, in the actual context of Jesus' life, I believe the Transfiguration experience was central. Importantly, it did include Jesus' upcoming death as the topic of conversation that Jesus had with two of his spiritual guides, Moses and Elijah. In this remarkable experience, Jesus took his inner circle of physical friends, Peter, James, and John, up a mountain to pray. Jesus' own spiritual and physic energy systems then became so radiant that they were visible to his three friends as "his face shone like the sun and his clothing became dazzling white." Next, they saw Jesus' spiritual friends, Moses and Elijah, talking with Jesus about his "departure" coming soon in Jerusalem.[16]

It is remarkable that commentaries do not address what was actually going on in this account. They discuss theological ideas present such as Moses representing the Law and Elijah representing the prophets. They speak of the theological implications of God's voice affirming Jesus. Nevertheless, one is hard pressed to find even one of the thousands of biblical scholars and teachers down through the centuries and today who ever talks about the elephant in the room: Jesus was having a connecting (subtle) state conversation with two highly revered men of the Jewish religion that had been dead for hundreds of years! Jesus needed guidance and encouragement to face the consequences of his attacking the oppressive religious, political, and social power structures of the day. He evidently received what he needed from the two heroes of his religious tradition who served as spirit guides for him.

It appears that, although channeling the dead is not popular in today's traditional religious circles, it was certainly acceptable to Jesus. It was also acceptable to Moses and Elijah. It is from writings attributed to Moses that we have dire warnings and prohibitions against consulting the "spirits of the dead."[17] Evidently Moses changed his mind after being dead for a while. This trans-worldly conversation ended with an auditory experience of God's voice telling Jesus and his three friends that he was a special channel of divine life whom they were to listen to closely. How reassuring for Jesus to hear from his Abba God that he was following his true spiritual path, in spite of outward appearances. Losing most of your followers and getting yourself sentenced to die as a criminal in the electric chair of the day was not what today is called the gospel of success.

Immediately following this transcendent state of consciousness is a crucial teaching about the results of spending time in altered state prayer. Jesus and his three friends came back down the mountain to find his disciples trying to heal an epileptic boy, but failing. Jesus heals the boy and the disciples ask him why they could not. Jesus responds by telling them they needed to spend more time in prayer. I imagine they immediately objected by saying they had been praying for hours for the boy. It must have been then that Jesus explained to them that it was not "praying for the boy" kind of prayer he was talking about. He was pointing them to the kind of praying he had just finished up on the mountain. This was "get away from it all" altered state praying that included connecting with spiritual realities that could provide the encouragement and guidance needed in order to transmit this kind of healing energy.

What did Jesus do in all that praying?

Jesus spent extended time alone in prayer.[18] What did he do in these long periods alone? Certainly he did not just keep repeating the "Lord's Prayer" over and over again. We know from his month-long experience in the wilderness and later in Gethsemane that some of his time alone was spent wrestling with his own ego, eventually resolving the struggle: "Nevertheless not my will but your will be done." I have called this the "connecting" level of prayer as Jesus connected with spiritual realities within himself.

Although there are no specific accounts of Jesus entering into the "being" level of prayer, we must assume that nights in prayer and days in the wilderness provided many opportunities for such deep awareness of his Abba for Jesus. I doubt that the writers of these narratives would have been aware of the two levels of connecting and being prayer since this was all new to them. Their accounts were exclusively about what could be reported in terms of actions. This was also true in the reported healings of Jesus which were always about visible healing. They would not have been able to record the healing of internal organs because there were no x-ray machines to show the healing.

Some scholars believe that at some point in his young life Jesus was instructed in various disciplines such as deep meditation or esoteric prayer practices. Even though there is no direct historical evidence for that for Jesus, it was a practice of Jewish mystics at the time and would have been available to Jesus.[19] It seems reasonable to assume he was at home with deep being states of consciousness where he could experience his identification with God. Whatever his spiritual practices, his model for us is that we, too, need enough time away from regular activities to sustain and nurture our inner spiritual lives. This only comes through zone prayer/mediation/worship practices both alone and with others.

Spirit from the inside out

One passage from the gospels provides an exceptional commentary on these zone encounters with the Spirit we have been describing. Jesus says those who come to him will experience "rivers of living water flowing from their heart."[20] This is a beautiful and accurate description of what happens in spiritual awakening of all kinds. It is a release of the already and always present Spirit that comes from deep within our being and results outwardly in what may be described as "living in the flow." It can also become a permanently accessible state of transcendence that is truly the "Spirit-filled" life.

The gospel writer then comments, "Now he said this about the Spirit, which believers in him were to receive, for as yet the Spirit had not been given because Jesus was not yet glorified."[21] Jesus' preceding statement was at a self-actualized transcendent level, describing an inner release of already present Spirit. The gospel writer's explanation was at a lower level, describing a Spirit coming from the outside which had not yet appeared. I suspect that this release of Spirit in these followers of Jesus seemed so dramatic in the intervening years between Jesus' statement and the early church, that it seemed to the writers that the Spirit actually was not around much before that. The Old Testament describes the Spirit occasionally "coming upon" various leaders and prophets. The prediction of the prophet Joel quoted by Peter on the day of Pentecost predicted that the Spirit of God would eventually be poured out on all flesh.[22] They saw this as the fulfillment of that prophecy.

The interpretation of these "Spirit experiences" by the early church writers may not be the one held by those at a higher level. To these early writers it evidently appeared that the Spirit was coming from "out there" to "in here." However, Jesus' own statement envisions a release from the inside and not a "coming upon" from the outside.

In addition, the early church was at an ethnocentric level, believing that only they had the Spirit and only those who came to believe in Jesus could gain the Spirit. However, at the integral level we can understand the Spirit as already and always present in everyone, regardless of their religion or lack of it. That does not mean they are aware of the Spirit's presence or manifest it. But it is still present deep within. Earlier in the Gospel of John, the writer makes it clear that the "life" in Jesus was the "light of *all* people."[23] The writer does not say *some* people, or a *few* people, or all *Christian* people. He uses the very powerful word "all." This is the "life" or Spirit that was released in a new way in Jesus' followers. In most religious and spiritual paths there is the recognition that the Spirit does need to be awakened to or released to "flow" in Jesus' words. As John states, Jesus, as embodied spiritual consciousness, is truly the light of all people, but all people are not aware of this light, regardless of the name by which it is called (Buddha consciousness, Krishna consciousness, Christ consciousness, etc.). Awakening to this awareness is the continuing work of the Spirit in the world in all religious/spiritual traditions.

Of the four New Testament gospels, John most strongly emphasizes Jesus' transcendent consciousness where he spoke from an elevated causal mode of awareness of his identification as Divine Being. This is seen in his "I am" statements such as "I am the light of the world" and "I am the bread of life."[24] In referring to these and other statements by Jesus, Stevan Davies argues that

> some of the 'Johannine style' sayings attributed to Jesus are as historically authentic as are some of the 'synoptic style' sayings attributed to him. . . . While in an altered state of consciousness, Jesus certainly said some things that were to be attributed not to him but to the Spirit speaking through him. As we have seen, the Jewish prophetic paradigm practically demands this.[25]

The Gospel of Thomas records Jesus speaking about the Light that was in and as him also being in us. "Jesus said, 'If you bring forth what is within you, what you have will save you.'"[26] What is already within us that will save us? The Spirit of God!

"Jesus said, 'I am the light that is over all things. I am all: from me all came forth, and to me all attained. Split a piece of wood; I am there. Lift up the stone, and you will find me there.'"[27] Is there anywhere the Spirit is not? No! Jesus said the light of the "I Am" Spirit was everywhere and in everyone.

Jesus said, "When you know yourselves, then you will be known, and you will understand that you are children of the living Father. But if you do not know yourselves, then you live in poverty, and you are the poverty."[28] Only by knowing our true self, the Divine Self within, can we know we belong to God. If we do not discover that which is already and always within, then we live in poverty.

Hear it clearly: Jesus was at home with mystical levels and transcendent states of consciousness. And he invites us to that same unfolding of experiencing and identification with divine reality.

CHAPTER 10

The Early Church in the Spirit Zone
"The other day, while I was in a trance . . ."

As a young, devout, churchgoing Christian, I made it through thousands of Southern Baptist sermons, Bible studies, and years of seminary courses without having ever heard a discussion of the New Testament idea of "trance." I grew up thinking trances were a New Age phenomenon and certainly not a practice of the early Christians. I was wrong. Trances are referred to by name three times in the book of Acts. Trances are another way of talking about the Spirit zone. Even more importantly, a trance state of consciousness led to the stunning breakthrough of the early church welcoming Gentiles into the Way of Jesus.

The book of Acts reports that "Peter went up on the rooftop to pray. He became hungry and wanted something to eat; and while it was being prepared, he fell into a trance."[1]

The event was so important that Acts records it again as Peter shares his experience with the church at Jerusalem: "I was in the city of Joppa praying, and in a trance, I saw a vision . . ."[2]

What is a "trance?"

The word "trance" here is the Greek word ἐκστασις, or *ekstasis*, from which we get our word "ecstasy." *Ekstasis* means an altered and deeply focused state of expanded consciousness where a person "perceives with his bodily eyes and ears realities shown him by God."[3] This is where " one . . . transported is full of God, or inspired, or gifted with power . . ."[4] This New Testament event appears perplexing to many Christians who want to have nothing to do with "trances." Therefore, it is usually ignored. This is an incredible loss. If one wants proof texts for altered states of consciousness, here they are! The Apostle Peter himself had a trance! And the Apostle Paul did, too, as he recounts, "While I was praying in the temple, I fell into a trance and saw Jesus saying to me, 'Hurry and get out of Jerusalem quickly.'"[5]

There is nothing to indicate these trances were unusual. What is being pointed out is not the trances but the life-changing events that transpired as a result of them. These were connecting-level zone experiences that led to decisive and life-changing actions.

New Testament scholar James Dunn talks about these ecstatic zone experiences, including "trance," in the New Testament, saying:

> By "ecstasy" I mean here an unusually exalted state of feeling, a condition of such total absorption or concentration that the individual becomes oblivious to all attendant circumstances and other stimuli, an experience of intense rapture or a trance-like state in which normal faculties are suspended for a shorter or longer period and the subject sees visions or experiences "automatic speech," as in some forms of glossolalia.[6]

What happened in Peter's trance?

The book of Acts recounts the details of Peter's zone experience:

> He saw the heavens opened and something like a large sheet coming down, being lowered to the ground by its four corners. In it were all kinds of four-footed creatures and reptiles and birds of the air. Then he heard a voice saying, "Get up, Peter; kill and eat." But Peter said, "By no means, Lord, for I have never eaten anything that is profane or unclean." The voice said to him again, a second time, "What God has made clean, you must not call unclean." This happened three times, and the thing was suddenly taken up to heaven.[7]

Notice that the Spirit used Peter's hunger and the smell of the food being prepared downstairs. Perhaps Peter had often smelled the meat of these animals he saw in his trance being cooked by the Gentiles as he passed by and wondered what they tasted like. The smells might have been very enticing. God uses whatever alphabet we have at hand to communicate with us. Peter did not discount the reality of his vision, as we are inclined to do: "Oh, I was so hungry I began hallucinating about food."

The religious rules, given in the Torah, were deeply ingrained in Peter. They prevented him from doing what God requested. This was "dirty" food according to the purity language of the Old Testament food laws. It took three times before Peter was willing to even think about what this meant. I am so glad God keeps repeating things to us until we get it.

Cornelius, a Gentile who was not a follower of Jesus, also has had a vision from God while praying that prepared him for a visit from Peter. (Yes, those who don't follow Jesus can have visions straight from God, too!) Peter goes to talk about Jesus to Cornelius' friends and relatives. This is a remarkable crossing of racial, religious, and social barriers since the Jews would normally not associate with the "unclean" Gentiles. In a dramatic event, "while Peter was still speaking, the Holy Spirit fell upon all who heard the word . . . for they heard them speaking in tongues and extolling God."[8] Peter's trance, along with Cornelius' trance, resulted in another trance-like experience of worship for the Gentiles. Here was the remarkable spread of the message of Jesus and the experience of exalted Spirit release in the new converts, all stemming from three experiences of a connecting state of awareness. Trances!

How did all of this come about? Why did these altered-state experiences occur so often?

The church began in the Spirit zone

The "church" is traditionally thought to have started in the event of Pentecost. This is described in Acts 2 where a remarkable Spirit zone experience occurred. Jesus' disciples were gathered in one place waiting for the predicted coming (release) of the Spirit in a bold, new way.

Suddenly they heard the sound of a fierce wind, saw flames of fire resting on those present, and joyfully expressed themselves in praise and prayer in "other languages." In addition, those in the crowd gathered to observe these things reported that they were able to understand the sense of whatever was being vocalized in their own native language. The church began in a blaze of altered-state experiences!

Inspired states continue

Acts describes the boldness of Peter and John in speaking publicly and transmitting spiritual energy to those they prayed for. "When they had prayed, the place in which they were gathered together was shaken; and they were all filled with the Holy Spirit and spoke the word of God with boldness.[9] This group experienced the Spirit zone together with physical sensations of shaking and an unusual level of confidence and authority in speaking out publically.

Spirit transmission

In Chapter 8 of Acts, Peter and John went to pray for the new believers in Samaria. They laid their hands on the new converts and they "received the Spirit." When a man watching them saw what happened to these new followers of Jesus when Peter and John laid their hands on them, he offered them money to gain the same ability. He was soundly rebuked by Peter. What is remarkable is that the altered state of "receiving the Spirit" was so powerful that it was dramatically and immediately observable. Most likely it was the same kind of elevated inspired states of consciousness that were reported previously in Chapter 2 and later in Chapters 10 and 19 of Acts. The believers prayed and praised God in both unintelligible words and understandable language as they channeled the Spirit.

Paul's life changing altered-state experience

In Chapter 9 of Acts, Paul had a dramatic and life-changing trance-like experience as he saw a heavenly light around him, fell to the ground, and heard the voice of Jesus. He was led, blinded, to

Damascus, where Ananias, as instructed in another vision, went to visit Paul and pray for him that his sight would be restored and he would "be filled with the Holy Spirit." Paul began his journey of following Jesus with an altered-state event. It was normal for him to continue to have these Spirit zone experiences which the New Testament reports as "being filled with the Spirit."

Paul continues to have visions

Paul recounts, modestly in 3rd-person language, another experience of trance or altered consciousness: "... I will go on to visions and revelations of the Lord. I know a person in Christ who fourteen years ago was caught up to the third heaven—whether in the body or out of the body I do not know ..."[10]

Later, Paul says, "While I was praying in the temple, I fell into a trance and saw Jesus."[11] Paul does not indicate that falling into a trance was unusual. Rather, it seems to be a normal occurrence for Paul, as with Peter. The trance allowed Paul to see Jesus and get some practical advice—"get out of Jerusalem quickly."

Christians throughout the New Testament and church history have had trances with visions. Many Christians today experience them and they are quite common in the church where I have taught for the last 45 years. Yet to many, if not most, Christians they sound strange. They would sound normal if we had understood that elevated zone states have always been a normal and vital part of the Christian life.

More prayer language and Spirit channeling

Chapter 19 of Acts recounts an uplifted and expressive state of consciousness entered into by a dozen people: "When Paul laid his hands on them, the Holy Spirit came upon them, and they spoke in tongues and prophesied."[12] This follows a common pattern recounted throughout the book of Acts where those who have already had direct experiences with the Spirit met with, and usually touched, those who wished to have a release of the Spirit within them. This "baptism in Spirit" was the merging of the Universal Mind with the individual mind. These early Christians rather suddenly awakened to the reality that they were one with God. This transitory but life-changing transmission resulted in a peak experience of overwhelming joy and contact with potent spiritual realities. That experience is still available today as witnessed by mystics of many traditions throughout the centuries.

The most reported outward responses in these early church cases were a joyful expression of prayer and praise directed to God in a verbal but transrational form (called "tongues" in many Bible translations) and spontaneous, intelligible words of encouragement, comfort, and challenge attributed to the inspiration of the Spirit (called "prophecy" in many translations).

Prayer languages, then and now

Thus, one of the seemingly strange, altered-state experiences frequently reported in the book of Acts is what is today commonly called "praying in tongues."

A recent survey of adults in the United States showed that about one in ten Christians pray weekly or more often in their own personal languages of prayer and praise.[13] The charismatic movement of the 1960s has made more people aware of this practice. Today, 36 percent of Americans claim to be charismatic or Pentecostal Christians. That corresponds to approximately 80 million adults.[14]

As of 2008, according to Barna surveys, one out of every four Protestant churches in the United States is a charismatic congregation. A slight majority of all born again Christians are charismatic. Nearly half of all adults who attend a Protestant church are charismatic. Seven percent of Southern Baptist churches and 6 percent of mainline churches are charismatic, according to their Senior Pastors.[15] These are striking statistics that indicate a widespread involvement of ordinary Christians in some form of altered states and particularly in personal languages of prayer and praise.

The most rapidly growing segment of Christianity worldwide is pentecostal/charismatic Christianity, placed at about one-quarter of all Christians.[16] A central feature of these groups is an emphasis (sometimes an overemphasis) on prayer language.

Early Christianity began in a blaze of both elevated rational and transrational symbolic speech, called "prophecy" and "speaking in tongues," respectively. This experience was so widespread on the day of Pentecost when the first followers of Jesus gathered in Jerusalem, that the writer of Acts claimed that they all "began to speak in other tongues."[17] This experience continued as more were converted to become followers of Jesus. We know that Paul, the brilliant scholar who was the primary shaper of what became Christianity both then and now, was also a practitioner of "tongues." He pointed out to the Corinthian church that, "I speak in tongues more than all of you."[18]

What is "tongues?"

This practice appears very strange to many today in spite of its one in ten prevalence in spiritual life in our culture. Using the archaic term "tongues" to translate the Greek word *glossa* makes it stranger still.[19] The contemporary term "glossolalia" is the combination of two words in Greek meaning "language speaking."[20] The word "glossolalia" is about as weird sounding as "tongues" except the word itself rather sounds like what we might imagine this phenomenon to sound like. I do not normally use either term.

I usually call this "a language of prayer and praise." More technically, *I understand "glossolalia" as the expression of a special, personal, transrational, symbolic language of prayer and praise to God flowing from an elevated state of spiritual awareness.* Let's unpack that definition.

It is "special" in the sense it is not used for normal discourse or in other linguistic fashion.

It is "personal" in that the expression itself seems to be unique to each person. In my experience, one person's language of prayer and praise is never duplicated by another person. It is one of a kind.

It is "transrational" in that the verbal symbols go beyond the rational, similar to what we find in other forms of spontaneous artistic expression such as jazz, free-form dance, or perhaps some music and painting as it is being composed.

I believe it is helpful to think of glossolalia as a "symbolic language." The words of traditional languages are, of course, themselves symbols. Glossolalia is symbolic of language itself, rather than the actual words of a known language. This symbolic language serves to express awe, gratitude, adoration, surrender, and other heartfelt feelings in praying to and praising God. It is like a language in the sense of repeated, symbolic, verbal expression. However, symbolic language does not have to stand the test of rational speech, syntax, proper pronunciation, and all the other things we have learned about speaking properly in many years of formal schooling. Therefore, one can use the wonderful means of "language" to most freely express oneself, without having to be limited by all the qualifications of an actual known language that must conform to certain rules.

This linguistic expression arises from within a person's Spirit as a Spirit zone manifestation of prayer and worship directed toward one's Ultimate Source. It is not limited to Christianity but is also found in other religious traditions.

I suspect that praying in this way often connects us with a sense of elevated consciousness and flow because of the way our brains are wired. The vagas nerve, when stimulated by feelings such as gratefulness, praise and adoration, may create a sense of upward movement in the throat. Also, the speech center is located in the left brain, which deals with the practical details of life. The right brain centers on the more creative, intuitive, flowing elements of consciousness. Trances occur from right brain activity. Praying with one's Spirit, to use the Apostle Paul's phase, connects the boundary-oriented activity of the left brain speech center with the loss of boundaries of the right brain. This gentle synchronization of the two brain hemispheres produces a sense of integration and wholeness as the sense of "humanity" of the left brain connects with the sense of "divinity" of the right. Our human individuation melds into an atmosphere of universal divine oneness. The Universal Mind unites with the individual mind.

There are six references in the New Testament to this form of non-ordinary, altered-state prayer and praise:

- At Pentecost ("and they all began to speak in other languages." Acts 2:4)

- With the Gentiles ("for they heard them speaking in other languages and extolling God." Acts 10:46)

- With the new converts at Ephesus ("and they spoke in other languages and prophesied." Acts 19:6)

- The widespread use in the Corinthian church (1 Corinthians 12-14)

- Paul's openness about his own prayer language ("I thank God that I speak in other languages more than all of you." 1 Corinthians 14:18)

- The reference to Spirit intercession ("that very Spirit intercedes with sighs too deep for words." Romans 8:26)

Because of this pattern, we can consider this elevated prayer and praise a widespread, if not universal, phenomenon in the early church. I will go into more detail with the hope that it will throw light upon the whole idea of spiritual state experiences both in the early Christian church and now.

The Apostle Paul makes six insightful claims about these languages of prayer and praise in 1 Corinthians.

(1) The purpose of these languages of devotion is to address God, not other people. (14:2)

(2) They are unintelligible to others and a mystery. (14:2)

(3) Those who express themselves to God in this way strengthen their inner selves. (14:4)

(4) This is a form of prayer that uses one's spirit and not one's mind. (14:14)

(5) Paul encourages others to pray and sing to God at times with their spirit and also to pray and sing to God at times with their mind. (14:15)

(6) Praying and singing with one's spirit is not to be forbidden. (14:39)

It is interesting that many of those churches who are most ardent in their belief that every word of the Bible is from God and practical for us today are also the ones who seem to totally disregard these six statements by the Apostle Paul. Others at the modern level dismiss this practice as foolish emotionalism. Both are wrong.

Paul's solution to the hubbub of the Corinthian church's meetings where everyone was speaking and praying at the same time was to limit what was spoken in "tongues" in a worship gathering to two or three times at the most. This was further limited because someone must be present who could interpret the sense of what was being said in the common language of the people gathered. When he claimed to personally practice "tongue speaking" more than most, he was certainly referring to his use of this spiritual practice in private.[21]

A language of prayer and praise is like a gentle, spiritual "buzz" that allows the intoxicating Spirit to loosen us up. It is one of the avenues that can both release and express the flow of the Spirit from within. That's one reason why Pentecostals love it so.[22]

Theologian Krister Stendhal, former dean of the Harvard Divinity School, says,

> As I read Paul it seems to me crystal clear that if the Presbyterians and the Episcopalians, the Lutherans and the 'proper' Christians, including the Catholics, did not consciously or unconsciously suppress such phenomena as glossolalia, and if other denominations did not especially encourage them, then the gifts of the Spirit—including glossolalia—would belong to the common register of Christian experience. . . . Glossolalia is a facet of what I like to see as high voltage religion. It is obvious to me that to some people and in some situations, the experience of God is so overwhelming that charismatic phenomena are the "natural" expression. In the history of religions and of the church there is an honorable place for ecstasy. Who said that only rational words or silence would be proper?[23]

What is "prophecy?"

The earliest mention of prophecy in the New Testament is the Apostle Paul's statement, "Do not quench the Spirit. Do not despise prophecies, but test everything. . ." [24] The statement tells us, among other things, that people were already doing what he cautions against —"despising" prophecies. We see it reported in the books of Acts and discussed at length in Paul's first letter to the Corinthians. What is this "prophecy"?

"Prophecy" may be best understood today as channeling the Holy Spirit. It seldom has to do with predicting the future. Prophecy is what Jesus was doing when he spoke "as" God in the "I am" sayings of John. During the Transfiguration, he was "channeling" Moses and Elijah, his spiritual guides. Channeling God's Spirit occurs when someone internally tunes in to the Spirit in such a way that he or she moves to a non-ordinary state of consciousnesses and begins receiving inspired impressions, words, or images. This may then be expressed in speaking, writing, or even creative drama, art, music, and dance. Paul is adamant that "prophecy" or channeling words from the Spirit is an incredibly valuable spiritual gift and we are *all* to strive for it. "Strive for spiritual gifts, and especially that you may prophesy . . . those who would prophesy build up the church.[25] While his lists of spiritual gifts vary, prophecy is in every one of them.

As stated above, he expressly says that channeling the Spirit should not be "despised."[26] Despising prophecies is very popular today in many churches where altered-state words from the Spirit are effectively trashed by teaching specifically against them. "All of that ended with the Bible," some say. "That is just New Age channeling which is forbidden by God." It is ridiculed by both those outside and inside the church. "He thinks he speaks for God." Or it is simply laid to rest by neglect.

While it is considered a special gift at times in Paul's writings, the ability to hear from God also seems to have been available to everyone at some level.[27] This is the difference between creative expressions of the Spirit that are unusually strong in some people and the more ordinary use, which is available to everyone. For instance, some people seem to have a "gift" of teaching, but most of us can explain something to others when needed. Some people seem to be able to transmit healing in a powerful and unusually "gifted" way. But everyone can send healing energy to others at their level of faith. Sometimes this is spoken of as the difference between a gift and a role. Only some people have a ministering skill at a gift level, but most everyone can have it at a role level. The church needs both. Everyone can learn to hear internally from the Spirit of God.

Some have such an incredible ability to hear from God for the sake of others that they were called prophets in the New Testament. Theologian Eugene Boring says:

> The early Christian prophet was an immediately inspired spokesperson for the risen Jesus, who received intelligible messages that he or she felt impelled to deliver to the Christian community or, as a representative of the community, to the general public. . . . all prophets function with the conviction that they receive direct revelations from the deity. Such revelations are received in a psychic state . . . which embraces the entire spectrum between an ecstatic trance, in which consciousness and volition are lost, and strong intuitive certainty, in which the prophet is in full possession of his or her reflective and volitional powers.[28]

Boring believes that parts of the four gospels of the New Testament are sayings of the historical Jesus and some are the Risen Jesus speaking through the prophets. He says, "The church always finds itself with the double-task of bearing witness to the once-for-all-revelation given the world in the there-and-then event of Jesus of Nazareth, *and* of mediating the continuing voice of the living Lord."[29]

Nothing in the New Testament indicates that the Spirit has stopped speaking. Just the opposite happens. Jesus explicitly says the Spirit will *not* stop speaking but will continue to speak.[30] Paul makes prophecy the most useful of all of the gifts in building up others.[31] The witness of the rest of the New Testament is precisely that—the Spirit keeps on speaking, back then and now, too.

Are the words from God or not?

With all words that are claimed to be from the Spirit it must be discerned as to whether they are from God's Spirit or not.[32] Or, more practically, whether they are high level or lower level. This is because we can "channel" from beings other than the Spirit or from lower entities rather than higher ones. This means that whether you are reading Donald Walsh's *Conversations with God*, having a session with a psychic, hearing the preacher soar to eloquent heights, responding to what someone says they heard from God for you, or wondering if the words that came into your head in prayer are from the Spirit—you must discern whether this is from the Spirit or not. The more likely scenario is one where we must discern how much of it is from God and how much is from our own or another's ego. We must always do the work of "testing of the spirits."

Hearing authentically inspired words from the Spirit or higher spiritual guides is one of the most strengthening, encouraging, comforting, and challenging of all spiritual practices and expanded state experiences.[33] We are not supposed to be able to have real church without these profound elevated states of consciousness.

The early Christians knew a spiritual experience when they saw one

The earliest Christians defined themselves not as much by a set of doctrines but by what they had experienced. As followers of Jesus, they had experienced God. For instance, Peter was convinced the Gentiles had become Christians because they had experienced the Spirit, not because they declared their assent to certain doctrines.[34] We know from early church history that beliefs in the early churches were all over the place. The many diverse groups of early followers of Jesus included the Gnostics (emphasizing a form of knowledge), the Thomasines (following the Gospel of Thomas), the Ebionites (staunchly Jewish), the Marcionites (staunchly anti-Jewish), and those whom Bart Ehrman calls the Proto-orthodox (those who came to eventually define orthodoxy or what is primarily today's version of Christianity).[35] But they all seemed to know a spiritual experience when they saw one, and the early Christians saw lots of them. Even the Proto-orthodox group, which emerged as the dominant version of Christianity, had an incredible history of spiritual experiences. Read the book of Acts and you can see that Christianity began in a blaze of experiencing God. And before that, read the gospels and see that Jesus lived a life filled with the intimate, transforming, direct experience of God. It was only later, as the direct experience of God began to wane and institutional and political factors took over, that beliefs came to be the primary defining mark of Christians.

It is not that our level of understanding of the Spirit is unimportant. Not at all. Understanding the teachings and life of Jesus are critical to our understanding the Christian life. It is that cognition cannot replace the experience of the Spirit. Stages cannot replace states, and states cannot replace stages. Both are crucial to the evolving Christian and the evolving church.

The purpose of the church is to accelerate our growth in both *stages of understanding* the spiritual life *and states of experiencing* it.

The royal road to experiencing God

Transcendent experiences of spiritual awareness are not just another level of consciousness or interesting phenomena. *They are the royal road to experiencing God.* The awareness and practice of higher states of consciousness is crucially important in integral and beyond church. These expanded states have been so neglected by churches today that they must be newly explored and encouraged if we are truly to evolve.

The Spirit zone in the Bible is neglected today

As I have said, scholars have generally ignored the altered-state spiritual experiences of the Bible. They may derive some theological significance from them but little practical understanding, such as the possibility that these experiences are still available to us today. In integralist (or whatever signifies what I am advocating comes to be called) church practice, not only are they available, but they are seen as intrinsic to the spiritual path that Jesus demonstrated.

This lack of understanding of the practice of elevated spiritual states seems to come from the fact that most academics have never been around these experiences, either in charismatic, Pentecostal or other settings. They may have read the works of mystics of the Christian faith down through the centuries that describe the Spirit zone states in incredibly beautiful and eloquent terms. However, they have never had anyone personally encourage them to explore altered states themselves. Instead they are left only to derive theological considerations from the biblical accounts of altered states, while never considering the possibility that they themselves could actually have these experiences today. Perhaps those who move freely in such experience are less likely to pursue the rigors of academia and, therefore, scholars are self-selected thinkers rather than thinker/experiencers.

The challenges of the Spirit zone

Psychologist Abraham Maslow said, "The very beginning, the intrinsic core, the essence, the universal nucleus of every known high religion ... has been the private, lonely, personal illumination, revelation, or ecstasy of some acutely sensitive prophet or seer."[36] What a great description of Jesus! But then the followers of the "prophet or seer" become involved and things get messy. They got messy in the early church very quickly. The founder's vision and experience begins to be dumbed down. Eventually, it may become so distorted as to be unrecognizable when compared to the original vision.

Among the first books of the New Testament to be written, probably sometime between 53 and 57 c.e., is Paul's first letter to the Corinthians. Here we find elevated and transcendent states in church gatherings graphically described from the very beginning of the early church.

The occasion for Paul to write to the Corinthian church in such detail about these state experiences was confusion in their worship services. The power of exalted states of consciousness in focused devotion, worship, prayer, and union with God pushed the early Christians in Corinth to gatherings that were sometimes beyond their ability to stay grounded.

We may have genuine elevated state experiences, but we always interpret and express those experiences through our stage of development. Intense spiritual experiences for those at lower growth stages can actually invite them to become more insistent that only they have the truth and everyone else is wrong. Or they can foster elitism with the claim that "my experience is bigger and better than yours, so I must be more spiritual."These very divisions, quarrels, and elitisms existed in the Corinthian community, partly as a testimony to the energizing power of transcendent states in those who were not used to them and their difficulty in handling them.

At the higher levels of spiritual development such as integral and beyond, these inspiring and even ecstatic states lead to unification, harmonization, and interconnectedness.

Quiet, meditative zone states

The incidents of altered states reported in the New Testament tend toward the reportable. That is, they are accounts of things which usually happened in public and that could be observed by others present. What these reported experiences most certainly leave out is the quiet, more meditative and profound devotional practices of the early Christians. We do not get detailed accounts of the deep prayers that, for instance, lead Peter and Paul into trances, until we come to the later Christian mystics. The centuries of experience in the Eastern traditions have something to teach us about con-templative states, along with those of the classical mystics of the Christian church such as Saint John of the Cross, Meister Eckhart, Saint Teresa of Avila, and contemporary mystics such as Bernadette Roberts and Jim Marion.

Normal and available

My purpose in describing these elevated state experiences in the New Testament is twofold. The first is to make the emphatic point that such experiences were a normal part of Jesus' life and those of the early Christians in their church life. The second is to suggest that at least some, if not all, of these state experiences and practices are available and important for us today. The claim of those in the traditional church that these experiences have ceased with the clos-ing of the biblical canon has no biblical, historical, or experiential basis. The similar claim from those in the modern church that these experiences are not important has no basis either.

I would advise three qualifications in the use of these practices today: (1) they are best interpreted in ways that move them beyond the magical/traditional/mythic levels. (2) They should be open to rational investigation and reflection by those who take the time and energy to experience them. Most of all, (3) they should lead to the strengthening and transformation of ourselves and others.

CHAPTER 11

In the Spirit Zone Today
My Journey

My first time

My first transcendent, altered state experience occurred when I was 23. Two weeks before, I had attended a weekend Episcopalian prayer retreat. I felt safe with the Episcopalians because they appeared theologically respectful and reserved, just like I thought of myself. Although I was Baptist born, Baptist bred, and expected to eventually be Baptist dead, I really liked Episcopalians. Episcopalians will do anything for God as long as it's not tacky. It seemed to me, back then, that Baptists would also do anything for God, especially if it is tacky.

However, these were not your ordinary Episcopalians. Back then they were called "neo-pentecostals." They were part of the underground early charismatic movement that "bootlegged" experiences of the Spirit into camp and retreat settings. At one point in that retreat those who wanted to be prayed for to receive a new release of the Spirit were invited to sit in a chair in the center of the small group as the others gathered around and prayed for them. At their invitation, I hesitantly and fearfully agreed to be prayed for. I almost jumped up and ran out when a very large and enthusiastic African-American woman clapped her hands and said, "Oh boy, we got ourselves a Baptist preacher!"

I was duly prayed for with quiet, intelligible prayers and other quiet, but unintelligible, prayers. As far as I was concerned, absolutely nothing at all happened to me. And that's exactly what I planned on.

I lived with my emotional brakes on and I certainly wasn't going to have an emotional or spiritual "experience" in front of anyone else. After all, I was a "minister" and already had everything I needed, thank you. That seemed to be fine with everyone. I think they were used to my kind and knew it just took a little time.

It was two weeks later, as I was in bed at night reading an Agatha Christie murder mystery, that I began to have an extraordinary feeling. Being a good Baptist, I had never been intoxicated, but later I thought this must be what it feels like for those who appear to be "happy drunks." I was suddenly in love with everyone and everything. I loved the walls of my room. I loved my parents, quite shocking at the time. I loved Agatha Christie. I loved the Catholics (Baptist preachers did not love Catholics back then). And I even loved God. Up to this point, I had majored in serving God, and did so with great enthusiasm. But the experience of being loved by and loving God was pretty much absent. This experience, which years later I would describe as a mystical union with all things, lasted several hours. The effects have lasted a lifetime.

It was a temporary merging of the Universal Mind with my mind. For some days afterward I felt and perceived things from a new and higher perspective. Later experiences and my evolving spiritual practices continue dimensions of that experience today even as I write this book. It was tangible, potent, and life-changing.

Spiritual intoxication

Sometime later, I saw, in a new way, this New Testament passage: "Don't get drunk with wine but be filled with the Spirit."[1] This had always sounded to me like a nice little moralism, something like, "Don't go to the bar and get loaded. Instead, stay at home and read the Bible." Or "Don't get drunk, go to church instead." But Paul was quite specific in his advice. Instead of filling up with alcoholic spirits, fill up with God's Spirit. What possible connection is there between getting drunk and being filled with the Spirit? In the experience of the early Christians, there was a whopping big connection. At Pentecost, when the Spirit came upon Jesus' followers *en masse*, they became so happy they were actually accused of being drunk! And now I related it to my own intoxicating mystical experience.

Jesus put it this way in the Gospel of Thomas, "Because you have drunk, you have become intoxicated from the bubbling spring I have tended."[2]

Years later I read William James's observation:

> The sway of alcohol over mankind is unquestionably due to its power to stimulate the mystical faculties of human nature, usually crushed to earth by the cold facts and dry criticisms of the sober hours. Sobriety diminishes, discriminates and says no; drunkenness expands, unites, and says yes. It is in fact the great exciter of the Yes function in man. It brings its votary from the chill periphery of things to the radiant core. It makes him for the moment one with truth. Not through mere perversity do men run after it.[3]

In my ardent search for theological understanding, I found that the former dean of the Harvard Divinity School, Krister Stendahl, had written,

> Opening up the full spectrum of religious experience and expression is badly needed in those churches that have suppressed the charismatic dimension. Flashlight-battery-voltage Christianity is certainly not strong enough for fighting the drug habit. And no religious tradition can renew itself without the infusion of raw and fresh primary religious experience.[4]

More recently, Ken Wilber's comment on these kinds of mystical experiences, using his specialized integral vocabulary, rang true for me.

> Right now, spiritual state-experiences are often disallowed by the dominant mode of discourse of many orthodox religions, and thus are forced elsewhere. . . . When spirit states do surface in religions, they are often pushed into evangelical revivals and Pentecostal ecstatic gatherings, which are usually subtle-state experiences and altered states that

are, in fact, of an occasionally deep nature—reaching into Underhill's state of illumination and grace—but they are usually kept segmented into red [warrior] and sometimes barely amber [traditional] stages of development. . . . The sooner spiritual traditions begin offering both higher states and higher stages, the sooner religion can step into its new role in the modern and postmodern world; the role of the great conveyor belt of humanity at large.[5]

Hanging with the mystics

I had been in biblically focused Southern Baptist churches all my life and had a Master of Divinity in New Testament and theology from a Southern Baptist seminary. In all of that time, spiritual-state experiences were strongly "disallowed." Pentecostals were dismissed with putdowns and laughter. No one ever instructed me about any of the altered states of consciousness so frequently and explicitly described in the Bible in which these same Baptists so ardently "believed." Here I was, with a graduate degree called a "Master of Divinity," having mastered very little about my divinity!

Meanwhile, now in my late twenties, I began exploring the religious world's then-secret underground network of camps, retreats, and meetings of what were called "neo-pentecostals" back then. There we could hear teaching about and experiment with elevated spiritual states. In the '60s, '70s, and '80s I spent much time with charismatic leaders such as Frank Laubach (Founder of "Each One Teach One" world literacy movement and author of *A Modern Mystic*), Agnes Sanford (founder of the "inner healing" movement), Bob Mumford and Derek Prince (both internationally-known Pentecostal teachers), John Wimber (founder of the "Vineyard" movement), Ruth Carter Stapleton (President Jimmy Carter's sister and charismatic teacher), Tommy Tyson (charismatic Methodist preacher who became my mentor) and Francis McNutt (Catholic priest, charismatic renewal leader, and author of many books, including *The Nearly Perfect Crime: How the Church Almost Killed the Ministry of Healing*). Francis McNutt and I attended the same

Agnes Sanford retreat where he was first "zapped" with the Spirit. I led retreats along with Ruth and Tommy, and the two of them along with Francis were frequent speakers at my church in the 1970s and '80s. I treasure those experiences even as I now understand them in a more integral framework.

I had begun to see that God was not a concept or a belief but an experiential reality. At one point I realized I was a fledgling Christian "mystic" who hung out with other Christian mystics wherever I could find them.

What's a Christian mystic?

Karl Rahner, the noted Catholic theologian, is widely quoted as saying, "The Christian of tomorrow will be a mystic, or not a Christian at all."[6]

A mystic is someone who seeks a direct and intimate connection with God. In the mystical state, the distance between God and ourselves vanishes. Mysticism is the practice of being one with God.

Wilber, using his specialized integral vocabulary, says,

> . . . one can take up meditation, contemplation, Pentecostal experiencing, or centering prayer whether one is at red, or Amber, or orange, or green, etc.[various stages], and be plunged into authentic gross, subtle, causal, and nondual religious states.[7]

Jesus, the founder of what has become today's Christianity, was first and foremost a mystic. He was a very rational mystic, but still a mystic. Ken Wilber's version of integral philosophy is observably mystical. *It should be no surprise that integral and beyond Christianity is essentially a mystic's Christianity.*

Mystical experience is available to everyone. It is a natural, normal part of our humanity until religion and society drive it out. Mystics are the normal people. It's the non-mystics who are abnormal!

Wilber says, "A mystic is not one who sees God as an object, but one who is immersed in God as an atmosphere."[8]

For the mystic, God is present in nature, friendship, love, art, music, dance, laughter, suffering, pain, the poor, and the oppressed.

We all have the potential to be modern-day mystics. It is already there deep inside of absolutely everyone. We can cultivate that awareness so that which is already true can become present in our awareness and constantly available to us.

A Christian mystic is someone who most likely got to the mystical by looking at the life and teaching of Jesus. Others look at Buddha, or Krishna, or, as we all end up, looking inside.

Mystical spirituality is not a nostalgic look at the past but an exciting foray into the future. The Spirit comes to us from the future —not the past.

The mystics ask you to take nothing on mere belief. Rather, they give you a set of experiments to test in your own awareness and experience. The laboratory is your own mind and heart, the experiment is prayer and meditation, or whatever connects you to the Spirit. You, yourself, try it and compare your test results with others who have also performed the experiments. And the exhilarating thing you will find out, according to the mystics, is that in the very core of your being you are God. This is what I have discovered in my own life.

Wilber says:

> Mysticism is transrational and thus lies in our collective future, not our collective past. Mysticism is evolutionary and progressive, not devolutionary and regressive, as Aurobindo and Teilhard de Chardin realized. And science, in my opinion, is stripping us of our infantile and adolescent views of spirit, is stripping us of our prerational views, in order to make room for the genuinely transrational insights of the higher stages of development, the transpersonal stages of genuine mystical or contemplative development.[9]

Matthew Fox gives us what he calls "twenty-one running, working, experiential definitions of mysticism." Their titles are:

> Experience, Nondualism, Compassion, Connection Making, Radical Amazement, Affirmation of the World as a Whole, Right-Brain, Self-Critical, Heart Knowledge, Return to the Source, Feminist, Panentheistic, Birthing Images, Silence,

Nothingness and Darkness, Childlike Playfulness, Psychic Justice, Prophetic, Being-With-Being, True Self, and finally, Globally Ecumenical.[10]

A mystic is someone who has a direct experience of God, or with whatever we call the sacred or that which gives ultimate meaning. In that respect, all mystics seem to have similar experiences even though they use different concepts and words to describe their experience.[11] "The essence of mysticism is that in the deepest part of your own being, in the very center of your own pure awareness, you are fundamentally one with Spirit, one with Godhead, one with all, in a timeless and eternal and unchanging fashion."[12]

Presbyterian minister David Garnett echoes many of our hearts when he reported on a denominational meeting, saying:

> I kept wondering in Denver: Where are the mystics in our church? I see plenty of lawyers. Where are the artists, the dreamers, the lovers? I wonder if our time would have been better spent sitting in silence together, praying silently, creating empty spaces, hospitable spaces, where we could make room for each other in all of our differences and passions, giving up that terrible need we all have to some degree to control others instead of love them, and then breaking down into twos and threes and fours and telling the Biblical stories and our own stories, and listening to music and poems and dreams, and pondering art, and connecting and networking with one another, sharing our dreams and joining our dreams with others.[13]

The Psalmist was a mystic: "As the deer longs for flowing streams, so my soul longs for you, O God. My soul thirsts for God, for the living God. When shall I come and behold the face of God?"[14]

The Gospel of Thomas uses strong words about the importance of being open to Spirit: "Jesus said, 'Whoever blasphemes against the Father will be forgiven, and whoever blasphemes against the son will be forgiven, but whoever blasphemes against the holy spirit will not be forgiven, either on earth or in heaven.'"[15]

This mystical saying uses the language of the later Trinitarian religious culture of the time in which it was finally formulated. It dramatically declares that we don't have to get what we think about God ("the Father") right. We don't need to get what we think about Jesus (the "son") right. But if we can't be open to Spirit, we can get stuck for a really long time, now and later.

Pointing out that the mystical is not prerational magic but transrational reality, Wilber says,

> Magic never in its wildest dreams thought that it would be trumped by mythic. And the mythic gods and goddesses never imagined that reason could and would destroy them. And here we sit, in our rational worldview, all smug and confident that nothing higher will sweep out of the heavens and completely explode our solid perceptions, undoing our very foundations. And yet surely, the transrational lies in wait. It is just around the corner, this new dawn. Every stage transcends and includes, and thus inescapably, unavoidably it seems, the sun will rise on a world tomorrow that in many ways transcends reason.[16]

The Restaurant of Life

Christians have sat down at the Restaurant of Life and the waiter has come to give us our particular designated menu, the Bible. Christians have studied their menu in every detail until they have understood what was offered. And, for hundreds of years, they have not ordered from the menu. *Instead, they have tried to eat the menu!* No wonder they have been grumpy, undernourished, and doctrinaire. Eating the menu instead of ordering from it is the traditional church's idea of having a spiritual experience (except for a conversion experience among evangelicals and worship among charismatics). When we learn how to order from the menu we can get a nourishing, great-tasting, wonderful meal. A cognitive framework is of great help and encouragement, but it alone is not enough. The map is not the territory. The menu is not the meal.

Mystical experiences

Marcus Borg says,

> A Spirit person or religious ecstatic is one who has frequent and vivid experiences of the sacred. Most of these experiences involve non-ordinary states of consciousness such as visions, shamanic journeys, mystical experiences, or enlightenment experiences.[17]

Becki Jayne Harrelson, a Christian artist friend of mine, has six of her works on permanent display in our church gallery of 240 images of Jesus from around the world. Here is how she paints:

> I go into an altered state of consciousness, a quiet ecstasy when I conjure these ideas up... or maybe I should rather say when I am given these ideas for they appear in my mind's eye effortless, in a twinkling of an eye. They make me giggle sometimes and a feeling of joy I can't fully express. It takes me a while to calm down to ordinary life. I feel as though I could ascend.
>
> In 1991 I had what some would call an emergency stage, a breakdown (but I think of it as a breakthrough), when memories I had kept at bay of having been sexually, emotionally, and physically abused as a young girl came flooding back with intensity. During that time, I prayed a lot.... And that's when Jesus, Mary, and a great pillar of white light began to appear to me, sometimes in dreams and sometimes in meditative states. Eventually, they began instructing me on the art. I asked the Light why was I given this artistic talent and what was I to do with it... And the answer was as clear as driven snow... "Love. You asked and Love answered." So I have endeavored to be true to Love's call.
>
> I practice meditative painting—my mind is blank when I paint—and sometimes that still small voice whispers, "Try this." For example, when I added money into the hand of one of the apostles in The Last Supper. I quit questioning the guidance long ago for I dedicated the art to Service for

the highest and best and that doesn't always jive with my perceptions or knowledge. I give the power to the still small voice within me, that wise Holy Spirit that abides in us all when we acknowledge It, and funny how It has blessed me with unique imagery and hopefully... May it serve to heal.[18]

Wilber points out that the "contemplative core" of all the world's religions is "a series of direct mystical, transcendental, meditative, contemplative or yogic experience—*not sensory and not mental*, but transsensual, transmental, transpersonal transcendental consciousness—data seen not merely with the eye of the flesh or with the eye of the mind, but with the eye of contemplation."[19]

Except for Pentecostal and openly charismatic churches, these experiences have often been successfully domesticated or eliminated altogether. In Pentecostal and most charismatic churches the mystical has been confined to certain expressions such as glossolalia and prophecy, and limited by a traditional theology. An integral approach will carefully discern the value of these experiences and include them while transcending the sometimes limiting practices and theology that accompanies them, such as that praying in "tongues," is proof of having the Spirit, or that only Christians can experience the Spirit of God.

In what Christian seminaries today are there courses on direct experiences with the Spirit? Where are the professors who are at home with this and not only teach but mentor and impart to their students this awakened capacity within them? It is clear from the book of Acts that impartation and transmission of some sort from awakened leadership is an important element in spiritual development. It is absolutely foundational in the Eastern traditions. But when there is no training, practice, or community understanding of this, the capacity for expanded state consciousness lies dormant in the Christian tradition.

In postmodern theologian Marcus Borg's account of his own spiritual journey we see a remarkable evolution of his spiritual growth. He began as a youth with a traditional background in the Lutheran church. In college and seminary he moved to a modern rational altitude where he did not know what to do with the notion of God. Then he moved to the postmodern state of not only seeing Jesus as a Spirit person but having his own ecstatic state experiences. Here is his account of these:

> In my early to mid-thirties, I had a number of experiences of what I now recognize as "nature mysticism." . . . In a sense, these experiences were nothing spectacular, at least not compared with those described by William James almost a century ago in his classic *The Varieties of Religious Experience*. Yet the experiences fundamentally changed my understanding of God, Jesus, religion, and Christianity.
>
> They were marked by what the Jewish theologian Abraham Heschel calls "radical amazement." They were moments of transformed perception in which I saw the earth as "filled with the glory of God," shining with a radiant presence. They were also moments of connectedness in which I felt my linkage to what is. They seemed similar to Rudolf Otto's description of experiences of the "numinous," the awe-inspiring and wonder-evoking "holy," the *mysterium tremendum et fascinans* (the tremendous mystery that elicits trembling even as it also attracts us in a compelling way). They involved a rediscovery of mystery—not an intellectual mystery, but an experience of holy mystery.
>
> These experiences, besides being ecstatic, were for me "ah ha" moments. They gave me a new understanding of the meaning of the word "God." I realized that "God" does not refer to a supernatural being "out there" (which is where I had put God ever since my childhood musings about God "up in heaven"). Rather, I began to see the word "God" refers to "the sacred" at the center of existence, the "holy mystery" which is all around us and within us. God is the non-material ground and source and presence in which, to cite words attributed to Paul by the author of Acts, "we live and move and have our being" (Acts 17:28).[20]

Pushing the mystics out of the church

As we have seen, spiritual state experiences were a regular occurrence in the life of Jesus and the early church. Over these last two thousand years these illuminating state experiences have been ignored or been a victim of "that only happened back then" reductionism. The spiritual path of Jesus has been taken over by the institutional church. It has moved from freely offered religious experience to required religious concepts which often include prohibitions against the very religious experiences Jesus modeled. Here are some of the claims that I have heard many, many times.

- "Those experiences were only necessary at the beginning and ceased with the early church."

- "They really happened then but we only study them now."

- "We don't need such experiences anymore because now we have the Bible, the church, and our creeds."

- "Seeking religious or exotic spiritual experiences is a very immature form of Christianity."

- "Don't go off the deep end with that religious stuff."

- "What is important is what Jesus taught and his actions against oppression, not mystical experiences."

- "These fanciful mystic experiences he was supposed to have had were probably added by the writers to enhance his image."

- "What you call mystical experience is just New Age gobbledygook."

- "We should not seek emotional experiences but rather try to live the right kind of life."

- "What is important is ministering to the poor and working for world peace. You're into too much navel gazing and mystical mush."

Such messages go on endlessly, dampening or preventing the very direct experiences with Spirit that can actually help us live life more abundantly and minister to a needy world.

Psychologist Abraham Maslow studied spiritual experiences extensively and pointed out that the main thesis of his book *Religions, Values, and Peak-Experiences* is this: "Organized Religion, the churches, finally may become the major enemies of the religious experience and the religious experiencer."[21]

It seems to me that has not only happened today, but it began happening within a hundred years of Jesus sharing his own spiritual experiences with us. *Christianity, which began in an outburst of life-changing spiritual experiences, is now the primary opponent of such experiences!*

Inviting the mystics back into the church

How do we integrate the dynamic direct experience of Spirit in the accounts of spiritual experiences throughout Christian history into our church experience today? How do we today include the authentic, biblically reported, direct experiences of Spirit which have been repeated and validated by the saints and mystics throughout two thousand years of church history? How do we also transcend the emotional excesses, manipulation, sensationalism, and mythic theology that has also been associated with such experiences?

Integral church does this by teaching, modeling, and encouraging both higher stage understanding and higher state experiences. It includes the charismatic experience of the early church and the mystical experiences of the saints through the centuries and today. It learns from the mystics of traditions other than Christian, such as Jewish, Buddhist, Hindu, and Sufi. In putting these into an integral framework, it also transcends some of the theological and cultural attachments of the traditional/mythic state that confuse the symbols of the mystical with that reality itself.

Jim Marion provides the best explanation in a Christian context that I have seen of these mystical levels of consciousness in his seminal books *Putting on the Mind of Christ* and *The Death of the Mythic God*. He discusses the four state-stages of psychic, subtle, causal, and nondual. I highly recommend both books for further exploration of many crucial aspects.

Pentecostal/charismatic churches

Chapter 10's description of inspired states in the New Testament may have sounded rather Pentecostal or charismatic. So let's be honest—they may be on to something. If Paul and Peter visited our churches today with their staid and stuffy services filled with a little congregational recitation followed by much sermonizing by professional clergy, while most of the people sit still and listen, they would have wondered if they were really in church.

There are 543 million Pentecostal/charismatic Christians in the world. [22] They make up about one-quarter of the world's 2.1 billion Christians. Allowing for the kind of adherents in all religious groups who are not really involved, this still remains an incredibly large number of Christians who have, or are around, mystical experiences within a traditional level religious worldview. They are the most rapidly growing group of Christians in the world.

Charismatic Christianity, ancient and contemporary, is at home with:

- Directly experiencing God through higher states of consciousness

- Momentary glimpses into other realities, often called "visions"

- Channeling words, images, or inner sensing that communicate divine wisdom and encouragement to us today

- Personal languages of prayer and praise

- Passionate corporate and private worship

- Transmission of the healing energy of the Spirit

Oral Roberts, Pat Robertson, and other traditional Christians may have higher states experiences that are similar to altered states of the Dalai Lama and Sufi and Christian mystics. It is their expressions and interpretations of those experiences which are quite different. All of us manifest and interpret our state experiences in terms of our own stage of consciousness.

The transcendent, "charismatic" type of altered states of the subtle consciousness that are so prevalent in the New Testament have also been neglected in the integral movement because the current leaders there are not familiar with them. Meditators tend to try to aim only for the causal state of formlessness. They are often not familiar with subtle state visions and forms. I believe that integral practitioners often shy away from these experiences because they do not want to be indentified with crazy Pentecostals or magic-oriented New Agers, or prerational stages. Or they simply aim only for the deep causal states without form. This is a great loss.

For the specifically Christian path, it is also a great loss. *We have yet to see what would happen if the Christian series of escalators offered Pentecostal/charismatic believers higher stages of understanding without disparaging their already sometimes higher states of experience.*

My experience with numinous connecting states

While I was in college a deeply spiritual deacon and businessman in the Baptist church, where I worked as minister of music, adopted me as a "spiritual son." It was his invitation that got me to the prayer retreat I described earlier. He would often invite me to other such gatherings where I observed Christians who seemed to have a spiritual energy and connection to God that I had not experienced in others or myself. I knew that I had read about such spirituality in the New Testament and other books, but here it was in living color. I was fascinated intellectually and hoped to experience more of this stream of spiritual life myself. But I am a very slow learner. Gradually over the years, as I began to pray for others as I had been prayed for at the Episcopalian prayer retreat, I would see them experience a refreshing of the Spirit, sometimes physical healing, and quite often inner healing and the experience of deep resting which some of us call "resting in the Spirit." Interestingly enough, back then, I never felt much of anything myself except the satisfaction of blessing others.

At one point I saw how "normal" the practice of a personal language of prayer and praise was in the early church. I decided one day that I would pray with any words that came to my mind except those I had already learned in actual languages. This excluded English, Latin, Hebrew, and Greek. I made sure I was alone—after all, this was probably going to be embarrassing. I just said some strange sounding "words" aloud. It *was* embarrassing. I told myself things like, "You're really crazy doing this. This has nothing to do with God. You are making all of this up. What if other people found out?" Nevertheless, I continued this practice over the weeks until the criticizing internal messages stopped. After a few months of this devotional practice, these disparaging messages were pushed away by the increasingly focused elevated state I experienced whenever I prayed this way. These negative messages have never returned in the last 40 years.

I find a gentle sense of elevation in the center of my chest flowing up to my throat which expresses itself in silent or softly spoken sounds which feel satisfyingly like prayer and praise directed toward God. Sometimes I pray this way first and it is followed by that gentle sense of inner welling up of gratitude and thanksgiving. Almost always in times of corporate (congregational) worship I find myself silently expressing myself to God in this way. I experience this as a gently transcendent state of focused prayer and praise which is usually filled with feelings of gratefulness and joy for God's nearness without and within.

University of Virginia moral psychologist Jonathan Haidt says, "Powerful moments of elevation sometimes seem to push a mental 'reset button,' wiping out feelings of cynicism and replacing them with feelings of hope, love, and optimism, and a sense of moral inspiration."[23] I experience this often.

Next, I began exploring channeling the Spirit. What worked best for me in stirring that up within me was to ask the Spirit specific questions about myself, others, or situations about which I was praying. I learned to "catch" the thoughts, words, sentences that came to my mind before I talked myself out of them. They often seemed to be from a source of higher wisdom, inspiration, and guidance than I would normally be aware of.

Most often I would write down the words, phrases, or short sentences that I heard inwardly. I have practiced "listening to the Spirit" for 35 years now. Most every morning I will take just a brief minute or two upon waking or later in the morning to sit with pen and paper and simply ask, "God, is there anything you want to tell me today?" Then I quickly write down the words, usually just a few, that come to my mind. I do not hear an audible voice, but rather these words just come up from within me. It took a while to learn to trust them and sometimes I am aware they are just random thoughts. At other times they are deeply helpful to me. Often I will write down, in one word, the name of a person or situation I am seeking guidance about. Then I mentally ask the Spirit about that person and write down what comes to my mind, usually just a word or two. The last time I did this was just a minute ago when I asked if there was anything the Spirit wanted to tell me about writing this chapter. I heard, "Go with the flow from within you." That sounds reasonable, simple, and just like good advice. I take it for that and also as an authentic word from God. Just because it is not strange, striking, or unusual doesn't mean it does not come from the Spirit. I think God is usually very reasonable and simple in communicating with us because that is mostly what we need.

I also see or hear things when praying for others in a time of healing prayer. This channeling of words and pictures is not as prominent in my experience as in, for instance, my friend and co-pastor at Broadway, Marcia Fleischman's. She has an uncanny gift of hearing from the Spirit when praying for others or even just being with them. She will often hear words and see pictures for me and others that are amazingly insightful and healing.

I take an hour or more on most days of the week to have a more extended time for spiritual reading (not study), being quiet, listening, and, most of all, deep "zone" prayer. I only occasionally ask for things. In praying for others I might make a simple request in my mind or I might intentionally sense God's Spirit, then the spirit of the person I am praying for, and then just see them both coming together. I don't know what people really need, but God does.

In worship services, especially at my church but also in visiting others, including Catholic, Protestant, and Pentecostal churches, I move into an elevated state of experiencing the Spirit within. Sometimes it takes a while to let go of the busyness of the day or, at my church, thinking about whatever part I have in the service. As I sink down into myself, letting the music, architecture, or liturgy move me into worship, I begin to sense the Spirit.

For almost 50 years now, I and many others in our church, have practiced "hands on" praying for others in small groups, healing services, and ministry times. I have prayed for literally hundreds and hundreds of people over the years, often with Marcia. She uses her gift for channeling healing words and images from the Spirit for others. I mostly just send the energy of the Spirit through my hands to others.

In these years I have seen remarkable things happen as we pray, and afterward, too. I am so immersed in this way of praying that I don't know what other pastors and church people do who don't experience this on a regular basis. Whether I am praying or getting prayed for, I get filled up and blessed with energy to be more of who I am in Christ and do more of what I am called to do in ministry.

The last few years at Broadway a small group has gotten together in what we call "Experiencing God." We usually begin with a guided meditation. Then we put a chair in the middle and all who wish to can take a turn sitting there and receiving prayer energy from the rest of the group. We hear words, see pictures, and send healing energy to one another. We will often say something like, "I don't know what this means but here is what I am seeing or hearing. Does that mean anything to you?"

This is all quite remarkable as we get "filled up" with the Spirit. The Apostle Paul's admonition "not to get drunk with wine but be filled with the Spirit" seems to take on a reality that is life-giving. Sometimes we get drunk with giggles, laughter, crying, or "resting in the Spirit," the shutting down of our external circuits so that we cannot stand but end up resting in a chair or on the floor while we experience God's presence and peaceful healing.

Spiritual guides

I have begun having another kind of transforming connecting state experience for the last six years. After pondering Jesus' transfiguration experience, I decided if Jesus needed the kind of guidance he got from Moses and Elijah, then maybe I do, too. I am not saying I have had any kind of experience quite as dramatic as what Jesus had. I have not yet glowed and radiated visible white light that could be seen by others. And my guides do not presently appear in the visible spectrum as they did with Jesus and his three friends. Here is how this transforming journey began for me.[24]

At the time of writing this book, I have been meeting weekly for over ten years now with Dr. Patricia Searing. A PhD from Fielding Graduate University and an ordained minister, she is an energy healer who touches my physical, emotional, mental, and spiritual bodies. For an hour every week I lie on her massage-type table while we talk and as she moves her hands over my body. Constantly collecting information from my own energy field and spirit, she interacts with me at many levels. All four of my "bodies" have massively evolved further through these sessions. Although she only mentions this kind of spirit guidance if directly asked, one time six years ago I did just that. I asked about her experiences with guides from the other side, telling her that I was interested because of studying Jesus' experience with Moses and Elijah. She encouraged me to think about who I was drawn to in my life that might serve as a guide. I asked, "Do you really mean anybody?" She responded, "Of course." I said, "I have always been fascinated with the disciple of Jesus named John." She suggested that I ask John if he would be one of my guides. I said, "Well, surely he would not be available. He's pretty famous and must be very busy." I guess I thought his time would be filled up by now. But Patricia said, "You'll never know unless you ask him." She invited me to ask John, out loud, if he would serve as a guide for me. I did so and instantly heard inside of me, "Yes, of course. I have been with you already for a long time. That's why you were interested in me to begin with." I broke out crying with overwhelming gratitude. (I am getting over being an emotionless rock nowadays.)

That began a relationship with someone whom I presume to be

the Beloved Apostle John that is incredibly enriching. After some initial conversations, which I have kept in my computer journal, John told me that my relationship with him was not primarily going to be one of words. I had lived so long only in my head that my body gets fairly disconnected. John told me I would simply sense his hand on my right shoulder, and he would be present to my right and slightly behind me. I felt that hand immediately then and do now every time I connect with him. He also told me that I was not going to be able to see or visualize him in my mind because that would also distract me from my body. Smart guy! That was exactly what I needed and his touch often calls me back into my body, as it is doing right now as I write sitting at my computer.

In the following months I asked Mary, Jesus' mother, if she would be a guide. She said, "Yes," and appeared on my left. There is an ancient scholar named Michael (not the angel, as far as I know) who now appears to my right, and, of course, Jesus, who appears directly in front of me. I say appears, meaning on the screen of my mind, not with my physical eyes. In more recent years, a group of mystic followers of Jesus from the fourth century, known by me simply as "the teachers," have appeared and communicated with me.[25]

Seeing spiritual realities

I would like Christians who take the Bible seriously to take what I am presenting in this book seriously. Therefore, I hesitate to talk about this last topic because it sounds like more New Age mumbo jumbo. As I have previously pointed out, a significant part of the New Testament sounds like what we commonly think of as New Age paraphernalia, too. In the New Testament there are trances, speaking under the influence of the Spirit in unintelligible sounds, talking to the dead, healing energy, channeling messages from the Spirit, and other paranormal phenomena. I wish the Christians who attack the New Age with such paranoia would first deal with these things in their own Bibles before they are spooked by it from New Agers. Everyone who is serious about Christianity has to decide how they will deal with the biblical manifestations which are there attributed to the Spirit of God. The need for discernment is extremely important today because not everything in psychic and other altered realms of consciousness is from the Holy Spirit. God's Spirit offers only high level resources of love and healing for us. Other quite manipulative and unloving spirits from lower astral levels can offer everything from silliness to really bad advice under the guise of sounding "spiritual."

Several years ago I began seeing people's auras, probably in the form of electromagnetic energy around bodies, with a larger area around people's heads. That may be the origin of the golden halos which artists seem to favor painting around the heads of Jesus and other saintly people.

Three years ago I began to see images when I was praying and/or meditating with my eyes closed or opened in a dimly lighted room. It began with what appeared to be the black cosmos with a multitude of twinkling stars, similar to looking at the sky on a totally dark night away from all other light sources. Later it appeared that I was having an out of body experience floating in outer space. Next, I began to see colorful lines moving in precise geometric patterns, brilliant and beautiful toroidal-shaped lines in front of me, radiating lines, spirals, whirling pinwheels, and other patterns in blue, red, green, violet, and gold. Then waves of color and, most often, a glowing golden cloud of light which approaches from the dark distance and rapidly moves toward me until it almost fills my visual field, and then disappears. On one occasion I entered the golden cloud and was visibly and bodily in a tunnel with golden walls. I felt myself touch the quite solid, ridged, dull gold walls in this immensely moving experience.

Next I was seeing images such as a television screen with pictures on it in front of me. Then I began seeing maps of the world fly past on my visual field. This has now moved to what appears to be traveling effortlessly and outside of my physical body rapidly around the world in the lower atmosphere as I watch the oceans, tall buildings in city skylines, and even people in various countries. It feels like I could reach out and touch them.

The strangest thing that has happened a number of times is that with my eyes closed and completely covered by a sleep mask[26] I can see objects around me. Several times I have put on the blindfold at the park where I power walk and looked at a tree up close, seeing the bark quite clearly, as well as other objects. I should do a magic act. Weird.

Those who take psychedelics or dissociative anesthetic drugs may experience what are called CEVs (closed eye visuals) similar to this. It is also not unusual in deep prayer/mediation to have similar visual experiences. I only report these things so that if something similarly "weird" happens to you in your spiritual path, you will neither worry about it, be blown away by it, or discount it, but rather discern it. I always share these things with a few others to make sure I am not dropping off the deep end. But then the deep end may be where the good stuff is.

Finally, I am reminded of the monk who excitedly told his superior that he had started levitating during his prayers. His superior casually replied, "Yes, but don't let it interfere with your praying." Good advice.

Brain entrainment technology

I have tried many ways of praying. For the last six years I have experimented with listening to specially produced CDs that help open me up to deeper states.[27] These recordings often have the sound of rainfall or gentle music. As one listens with a stereo headset, underneath the audible sound is an almost inaudible tone which differs slightly between the left and right sides. This produces a binaural beat leading to what is called brain wave entrainment. The tone elicits a meditative state, moving one progressively from beta into alpha, theta and delta brainwave states. Several times a week I do one-hour sessions that are both relaxing and invigorating.

After I put on my headphones and start listening to an entrainment CD, I often begin my zone prayer time with the Three Faces of God Invocation (see Chapter 12). This is followed by a grounding ritual involving my seven primary vertical energy centers, which helps me focus and become grounded. Next is usually a time of "connecting" state prayer involving the striking presence of Jesus and others and spontaneous imaginative visualization and out of body experiences (all "connecting" states). At some point this normally leads to deeply abiding ("being" state—without forms) in God near the end of my hour.

Other times during the week I take from five to 30 minutes, usually in the morning, to center my attention on spiritual realities. I sit quietly, sometimes reading from the New Testament gospels or the Gospel of Thomas. Sometimes I read Rumi's or Hafiz's poems. I pay attention to my breathing, becoming grounded and centered. I may worship for a time in both English and my prayer language, expressing adoration and gratefulness. This almost always gets my spiritual juices going. Often I will write down what I hear when I ask the Spirit about various people or situations in my life. The question is usually, "Is there anything you want to tell me about _____?" I write down the word or words that I hear. They are amazingly helpful and encouraging. Sometimes the thoughts begin to flow and I go over to my computer and enter them. Sometimes I will repeat affirmations and verses that are especially meaningful to me.

An observation about meditation

The point in describing some of my own practices and experiences is to encourage you to actively find and pursue the spiritual practices that fit for you. I am not suggesting you try mine unless you are attracted to them. Try anything that seems interesting and which you discern may be of a significant spiritual level. Do the practices that accelerate your growth in both states and stages. The goal of all spiritual practice is to awaken to the Divine Self within and to connect with the kinds of spiritual realities that Jesus, the early church, and other saintly mystics down through the centuries have experienced.

I am aware that some people who meditate are only trying to move into a "being" state with a total relinquishment of all attachments and forms. It can take many years of meditation to come to this depth. The first experiences of the early Christians were "connecting" state experiences. This was because they are easier to come by. I believe many in the meditating community, whether Buddhist, Christian, or nothing, tend to skip subtle state connecting experiences because they are not familiar with them. They are not encouraged in them, but rather discouraged from them. Some forms of prayer and most forms of mediation focus on *not* having such experiences, which may be seen as distraction or even superficial. I believe connecting state practices can jumpstart the path of spiritual experience. They can then open the door to the "being" state of deeper realization. They can also refresh and intensify other practices. I encourage you to have an active time talking to God and listening for a response. Actively state your intention. What do you want from your time? Get in touch with what moves you. Be open to images and sensations. Fully engage in pouring your heart out to God. Let hurt and sadness flow. Let praise flow. Let deepening silence flow. Don't hesitate to move around physically if that helps. There is no need to be passive in the connecting state. A treasure trove of rich experiences waits for each of us there.

Rivers of rubies from your heart

Jesus said that rivers of living water shall flow from our hearts.[28] I close this chapter on that intoxicating, mystical flow of the Spirit with these striking lines from the mystical poet Hafiz's "The Great Secret":[29]

God was full of Wine last night,
So full of Wine
That He let a great secret slip.
He said:
There is no person on this earth
Who needs a pardon from Me—
For there is really no such thing,
No such thing
As Sin!

The Beloved has gone completely Wild—
He has poured Himself into me!
I am Blissful and Drunk and Overflowing.
Dear world,
Draw life from my Sweet Body.
Dear wayfaring souls,
Come drink your fill of liquid rubies,
For God has made my heart
An Eternal Fountain.[30]

PART III
STANDPOINTS

Standpoints are the places where we stand to view everything in our lives—every object, event, moment, person, including God and spiritual realities. They are the perspectives we bring to all things. The three primary perspectives or standpoints are reflected in all modern languages as 1st-person, 2nd-person, and 3rd-person. We can look at any and all things from how we personally see them (1st-person), how others see them (2nd-person), and from the point of view of the objective facts about them (3rd-person). In linguistic terms, the 1st-person is the person speaking *as* him- or herself—the subjective "I" realm. The 2nd-person is the person being spoken *to*—the intersubjective realm of "You." The 3rd-person is what is being spoken *about*—the objective "It" realm.

These three perspectives are each different and each crucial. You cannot look at any reality from one standpoint and see what you can see from the other two. Anything less than all three and we miss seeing the full picture.

CHAPTER 12

The Three Faces of God
God in 3D

Would we recognize God if we saw her? We may have a spiritual form of prosopagnosia, the technical word for face blindness. Recently scientists have found that face blindness seems to be genetically based and is surprisingly common. It afflicts, in some form, about one in every 50 people. That is more than 5 million in the United States alone. For most, it is about having difficulty recognizing the same face when you see it again. That means it gets complicated trying to follow a movie plot or seeing someone you have met before. At the severe end there are people like Gaylen Howard, a 40-year-old homemaker in Boulder, Colorado. When she is standing in front of a mirror in a crowded restroom she makes a funny face so, as she says, "I can tell which one is me." Some with severe face blindness can't recognize their own children. Face blind people are often accused of being unfriendly or uncaring because they do not readily recognize faces they have seen before. However, it is just the way they are wired.[1]

Human beings have been trying to recognize God's face for a long time. Archaeologists have discovered cave wall paintings from thousands of years ago with religious symbols and drawings of our early attempts to see the faces of the gods. Unlike face blindness, which is a genetic disposition, scientists are discovering that we are biologically hardwired for the spiritual life. We actually have a natural capacity to recognize the sacred and transcendent. As evolution moves to more physical complexity in an organism, the more capacity that organism has for consciousness and for spiritual awareness.

Of Earth's creatures, it seems that we humans are able to be most conscious of the face of God. However, our preconceptions, lower level understanding, and lack of coaching hinder us from recognizing when we are seeing, feeling, hearing, tasting, or sensing God.

How did Jesus relate to God?

How did Jesus, the inspiration for the spiritual path we call Christianity, see the face of God? *The point of the Christian life is to have the same kind of relationship with and understanding of God that Jesus had and express it in the world as he did in accordance with our gifts.* So, how did Jesus see God?

Jesus spoke of God in three distinct ways: **Jesus spoke *about* God, *to* God, and *as* God.** This nine word sentence is an unparalleled revelation about God as understood and experienced by Jesus. It can guide us into a new and higher path in following Jesus. I will spend these next two chapters unfolding it. First, a brief summary:

- **Jesus spoke *about* the *Infinite Face of God*.** All of his life he thought and reflected *about* God. In his small town of Nazareth, so directly in contact with nature, he had many opportunities to notice the beauty and character of creation. The Psalmist taught him that the whole Earth, nature itself, was filled with the glory of God. His Jewish religion was filled with stories about God revealed in the history of humankind. He talked about God in sayings and parables that revealed his deep connection with the awesome God of Abraham, Isaac, and Jacob. He pondered about life and God from his early years as revealed in exchanges with the religious teachers in the Temple at age 12. This was the objective, cognitive face of God where God was spoken about and reflected upon in deepest contemplation.

  This was the God Jesus was hinting at when he said, "God is greater than I."[2] This is the ceaselessly creative divine energy. *Divinity, as the Infinite Face of God, is a metaphor for the Source, Process, Expression, and Goal of Evolution unfolding in ever greater truth, goodness, and beauty.*

- **Jesus spoke *to* the *Intimate Face of God*.** He went off in the quietness of the night or the aloneness of the wilderness to talk *to* God, whom he uniquely addressed as Abba—dearest father, papa, or daddy.[3] His prayer life nurtured and guided him in all that he did. Talking to God in intimate personal terms was as natural as breathing for Jesus. In extended prayer times in the wilderness and Gethsemane he wrestled with God, agonized with God, and kept surrendering to God in the depths of his being. This is the intimate, relational face of God in deepest communion.

- **Jesus spoke *as* the *Inner Face of God*.** At some point in his life Jesus began to realize that deep within him was the very image of God. This presence of God was actually his own deepest, truest Self, his Supreme Identity. When the Gospel of John reports him saying, "The Father-Mother and I are one,"[4] he was reflecting his experience, not just his theology. He embraced his own inner divinity and walked on Earth *as* God. This was the internal, subjective face of God as his own deepest Self. Jesus was speaking *as* God when he said things like:

  > "I am the light of the world."[5]
  > "I am the way, the truth, and the life."[6]
  > "Whoever has seen me has seen God."[7]
  > "Before Abraham was, I am."[8]

The earliest Christian groups were quite diverse, but most were sure that Jesus was divine. Their differences were about *how* that was true. The later creeds, for all their limitations, accurately saw the truth of Jesus' divinity.

Jesus related to God in all three perspectives[9]

(1) Jesus spoke *about* God as an infinite and glorious object or subject. (2) Jesus spoke *to* God as his Abba, the motherly-fatherly One of intimate personal relationship. (3) Jesus spoke *as* God, as realized and manifested inner divinity in human form. These three faces

embrace (1) the "It" of study and reflection about the awesome and infinite God, (2) the "You/We" of the cherished and close Other, and (3) the "I" of the "I Am" inner identification with God.

Three Questions about your God

1. Is your God big enough?

It is easy for the modern mind to make fun of a God who is only a superman sitting "up" in the heavens. The God who is the "Man Upstairs" is not big enough. The perspective on a God who is big enough to both create, inhabit, and continue to evolve the galaxies of the vast cosmos is what I call the *Infinite Face of God.*

2. Is your God close enough?

If we only have the God of infinity, we are very limited. This may sometimes be the only recognizable face of God for some philosophers and deists, but it is not enough for the Jesus Path. The traditional "Man Upstairs" is not only not big enough, but he is not close enough. It is imperative that we give up this "in between God" who is neither big enough or close enough. Jesus revealed to us that the mysterious and unfathomable God of the cosmos comes to us like a close and caring parent, Abba mommy-daddy. I call this the *Intimate Face of God.*

3. Is your God "you" enough?

Jesus was a blueprint, showing us what it was like to gladly embrace being made in the image of God. He fully owned his own God Self and invited us to do the same. Jesus operated at the highest levels of manifesting his own divinity. As long as we hold to God as the "man upstairs" we cannot do justice to the Infinite Face of God or the Intimate Face of God. But it is the God within and as us which is most damaged by the "sky god" of previous stages. Jesus decisively modeled and manifested God within him and *as* him. His own Eternal Face was the Face of God, and he pointed to that same Divine Face within every person. I call this the *Inner Face of God.*

Jesus embraced all three faces of God—the Infinite Face, the Intimate

Face, and the Inner Face—as he demonstrated the fullest possible relationship to God. The soul of the Jesus path is that these three points of view are also a model for us in relating to God. These are the three most direct ways in which all of us can understand and experience God. The Spirit of God manifests itself in 3rd-person Infinite God, 2nd-person Intimate God, and 1st-person Inner God. These are the Three Faces of God.

Embracing the Three Faces of God is quite radical, amazing, and profound. I can personally testify that it will transform those who welcome and practice it!

The Infinite (Panentheistic) Face of God

When we are looking for truth *about* the Infinite God, we are viewing God from the 3rd-person perspective. The 3rd-person face of God looks like studying, reflecting, and speaking *about* the awesome God who is Creator of Heaven and Earth. Here God tends to be impersonal as Source, Evolutionary Impulse, ground of Creative Energy, or Being. God is seen as an object, an "It." Calling God "It" may seem devaluing, but this can be a way to distinguish the three standpoints from one another. Remember, God is infinite, beyond description and human comprehension. However, if we are to talk about God, we must use words and metaphors, as limited as they are. With that in mind, let's look at the three ways of thinking *about* God in the major religious traditions of the world that talk about God. (Buddha did not speak of God because he believed that it was not useful.)

(1) Theism

The way of picturing God that we are probably most familiar with is *supernatural theism*. God is considered an all-powerful, separate, person-like being in theism. This is the traditional stage way that the monotheistic religions of Judaism, Christianity, and Islam view God. This supreme being created a world that was entirely separate from its creator. God is far away and somewhere other than here, namely "out there" or "up there." This is the "Man Upstairs" who sometimes intervenes in the world to make things happen.

He, and this God is usually a "he," is very powerful and could wipe out the entire world (again) if he wanted to. He is like the Greek god Zeus sitting up in the sky on a throne running things. Sometimes he's loving and kind, and sometimes he's angry and vengeful and unleashes his wrath on bad people. But he's always righteous and just, even when he's punishing people, because God can't do anything wrong.

Where did we get these ideas from? Mostly from the Bible and then elaborations by early theologians like Anselm (1033–1109) and later Renaissance painters. The Bible saw a three-tiered universe. Heaven was up there beyond the sky, and that was where God lived. Then there was Earth, where we live, and underneath the earth was the land of the dead, the place Christians called hell.

Disillusionment with this kind of setup has been growing ever since Galileo (1564–1642) confirmed the theory of Copernicus (1473–1543) that Earth was not the center of the universe. Before that time, Christians believed the cosmology of the Bible—the sun and planets moved around the Earth, the stars were fixed in the heavenly ceiling, heaven was on the other side of that ceiling, and hell was underneath the flat earth. Jesus came down from up there where God was to tell us about up there. And he warned us about down there—hell under the earth.

When we talk about "God watching over us," we can simply mean that the Creator and Source of All That Is is inherently creative and caring. However, the supernatural theist often means that God is literally up there somewhere watching us like a big divine tracking satellite in the heavens. Here is the question: "Is that God big enough for our understanding today?"

(2) Pantheism

A second way of viewing God is pantheism, which is often associated with Eastern religions such as Hinduism. In pantheism, God is identical to the Universe, or Nature. God is the sum total of all that ever was, is, or will be. God is existence itself, or reality, or all that is. God is not separate in any way from God's creation, but rather God is all of creation. Pantheism has always seemed to Christians to be a quite inadequate way to understand the God which Jesus talked about.

(3) Panentheism

Panentheism is a third way of viewing the Infinite Face of God, with the emphasis on the second syllable "en." Pan*en*theism is *very different* from theism and pantheism. With theism, God is always separate from the universe. With pantheism, God *is* the universe and nothing else. With panentheism, God is *in* the universe, and the universe is *in* God. Theism sees God as a separate being, separated from everything. Pantheism sees God as everything, and God is limited to the everything of creation. Panentheism sees God both beyond everything and, at the same time, as part of everything. God is in everything, and everything is in God. God is more than us and yet also very close to us. God is within us and we are within God.

The Apostle Paul says, "For what can be known about God is plain to them, because God has shown it to them. Ever since the creation of the world, God's eternal power and divine nature, invisible though they are, have been understood and seen through the things that God has made."[10]

What does creation show us about God? We know now that there are more than 70,000 million million million stars in the known universe and even more black holes. These 70 sextillion stars (that's 70 followed by 21 zeros) are more than the number of grains of sand in all the world's deserts and beaches. Beyond the observable universe, the number of stars appears to be infinite.[11] By the end of your reading the next few pages the universe will have expanded a billion miles more in all directions and is speeding up all the time.

The size of the conventional God of theism of most churches has become much too small for a world of infinite cosmic dimensions and quantum measurements of time and space. Such a tiny god is hardly big enough to be worshipped. Panentheism includes a God that is as big and bigger than the cosmos, as opposed to theism and pantheism. Theologians use two words, *immanent* and *transcendent*, to say that God is both right here (immanent) and out there (transcendent). Panentheism is a way of saying that God is both right here and out there.

The Bible makes many attempts to describe this God who is both right here and out there.

> ". . . even the highest heaven cannot contain God."[12]

> "Where could I go from your spirit? Or where could I flee from your presence? If I ascend to heaven, you are there. If I make my bed in Sheol, you are there. If I take the wings of the morning and settle at the farthest limits of the sea, even there your hand shall lead me and your right hand shall hold me fast."[13]

> "Do I not fill heaven and earth? says the Lord."[14]

> "If these keep silence, the stones will cry out."[15]

> "All things came into being through the Word. And without the Word, not one thing came into being. What has come into being in the Word was life and the life was the light of all people."[16]

> "Jesus said, 'Split a piece of wood and I am there; lift up the stone, and you will find me there.'"[17]

> "In this one we live and move and have our being."[18]

> "In Christ all things hold together."[19]

> "Christ is all in all."[20]

> "God will be all in all."[21]

> ". . . the fullness of the one who fills all in all." [22]

> "There is . . . one God and Father-Mother of all, who is above all and through all and in all."[23]

> "God is love, and those who abide in love abide in God and God in them."[24]

Episcopal priest and theologian Barbara Brown Taylor says,

God is up there, down here, inside my skin and out. God is the web, the energy, the space, the light—not captured in them, as if any of those concepts were more real than what unites them—but revealed in that singular, vast net of relationships that animates everything there is.[25]

Theologian/philosopher Paul Tillich calls God the "being as being or the ground and the power of being."[26] This is God as the Ground of Being. God is the ground upon which all being is based and from which all being proceeds.

Enlightenment teacher Andrew Cohen puts another slant on it in his version:

> The ground of being is empty of everything. It is an objectless, spaceless, timeless, thoughtless void. But everything that exists has come from this no-place, including you and me. This empty ground that we all emerged from is the womb of the entire universe. When something came from nothing fourteen billion years ago, the nothing didn't disappear. That unborn, unmanifest dimension is the ever-present ground out of which everything is constantly arising.[27]

The work of Bernard d'Espagnat, a distinguished theoretical physicist and philosopher of science, on "veiled reality" is insightful here. It won him the 2009 Templeton Prize. He asserts that matter everywhere is entangled in a "veiled reality" that exists beneath time, space, and energy. Through science, he says, we can glimpse some basic structures of the reality beneath the veil, but much of it remains an infinite, eternal mystery. "There must exist, beyond mere appearances ... a 'veiled reality' that science does not describe but only glimpses uncertainly. In turn, contrary to those who claim that matter is the only reality, the possibility that other means, including spirituality, may also provide a window on ultimate reality cannot be ruled out, even by cogent scientific arguments."

At times d'Espagnat calls this veiled reality a Being or Independent Reality or even "a great, hypercosmic God." He says that it is a holistic, non-material realm that lies outside of space and time.

He believes that, since science cannot tell us anything certain about the nature of being, clearly it cannot tell us with certainty what it is not. "Mystery is not something negative that has to be eliminated," he said.

> On the contrary, it is one of the constitutive elements of being. . . . I consider I have sound reasons to believe in the ground of things I mentioned, lying beyond our ability at conceptualizing and which from time immemorial thinkers, less naive than was often thought, called 'the Divine.' I like conceiving it to be infinitely lovable and am therefore convinced that those among our contemporaries who believe in a spiritual dimension of existence and live up to it are, when all is said, fully right.[28]

How interesting that scientists sometimes sound more mystical than theologians.

God's presence in these qualities rings out in the Breastplate, St. Patrick's magnificent prayer, a soaring call to the universal presence of Christ, the uniquely Christian name for God:

> Christ be with me, Christ within me, Christ behind me, Christ before me, Christ beside me, Christ to win me, Christ to comfort and restore me. Christ beneath me, Christ above me, Christ in quiet, Christ in danger, Christ in hearts of all that love me, Christ in mouth of friend and stranger.[29]

The panentheism of the Bible certainly presents God as relating to persons and thus "personal," (immanent). This God is also infinitely beyond personality (transcendent). To communicate God's infinity, the Bible describes God in many non-personal images. Consider a few: *Sun* (Malachi 3:20), *Word* (John 1:1), *Rock* (1Corinthians 10:4), *Fire* (Hebrews 12:29), *Light* (1 John 1:5), *Waters of Life* (Revelation 21:1), *Wisdom* (Proverbs 1:20), and *Love* (1 John 4:8).

God's "person"-ality is also a metaphor for he/she/it. (All pronouns fail when contemplating Ultimate Mystery.) God is also as infinitely beyond being a "person" in the traditional sense as the One who created light is Light beyond light.[30]

God as a verb

Buckminster Fuller was the first person I heard say that God was a verb rather than a noun. I didn't know what to make of that years ago. Now I see it as a beautiful expression of the Infinite Face of God, the 3rd-person standpoint. God is less like an object and more like a process—the Creative Urge and the Evolutionary Impulse. This helps us not think about the "big guy in the sky" when we are imaging the Infinite Face of God. Carried on to the 1st-person standpoint, we then, as incarnated divine beings, are God's verbs—the voice, hands, heart, and feet of God's creative process in the world today.

Michael Murphy, co-founder of Esalen Institute, states,

> Evolutionary panentheism says that the divine is both transcendent to and completely involved in the evolutionary process of the manifest world. The emergence of new forms of existence throughout history, from inanimate matter to life to human consciousness, is seen as the unfolding of hidden divinity. As the spirit within all things progressively manifests itself, what is implicit is gradually made explicit.[31]

Therefore, God is not a "being" in the sense that he/she/it is one object among many objects. The limitation of the letters "en" of panentheism is that it may seem like we are talking about actual space and the way one object is in some part of space and another object in another part. God is not literally any kind of container. The idea of all things being in God is elegant but, as with all analogies, limited. Perhaps the poets may say it best:

> THEE, God, I come from, to thee go,
> All day long, I like fountain flow.
> From thy hand out, swayed about
> Mote-like in thy mighty glow.
> —Gerard Manley Hopkins [32]

Look at nature, science, the cosmos, and beyond. Reflect on atoms, quarks, and strings. When scientists study these things, they are exploring the glory of God. Contemplate the Great Mystery.

Look deeply into the Ground of all Being. You are considering the 3rd-person face of God, All That Is And More. This is the face of God to reflect upon in wonder and awe. Do not hesitate to find this Infinite Face of God wherever you look.

The Intimate Face of God

The Bible often speaks of God as the "other" because that is a natural way to also express worship and devotion in a 2nd-person, personal way. This is the Intimate Face of God, the Beautiful Other, the "Thou," of Martin Buber's "I-Thou."[33]

Jesus spoke about, in traditional translation, "our Father in heaven." Marcus Borg makes the point that for the Jewish people, heaven was not far away. The universe was very small, with the sun, moon, planets, and stars mounted on a dome not very far above the Earth. Jesus said that the Kingdom of Heaven was actually within and among us.[34] That's pretty close.

Traditionally, churches are most familiar with God in 2nd-person. This is the Divine in relationship to us. God is the Creative Intelligence who is present and with whom one may have a conversation. This sense of God is very personal and intimate as Jesus demonstrated in calling God "Abba"—"Papa," or "Daddy."

Some at the modern level are uncomfortable with thinking of God in this way because it reminds them of the mythic god of the traditional stage who is "up there." As I wrestled with this one day, I found these words coming to me from what I assume to be my inner spiritual guidance:

> You are a human being who relates to other beings in what you call "2nd-person." This involves a sense of external presence, words, seeing, and all the other particulars of what we call a relationship. You don't need to attempt to get along without this way of relating, because without it, you would be impoverished. Prayer is not just talking to All of Life (3rd-person). Prayer is not just talking to your Self (1st-person). Prayer is, at the least, talking to God as one being relates to another.

The Intimate Face of God is the Presence of God close to us.

That which is the 3rd-person Infinite Face of God comes alive in 2nd-person closeness:

- God of cosmos who rushes to hug and kiss us.

- Ultimate Reality that stands before us while we lovingly look into one another's eyes.

- Evolutionary Impulse that sits across the table, breaking bread and drinking wine with us.

- Divine Intelligence that appears on the sofa next to us and starts a conversation.

- Sacred Love that puts its hand on our shoulder and reassures us in the middle of the darkest night.

- Creator of Heaven and Earth who pauses to listen intently and hear our heart.

For 2nd-person awareness of God, look at whoever or whatever most reveals God to you as the Great Other. The Bible uses dozens of metaphors for this face of God, and so may we. Some of the names and metaphors for God that portray God in 2nd-person relationship are: Father (the Church's favorite name for God in 2nd-person), Abba (Jesus' favorite name for God in his native tongue, Aramaic, meaning Daddy or Papa), Mother, Creator, Spirit, Holy One, Jesus, Almighty, Grandmother, Grandfather, Lord, Savior, Higher Power, Big Mind Big Heart, Redeemer, Sustainer, Holy Spirit, Spirit of Jesus, Lord Jesus Christ, and My Beloved.

In 2nd-person we relate to the face of God as the Other *to* whom we speak. This is the face of God whom we worship and adore, and to whom we surrender—ego-humbling Divinity. In worship we sing this face's praises. Look into the face of Jesus and give thanks for this Intimate Divine Face. Raise your hands in surrender to this Divine One. Dance in whirling joy for praise of the Great Lover. Lift your voice in song to the Lover of Your Soul. When words do not suffice, use words beyond words to flow in ceaseless praise to the Lord Most High and Lifted Up. Let your heart reach out to the One who is always near to you. Give thanks to the One True Self, the Great Light. This Beautiful Other elicits emotions of gratitude, blessedness, love, surrender, and devotion. Whatever your spiritual path, do not hesitate to give yourself to your Beloved.

The poet Hafiz dazzles us with this face of God in "You Better Start Kissing Me":

> Throw away
> All your begging bowls at God's door,
> For I have heard the Beloved
> Prefers sweet threatening shouts,
> Something on the order of:
> "Hey, Beloved,
> My heart is a raging volcano
> Of love for you
> You better start kissing me—
> Or Else!"[35]

The Inner Face of God

This is the face of God which is least familiar to those of us in the Western spiritual traditions. It is a shocking idea to many Christians, sounding like heresy. Since it is so unfamiliar, I will devote the entire next chapter to understanding this from a biblical point of view. You may want to read that before you continue here. In knowing our deepest Self as divine, the boundaries between us and God dissolve so that we can know and feel our oneness with God as the divine spiritual being that we are. In seeking the face of God in 1st-person we look in the mirror and see behind all the ego and distortions. If we look deeply enough, we find the image of God *as* our True Self. We can begin to see the "baby" divinity within us.

This is not easily done. We have been taught we are sinners. We are terrible creatures doomed to hell. Unless we believe the right thing or do the right thing we are doomed because we are so bad.

On the other hand, our ego loves nothing better than to play god. As one sage directed at the man seeking guidance, "You have clearly lived a remarkable life, achieving great things. Do you think there's any chance of you getting over yourself?" That is why Jesus said that to find our true self we must deny our false self.[36] We are divine in exactly the same way that Jesus was divine. The difference is that Jesus knew and experienced this. We do not. The difference between us and Jesus is a matter of degree, not kind. Our divinity is buried under a bucketful of ego.

Jesus said that if one has seen him, one has seen God. He also said, "God is greater than I."[37] Jesus was not "all there is" of God. Neither are we "all there is" of God just because we are like God. These two statements from Jesus put it all together in the most beautiful and comprehensive way: "I am God." And "God is greater than I." This is true of us, also. We are God and God is greater than we are. We can put it in another form by using capitalization to emphasize the difference: We are god and God is greater than we are.

This way of writing it would put what Jesus was saying this way: "If you have seen me, you have seen god—little god. But God is greater than I am. That's Big God." Our god self is our Big Self. Sometimes I say it this way, "We are all pieces of God." Or we are all "baby divinities."

Dustin DiPerna says:

> As Christian followers reflected on the life and teachings of Jesus, less did they make him the example, and more did they make him the exception. Slowly, Christ's causal peak experience was placed on a pedestal. After time, it was only Christ who was allowed to claim identification with the divine. In the East, causal union or union with the divine, would remain available to all aspirants. In the West, Godhead was reserved, at all costs, only for Christ.[38]

No religious tradition has yet successfully recognized, integrated, and balanced all three faces of God. One day a parish priest in India went up to a group of schoolchildren and asked them, "Where is God?" Some of the children were Hindus and some were Christians. All the Christians pointed up to the sky (God is in heaven.). All the

Hindu children pointed to the heart (God is in the heart.). These are the two most common and different ways of understanding God, and they are both important. While the Christian children were probably at a traditional stage, at the integral stage, pointing up to the sky can mean both something of the infinite God in and beyond everything and, perhaps, the intimate God watching over us. Pointing to the heart is the inner God. Jesus pointed *everywhere*, both within and without.

Eastern religions seem reluctant to accept the 2nd-person face theologically, although in common practice they do. Buddha did not find talking about God helpful, although in everyday practice Buddhists often appear to relate to the Buddha as God. The religions of Christianity, Islam, and Judaism sometimes have difficulty with the infinite God of 3rd-person glory, instead settling for the "Big Man Upstairs." However, they have the greatest difficulty considering the 1st-person face of God. Even though most Christians believe that we should act like Jesus and be the hands, feet, heart, and voice of God in the world, *they would not dare to think that is actually possible!* This is because they believe Jesus was divine and we are not. What would happen if Christians changed their minds (called "repentance") and decided Jesus was right when he said that we are "all gods"?[39]

Since Jesus said that we are gods, it is legitimate for us to claim that personally by saying, "I am a god." However, a better way of saying that may be something like, "The I of my True Self is God." Both statements are true. However, the latter is a more diplomatic, nuanced, and less likely to be misunderstood.

Hafiz catches this in his poem "When I Want to Kiss God."[40]

When
No one is looking
I swallow deserts and clouds
And chew on mountains knowing
They are sweet
Bones!
When no one is looking and I want

To kiss
God
I just lift my own hand
To My
Mouth.

Don't leave out any of the Three Faces of God.

I consider the Three Faces of God to be the most significant advance in our understanding of God since the formulation of the Trinity in the fourth century. These three perspectives give us the fullest understanding of and relationship to God possible in this life.

When Jesus said that God was greater than he was, he was referring to the Infinite Face of God that is beyond our understanding. We attempt to speak about this "greater God" in 3rd-person language while realizing all of our attempts fall short. Yet we must reach for the widest, deepest, greatest understanding of God we can. To leave this out is to have a God that is too small. Leaving out the infinite divine consciousness limits our understanding of God. It denies us the use of our Spirit-given minds to contemplate God in the most profound ways possible.

When Jesus spoke to his beloved Abba-mommy-daddy, he was relating to the Intimate Face of God. This was the most meaningful way for him to connect in a personal, close way to God. In 2nd-person apprehension we can connect to God in whatever intimate way is the most meaningful, personal, and cherished for us. At the same time, we know that God is greater than this. Yet, we need this personal relationship to our Source because we are spiritual beings. To leave out this intimate, nurturing relationship to God is to be unconnected in any meaningful, personal way to God.

Leaving out the Intimate Face of God invites us to narcissism because we confuse our ego with our True Self. Our ego would like nothing more than to think of itself as God. As one fellow said, "I aced the narcissism test. I got every single question right!"

We need to surrender to the ego-humbling face of God as the Intimate Other. I saw a rather caustic T-shirt that parodies leaving out this intimate divine reality. It said, "Have you accepted yourself as your own personal savior?" When Jesus prayed in Gethsemane "Your will not mine be done," he was asking to be saved from himself, his own ego. Who was he praying to? Himself? Of course not. He was surrendering to the will of the Divine Other. Our ego loves to hide out in the 1st-person, pretending to be God. Only the sensibility of the Intimate Face of God can keep us from that deception.

When we come to have a personal relationship with the Intimate Face of God, our lives are most available for transformation. We come to know we are loved and cherished by our Beloved. We move into the dynamic of person-to-person transforming love. As one who aims to be a good theologian and scholar and yet also a mystic like Jesus, I gladly testify that this divine intimate love has transformed my life beyond measure. I am loved!

And finally, when Jesus said that if we saw him we saw God, he was relating to God in inner identification, the Inner Face of God. He modeled this truth for us so that we can also know that our deepest "I" is the "I" of God. To leave out this identification with the Divine is to reject Jesus' claim that we are the light of the world as he is the light of the world, divine children of God.

Leaving out our Inner Face of God denies us our very deepest and most precious identity as those who bear the image of God. The "I" of our True Self is God. We are baby divinities who have an infinity of growing up to do. But we are divine like Jesus was divine.

Putting it all together, our understanding and relationship to God is expressed most fully by embracing all three perspectives— Infinite Divine contemplation, Intimate Divine communion, and Inner Divine union.

How do the Three Faces of God fit with the Classic Trinity?

They fit wonderfully well. However, they are not the same thing. Let me unfold how an understanding of the Three Faces of God values, includes, and enlarges the classical understanding of the Trinity of "God the Father, Son, and Holy Spirit."

How we came to the Trinity

Let's trace the idea of "God the Father, Son, and Holy Spirit," the "Trinity," from its very beginning. God in the Jewish religion at the time of Jesus was "variously represented as one and unique, as creator, ruler and king, residing in heaven, all-powerful, all-seeing, omniscient, as father of Israel, as savior, as judge, as righteous, terrible, merciful, benevolent and forbearing."[41]

This was the awesome, fearsome, vengeful, and compassionate God of Abraham, Isaac, and Jacob. In a stunning breakthrough to "more stately mansions," Jesus saw this face of God in a radically new way. He called this God "Abba," "dearest father" or "papa," a term of respect and intimacy used both by children and adults.[42] Jesus taught his disciples to pray to God as this Abba. They were sure this was God—God the Father.

Next, there was the God the first Christians called *pneuma*, which, in Greek, means both "breath" and "spirit." This was the Spirit or "wind" of God that had moved over earth at creation.[43] They were familiar with stories of God's Spirit coming upon leaders and prophets in the Old Testament, giving them wisdom and guidance. Joel predicted that in the future the Spirit would be poured out upon all people.[44] They believed that this began to be fulfilled on the day of Pentecost as the disciples were gathered together, and the Spirit was released in and among them.[45] They felt God as the liberating, healing, joyful energy of the Spirit. They were sure this was God—God the Holy Spirit.

Something else was also happening. Jesus was so full of God that he began to look like God to the people around him. Jesus affirmed this when he said if you saw him, you saw God, even though God was greater than he was. This was perplexing for the first followers of Jesus, who were Jewish monotheists. They believed there was only one God, and that God was completely separate from humans. What was a human being doing acting and talking like God? The Jewish leaders who were not Jesus' followers called this blasphemy, and it was one of the things that got Jesus killed. In John 10 Jesus claimed to be God right there in front of them. Many, if not most, of his early followers were increasingly sure this was God—God the Son.

But how were they to understand what they were experiencing? Their strong belief was that there was only one God. "The Lord our God is one." So was God this "Abba" that Jesus prayed to and talked about? Or was God this person called Jesus of Nazareth? Or was God this creative, intelligent, "person-type energy" that swept over them and flowed from within them?

What a dilemma! As monotheists, they had to do something to reconcile their *experience* of three "Gods" with their *theology* of one God. So after reflecting on this for a couple of hundred years, early Christian thinkers began to arrive at a brilliant solution—as far as it went. They invented a new word, one that's not in the Bible at all— the Trinity—one God in three persons.

The three religions of Judaism, Islam, and Christianity are all considered monotheistic. However, Trinity is what may be called "soft monotheism," as opposed to the "hard monotheism" of Judaism and Islam which does not allow anything or anyone, including Jesus, to share in God's being. The word "Trinity" was first used by Tertullian (c.156-222), an early church leader.

Eventually, the early Christians held a meeting to make the idea of the "Trinity" an official doctrine. This meeting was the first widespread meeting of leaders of the early church as it was developing in Roman and Greek cultures. It was held in Nicea in Bithynia (present-day İznik in Turkey) and called by the Roman Emperor Constantine in 325 C.E. This gathering put the early Christian beliefs into the Hellenistic thought of the early fourth century and out of it came the more formal doctrine of God the Father, God the Son, and God the Holy Spirit.

The Trinity was a classical formulation that was a stage-appropriate understanding of the actual relational experience of the early Christians. They grew up knowing God as the "Lord" of the Torah whom they prayed to now as Jesus' *Abba*. Then they experienced God in and as Jesus, the Lord. He was both human and divine. They prayed to him, also. They experienced the mysterious, joyful breath of God the Spirit moving among and upon them as God. They prayed to the Spirit, too. They wrestled these three experiential relationships into a single understanding, inventing a word that we know as "Trinity." Here was another example of the Spirit teaching the church beyond the words of the New Testament to help them clarify a truth that was already there, building "more stately mansions."

This was a real breakthrough in spiritual understanding in the traditional stage of development these early Christians were in at the time. It was a good beginning of a fuller path in attempting to understand the God who is beyond our understanding. The Trinity has been a solid, accessible center of gravity for much of the Christian community for centuries.

The Spirit has even more to teach us here

What has seemed apparent to an increasing number of Christians today is that the first followers of Jesus left out or misunderstood some of who Jesus was and what he taught. They did this because they were at a lower level of spiritual development than Jesus was. Those with whom they were attempting to communicate were at an even lower level. This was nothing new. It has been a common occurrence for a brilliant and profound spiritual leader to inspire others to follow him and then be misinterpreted because his followers were not operating at the same stage of spiritual breakthrough that their leader was.

Another factor was that soon the growing cadre of official church leaders actually suppressed some of the early understanding of Jesus, especially the Sacred Center within us all, because it was threatening to their ecclesiastical power. If God is not limited to speaking through priests, then things could get out of hand—at least the priests' hands. At first, the early church did away with the priesthood. There were no priests in the early church like there had been in the Temple. Then the leaders of the version of Jesus and his message that had come to dominance reinvented the priesthood. This version, what we now know as traditional Christianity, prevailed partly because of the strength of this strong and official leadership. This helped Christianity to survive as an institution but in a distorted form.[46]

The limits of traditional Trinity

Today the doctrine of God, limited only to the Trinity as it is traditionally understood, represents a formidable block to spiritual growth beyond the traditional level. Believing that Jesus was the unique and only Son of God prevents us from recognizing our own divinity and acting as the fully human and fully divine Jesus in the world today. If Jesus is totally unique and unrepeatable, as we have been taught traditionally, then the face of God we have called 1st-person is not available to anyone else.

When Jesus got kicked upstairs he carried the divine identity with him.[47]

The problem is that Jesus modeled and taught something different. The concept of Trinity, as it is traditionally formulated, fails to take Jesus' life, teaching, and mission seriously in the area of self-identity. In particular, it invites us to stop with Jesus as the unique and only divine son of God. This leaves us as something less than participants in the divine nature, the divinity of our shared Sacred Center.

The traditional Trinity, taken alone, also lacks the higher, transcendent, infinite perspective of God as bigger than everything. The popular "Big Man Upstairs" image of God who sits "up there" in heaven directing the traffic of the cosmos is something of an understandable but inadequate attempt to have the glorious three "persons" of the Trinity encompass the also glorious infinity of cosmic space.

God, the Spirit, 3rd-person of the Trinity, may seem to have some elements of both infinite beyond and inner within. However, theologically and in practice, the Spirit is understood as personal, One with the Trinitarian community of Three, or sometimes seen as the love relationship between Father and Son. These are all 2nd-person standpoints. In addition, Spirit is traditionally understood as coming to live *inside* of us. This is definitely not understood as Spirit *as* us but rather someone inside of us to whom we relate and therefore another 2nd-person standpoint.

Just as the idea of Trinity came from the experience and understanding of the early Christians, so the Three Faces of God comes from Jesus' experience and understanding. Jesus, in 3rd-, 2nd-, and

1st-person apprehension (Infinite, Intimate, and Inner) spoke *about* God, *to* God, and *as* God. It also comes from our own evolving consciousness today. I believe we should honor and love the "Trinity" for what it is—the way the early followers of Jesus experienced God, which for many today, is the first step into the Three Faces of God. As a first step, it is true, helpful, wonderful, and incomplete. We can experience a transforming relationship with the Trinity as God the Father, God the Son, and God the Holy Spirit. We can know God as Abba, as incarnate in Jesus the Son of God, and as Spirit which flows upon and within us. Clearly, these are all relationships, and I personally and gladly embrace them. As relationships, they are wonderful expressions of the Intimate Face of God. However, that leaves us with the Infinite Face of God that is transcendently beyond personal (transpersonal) and the Inner Face of God, which is our own Sacred Face. Where do these fit in?

The Trinity beyond the Trinity: The Expanded Trinity

Revolutionary as it was, this Trinity of "God in three persons" who are close and caring is not enough. I need a divine face that is bigger and beyond big. If I want a larger understanding of God than these three "persons" of the Intimate Face of God, I must go *higher* than this traditional Trinity allows by recognizing the Infinite Face of God. This is the transcendent God that is beyond the personal or any personification—the awesome, mysterious face of God. This is Paul's "in whom we live and move and have our being." This is Tillich's Ground of Being. This is Borg's panentheism.

I also need to know who I am. Am I like Jesus or not? Is Jesus like me or not? If, like Jesus, I am to find an inside image of God as my own Original Face, I must also go *deeper* than the traditional Trinity. I must awaken to the Inner Face of God, my own True Self.

Therefore, I see the glorious traditional Trinity as the Intimate Face of God within the even greater and more expansive glory of the Three Faces of God Trinity. This is like a TV with the picture within the picture. The picture of the traditional Trinity shines within the fuller, larger, expanded picture of the Three Faces of God. This is the TRINITY beyond the Trinity. This is "a more stately mansion."

Some, like evangelical, charismatic, and Catholic Christians, have majored on the transforming Intimate Face of God. Some, like mainline Christians, may have focused mostly on the awesome Infinite Face of God. Some, like the Orthodox with their *theosis*, and the classical Christian mystics, seem to have had a more comfortable place than others with the radiant Inner Face of God.

I propose that we come together in a more integral space *and affirm all three divine highlights as true but partial.* Let's put the intimate God of some, the infinite God of some, and the inner God of some together into the Three Faces of God, a more complete and expanded Trinity.

Since this may be new mental, if not experiential, territory, let's review again. The three faces of God are:

(1) **"I" – The Inner Face of God:** God in 1st-person is the image of God as me, the Christ Self, the True Self, the Unique Self, Buddha-nature, the eternal "I am," Pure Awareness, Pure Consciousness, Original "I Amness."

(2) **"Thou" – The Intimate Face of God:** God in 2nd-person is the wondrously caring classical Trinity whom I speak to— Abba Father/Mother, our elder brother Jesus who is our Supreme Guide and Lord, and Spirit that flows in endless, joyful, creative impulse. There are also other namings for the Holy One who comes close to us as our Beloved.

(3) **"It" – The Infinite Face of God:** God in 3rd-person is the face of God that I speak about as the creative evolutionary process, the Web of Life, Ground of Being, the Great Mystery, and in specifically Christian terminology, Cosmic Christ of Colossians 2:15-20, who is the pattern that creates and holds all things together.

We need 1st-person identification *as* the Inner Face of God, 2nd-person devotion *to* the Intimate Face of God, and 3rd-person inquiry *about* the Infinite Face of God.

We receive something different and very practical from each

Divine Face:

- In the inwardness of the *Within Face*, Spirit abides *as* our own deepest Sacred Self, allowing us to speak, in our brightest moments, *as* the light of the world. As a participant in the divine nature, I am called to act and speak *as* the hands, feet, heart, and voice of God in the world today.

- In the intimacy of the *Warm Face*, Spirit comes so close to us that we can feel the moist breath of our Beloved, and we are propelled to love for all conscious beings.

- In the infinity of the *Wondrous Face*, Spirit manifests in the world of form and I reflect *about* God. In Hafiz's words, "God courts us with the beauty of this world."[48] We are entranced by the mysteries of the entire interconnected cosmos that exploration by science allows us to behold.

"And in that radiant awareness, every 'I' becomes a God, every 'We' becomes God's sincerest worship, and every 'It' becomes God's most gracious temple."[49]

Devotion in Motion—A new liturgical practice

The words of the traditional Trinitarian formula, "Father, Son, and Holy Spirit," have been echoed and repeated over the centuries until they have become embedded in our cultural and individual consciousness. When Westerners say the word "God" they most often mean the traditional Christian idea of Trinity. I believe we must intentionally adopt more evolved mantras to enlarge the beautiful, true, and limited idea of traditional Trinity. We desperately need a more inclusive linguistic framework that fits with a fuller understanding of who Jesus was and what he taught us.

"Father, Son, and Holy Spirit" is memorable and familiar. Infinite, Intimate, and Inner God is also memorable but certainly not familiar. However, that can change with time and practice.

I offer what I use in my own prayer meditation practice and what I teach my congregation as one way of doing this. I often begin my own private zone prayer times by affirming these three faces with the following ten-second "devotion in motion." At our church we also do the following exercise aloud and with motions as a congregation at times in our worship service as a liturgical practice in recognizing the Three Faces of God.

We look upward while holding our arms outstretched at our sides. This symbolizes the all-encompassing Infinite Face of God. We echo Paul's words in Acts by saying aloud, *"Infinite God in whom I live, and move, and have my being."*[50]

Then we move our hands forward and bring them together in front of us, palms and fingers touching in traditional prayer fashion and also in the familiar "namaste" posture. The namaste of the East is recognizing the divine in the other. In the West, this same posture represents prayer, or talking to the my Beloved. They combine beautifully in the posture of hands together in front of us in namaste/prayer. This symbolizes the Intimate Face of God standing close to us, in front of us, or holding us. We address our Beloved aloud, in the words of Jesus' promise to be with us always: *"Intimate God, you are always with me."*[51]

Finally, we place our open hands over our heart to signify the Inner Face of God within and as our True Self. In spoken voice, in the words Jesus revealed about us (and all people) so long ago we affirm, *"Inner God: I am the light of the world."*[52]

In this simple, threefold movement with words, we express the *wonder* of the Infinite Sacred, the *warmth* of the Intimate Sacred, and the *within* of the Inner Sacred. Here is how this "devotion in motion" or more liturgically, the "Threefold Faces of God Invocation," appears (See next page.).

God in 3D

Most Christians and churches have a one-dimensional image of God as the Divine Other, the Intimate Face of God offered in the Trinity. Some add a second dimension to their image of God with awareness of the Infinite Face, God in and beyond everything in ceaseless creativity. The infinite dimension is embraced by the modern church and the intimate dimension by the traditional church.

The Three Faces of God Invocation

1. "Infinite God in whom I live and
move and have my being."

2. "Intimate God, you are
always with me."

3. "Inner God: I am the
light of the world."

With the inner dimension mostly absent, that leaves us, at the most, with a two-dimensional image of God. Today's Christianity lacks the three-dimensional view of God that Jesus had. Seeing God in 3D is the most exciting way we have to embrace and speak of the Sacred Face in all three dimensions.

Wittgenstein said, "Language is the house we live in."[53] The traditional Trinitarian house is the only linguistic God-house that has been offered to Christians. It's not a bad house. This house with its three rooms used to seem spacious to previous generations. However, for an increasing number of us, our language house has grown larger because our consciousness has grown much, much larger. Now this traditional three-room house appears a little cramped when we try to crowd our expanding awareness into it. We have outgrown this house. We cannot fit into it any longer. It leaves out the infinite creation of the cosmos. Its obvious patriarchal bias leaves the feminine standing on the outside, making God linguistically two-thirds male. Even more exclusively, it leaves every person standing on the outside, except for Jesus.

There came a time when the Holy of Holies could no longer contain God and had to be opened up. Now God is too big to fit into our traditional Trinitarian house alone any longer. I believe we need a new house which builds on parts of the old house and assembles a new, vastly more spacious one. We can live and breathe and grow in this more stately mansion of fresh, expanded ritual and naming language.

I have initially offered the God-language of Infinite, Intimate, and Inner. I am now waiting on our poets to help evolve beautiful new liturgical language. All new religious language suffers from the lack of familiar warm and shared memories of meaning. However, we must begin somewhere. Therefore, in the meantime, I use attempts like the following examples to express God in 3D.

First, at our church we often write words for the Lord's Supper that follow a certain theme. One of the themes is the Three Faces of God. In our service, the worship leaders read the words while the congregation follows and participates with the projected words/images in the front of the sanctuary on the beautiful large white space between the radiating golden arches that meet in the center of the high-domed ceiling. Here is one such Communion liturgy:

Communion—Threefold Invocation

(Leaders)

Welcome to this celebration of Jesus' last supper with the disciples. People believe many different things about this time of communion with the Living Christ and with one another. Whatever you believe and whoever you are, you are welcome at this table.

(The cup and bread are lifted up at this point.)

In this moment, we acknowledge the Threefold Face of God who fills all creation.

Jesus spoke *about* the Infinite Face of God who is in this bread and cup and beyond,

Jesus spoke *to* the Intimate Face of God who is with us and as close to us as this bread and cup,

Jesus spoke *as* the Inner Face of God who is within us, even as we take and eat this bread and drink from this cup. And the bread and fruit of the vine becomes us.

Join us in the movement and words of this Threefold Invocation.

Infinite God,
In whom we live and move and have our being.

Intimate God,
You are always with us.

Inner God,
We are the light of the world.

(Leaders)

We lift up this bread and cup as symbols
of God's threefold reality
beyond us, with us, and as us.

Jesus turned no one away.
Neither do we.
Communion is offered to all who are here.

Whoever you are,
Wherever you are,
Just as you are,
You are welcome at this table.

(The elements are then served)

Here are four prayer/benedictions:

> May we contemplate God's Wondrous Face,
> In and beyond everything.

> May we commune with God's Warm Face,
> The One who is always with us.

> And may we live as God's Within Face,
> Giving light to the world.

> In the name of Infinite Being in whom we live and move
> And have our being,

> Of Intimate Beloved, the One who is always with us,

> And of Inner Beauty who is our deepest True Self within,
> The light of the world.

> May God bless you and keep you,
> May God's Countenance be lifted up upon you,

> That Infinite Face shining throughout the cosmos,

> That Intimate Face in gracious guiding presence,

> That Inner Face flowing from you like rivers of living water,
> And giving you peace.

> *(The following can be used with the hand motions*
> *as it is said slowly by the leader.)*

> In the name of our loving, infinite, intimate, inner God,
> Amen.

CHAPTER 13

Owning Our Divinity
Health, not heresy

Moving is such a hassle. It's especially difficult if you have lived in one place for many years. You have collected lots of "stuff," stuff you didn't even know you still had. Moving means packing it all up in boxes or going through that sometimes grief-filled experience of tossing out those collections of things that no longer seem worth dragging around with you.

I faced this in a new way when I moved from the big house my kids had grown up in to a small condo. My hobby, since I was 14, has been the art of magic. I had built a number of illusions such as levitations, dismembering boxes, apparatuses for appearing and disappearing assistants, and various other props for the full evening show I did once each year at Thanksgiving for the church. I had labored long and hard to build these illusions because I could not afford to buy them. They were cleverly conceived, meticulously crafted, and beautifully finished. They were also really big. They filled our two-car garage and there was no way to keep them. I made the heart-wrenching decision to give them all away to the local high school magic club. The teenage magicians were excited. I felt like I was giving my kids away.

It was the beginning of downsizing my life so I could travel more lightly. God evidently has had a similar problem in the past and even today. Let me explain.

God as a Moving, Evolving Target

As I have mentioned before, very early in the Bible, God was understood to live far away, usually on mountaintops as with Moses and his famous stone tablet writing session with God. But God would occasionally come closer, as in a burning bush, a pillar of fire by night, and a cloud of smoke by day. Eventually God came to live in the Holy of Holies in the Temple in Jerusalem. This must have been a very cramped one-room apartment when you were used to living all over the cosmos.

The Temple was massive, an incredibly grand masterpiece of visual splendor and architecture. It had been built five centuries before Jesus, and Herod had it renovated in 20 B.C.E. It was a series of courtyards that led progressively closer to where God dwelled in the innermost room called the Holy of Holies. In fact, the Temple was a series of partitions that were designed to keep people away from God!

The ancient historian Josephus gives a brief description of the layout of the Temple.[1] The Temple had four courts, each with restrictions on who could enter. The outer court was open to all, including non-Jews, except for menstruating women. (Talk about a good reason for PMS!) All Jewish men and Jewish women who were not menstruating were allowed into the second court. Beyond the second court was the third court into which ritually pure Jewish men could enter. Finally, the fourth court was restricted to priests who were properly attired, which means essentially priests who were on the job. The innermost room of the temple was a small empty space that could be entered only by the high priest. Once a year, on Yom Kippur, the High Priest dressed in his priestly clothing could enter the Holy of Holies and pray to God on Israel's behalf.

Later legend (not found in the Bible) had it that a cord was tied around his leg in case he fell or was incapacitated. The other priests could pull him out with the cord without having to run the risk of instant death by an unauthorized entrance into the Holy of Holies. True or not, it captures the idea of the awesomeness of the place.

The Temple courtyards represented both an increasingly accessible path to God and also the barriers that the religion of Jesus' day erected to keep people from God. When Jesus angrily tossed the moneychangers from the Temple, the "keeping people from God" setup was what got to him. The moneychangers actually provided an important service by changing everyone's currency into Temple currency. The problem was where they were doing their business. It was in the outermost court, the court of the Gentiles. It was the only place the Gentiles could come to worship the God of Israel, and it had become an incredibly busy marketplace. Jesus, quoting Isaiah 56:7, said, "My house shall be a house of prayer for all nations" as he was whipping around the marketplace.[2] Clearly, he was angry at the way the religious leaders and religious system had excluded the Gentile nations from worship. What a tantalizing prophet-style picture of raging divinity ensconced in raging humanity, all aimed at liberating the world!

But that was not the only exclusion. All women were excluded from the court of the men. Most men were excluded from the court of the priests. And the priests were excluded from the Holy of Holies except for the High Priest once a year. That was certainly a different time back then.

Wait! Come to think of it, all of that is still around today in many places! Only the pure ones, those whose sins are forgiven because they are of the pure group—Christians, can even get into the Temple. Women can't go where the men go and be priests. Most men can't be priests because only a few "special" men can be priests. And there is one priest who is always more important than all the others, whether called the Pastor or the Pope.

These courtyards and walls represented more than the actual Temple layout and rules. They were also a picture of the religious barriers that kept people from directly accessing God. As long as God lived in the Holy of Holies, surrounded by all the walls and rules, God was remote indeed.

At the death of Jesus, it was reported that the large curtain which separated the Holy of Holies from the court of the priests was torn in two, from top to bottom. What a stunning picture of God being released into the world.

Paul Tillich puts it this way:

This curtain cannot be mended any more, although there are priests and ministers and pious people who try to mend it. They will not succeed because He, for whom every place was a sacred place, a place where God is present, has been brought on the cross in the name of the holy place ...When the curtain of the temple was torn in two, God judged religions and rejected temples ...The curtain which makes the temple a holy place, separated from other places, lost its separating power ...[3]

In Jesus, the early Christians believed that God had moved out of the Holy of Holies to be near us. Jesus was called "Emmanuel," which means "God with us."[4] That's what Jesus meant to his followers. God had moved into the neighborhood in a new and amazing way.

Then Paul went on to write about God's second move, Jesus as the Christ consciousness living in us. "Christ in you, the hope of glory."[5] First, God had moved from out there to be close by—and then to "in us." That seems about as close as you can get to God, right? Wrong!

There was one more move God made (or an already and always-present reality we had yet to recognize) that the first followers of Jesus almost missed. Sadly, the church has nearly buried it completely since then.

The third move of God (and the next move for our spiritual consciousness) was from *in* us to *as* us. I understand that is what Jesus had in mind when he came to offer us a blueprint for this newest move of God. He came to demonstrate God *as* us.

One problem we have with this last move is that we seem to think God is still carrying around all the baggage "He" used to have. Fire, brimstone, earthquakes, revenge, mass killings, temples, priests, purity rules, lots of walls, some people in, some out, and so on. That appears to many reasonable people to be too much baggage to have come live inside us, much less live as us, even as badly as we act.

Jesus came to tell us that God has left all that baggage behind! Actually, God never carried that stuff around anyway. We just thought She/He/It did because we can only see what our worldview allows us to see. Most worldviews don't allow us to see God without baggage. Jesus came to tell us that God has no baggage whatsoever. God is love—and love has no baggage.

It now appears that God has moved three times. First, God moved from out there to close by. Second, God moved from close by to inside of us. Third, God moved from inside of us to *as* us. Each time we have to let go of a little more of that terrible baggage we have had God carrying around. Those who haven't let go of the old baggage around God still can't see God in them, much less AS them. Does God have any moves left? Oh, most certainly! I can't wait!

The greatest cognitive block to our spiritual growth

The greatest cognitive block to our spiritual growth is the belief that Jesus is the totally unique and only Son of God. (The other block is a psychological one—our emotional woundedness. See Chapter 16.)

Ken Wilber says, "The radically unique (and non-repeatable, non-reproducible) realization of the Nazarene blocks the final liberation of the soul in this body, in this life, on this earth."[6]

Jim Marion says,

> In Christianity, this mythic [traditional] conception of God has almost completely colored our understanding of Jesus and his teachings. Jesus has been primarily understood—not as a human being who realized his own divinity, but as a god or divine being who was sent down from the sky. This god then died on the cross to appease his Father, the Sky God, for the sins of humanity (supposedly incurred long ago by the first humans, Adam and Eve, in the Garden of Eden). This has been the central myth of Christianity. Until recent years, literal belief in this myth has been virtually a "given" among believers in all Christian countries.[7]

While much of Christian tradition teaches that only Jesus was divine, does the Bible really teach that? Was Jesus the example of the divine human, or the exception? Let's travel through Bibleland and explore our divinity.

Made in the likeness of God

The very first thing the Bible says about us is that, like Jesus, we are made in the image and likeness of God: "Then God said, 'Let us make humankind in our image, according to our likeness.'"[8]

What does it mean to be made in the image and likeness of God? Are we really like God? We have traditionally been taught that the biggest sin of all is to think we are like God. However, Genesis is not talking about our false self, but rather about our True Self. Our ego is the self we have created and endlessly attach to. Ego is anything that keeps us from being our real Self. Our authentic True Self is what God has created. We went on to embellish that first self by creating the ego attachments which cloud and distort our Original Self. I want to suggest that we should understand that Genesis 1:26 is saying that somewhere deep inside each of us we are the spitting image of God!

But Genesis doesn't leave that idea alone. Next, it predicts that we could actually become even "more" like God. The serpent said to Eve that if she ate of the fruit of the tree of good and evil, "your eyes will be opened and you will be like God, knowing good and evil."[9] Of course, they were already like God but did not know it because their spiritual eyes were not yet open.

Therefore, rather than a bad thing, awakening to the knowledge of good and evil was exactly what needed to happened if we were going to develop spiritually. We cannot evolve if our eyes are shut. People who do not know the difference between good and evil are considered sociopaths today. A basic facet of spiritual development is the growing ability to discern what is good from what is evil, what is loving from what is not. In effect, the serpent said, "You will awaken and you will discover that, indeed, you are divine like God."

We have been taught that the serpent was lying, and it was deceiving Eve. But the serpent was actually telling the truth! The man and woman went ahead and ate the fruit. Then God summed up the situation like this, "See, the man has become one of us, knowing good and evil . . ."[10] According to God, we had just joined the "plural of divine majesty." God affirms that we are like the Majestic Ones, like God's very Self. We are a part of the Divine Being.

Amazingly, Genesis states that the whole idea of not only physical evolution but spiritual "evolution" is something that God set into motion! We moved from being just "dumb" animals to humans who know the difference between good and evil and are like God. We began to wake up and see what we had not seen before. Yes, folks, Genesis graphically tells the story of both biological and spiritual evolution!

It is difficult for me to think (metaphorically) that God really did not want us to partake of the tree of knowing about good and evil. God did warn us about the pain and angst of growing up, but it was the very thing God had designed us for. I understand the first three chapters of Genesis not as a story of the *fall* of humankind but of the *emergence* of humankind. It tells how we are different from the animals because we know the difference between good and evil. It tells of our awakening to our divinity.

What does it mean to be like God? The traditional view is that we have a few "godlike qualities" such as free will, the potential to love, the ability to forgive, and the capacity to distinguish between good and evil. But what if we are like God in our essence? Instead of having a few divine qualities, are we intrinsically divine? How much "like" God do we have to be before we are really divine like God? There is great wisdom on this very question in the biblical passages I discuss below. The big question is "Did Jesus think we are divine like he was?"

"You are the light of the world."

Early in the book of Matthew, Jesus makes a stunning declaration: "Jesus said to them, 'You are the light of the world.'"[11] How could others be the light of the world when Jesus was later to say that he was light of the world?[12] This could only be possible if we, along with Jesus, are all the light of the world because we all hold the divine image of God within us.[13] But does Jesus teach this anywhere else? Or is this a lone passage standing apart from the rest of Jesus' teaching?

Doing what Jesus did

Jesus came teaching and doing marvelous works of healing. Then he taught us that, "Whoever believes in me will do the works I do, and even greater ones."[14]

We seldom take this seriously. We are more likely to believe the conventional emphasis on our sinfulness and inability to do much of anything. Nevertheless, Jesus had a different view of us. He believed that we could evolve to the spiritual level he inhabited and even beyond it. He not only believed this, he taught it. This picture of Jesus showing me the way to awaken to my own divinity is incredibly exciting to me.

What difference does it make? I like listening to pipe organ music. It's not that I particularly like organ music, although I love classical music. I listen for another reason. I play the organ, having been organist for several churches in the past.

So why do I like listening to organ music played on magnificent pipe organs? *Because I imagine myself doing the playing.* It feels great. It feels powerful. That is my foot on the pedal connected to the 64 foot thundering Diaophone Profunda pipe. That is my hand on the keyboard with the Trumpet rank blasting out majestic sounds. That is my pinkie on the sweetest Vox Humana pipe you have ever heard.

I recently asked myself if I ever think of playing life like Jesus did? When I see his power and wisdom and leadership, do I like to think about myself doing what he did? I have been taught that's not possible. I was taught wrongly. It *is* possible. According to Jesus, it is actually *inevitable*. It's only a matter of how long it will take us. We are baby divinities in the process of growing up. God has eternity to wait for us.

"If you have done it to the least of these, you have done it to me."

In Matthew 25 Jesus tells a story set in the apocalyptic imagery of his day. The nations are gathered before the King. Those who have treated others unjustly and with neglect will go into "eternal" punishment. Those who have treated others with justice and compassion will go to "eternal" life. The traditional stage has commonly taken this as a teaching about the fate of those who believe in Jesus over and against the fate of those who do not. However, this is obviously not the case, since the basis of the division has nothing to do with being a believer in Jesus or what religion one has embraced. According to Jesus' story, it is entirely based on how we treat one another.

However, there is a further truth that underlies Jesus' point about how we treat one another. He says that the way we treat one another is the way we treat him! "Just as you did it to the least of these, you did it to me."[15] How could that be? On what basis could treating someone else be just like treating Jesus? He is traditionally considered the only begotten Son of God, uniquely divinity incarnate. Traditionally, we are thought to be sinners who need saving. However, Jesus will have none of that. He knew that each person was like him, made in the same divine image of God and possessing the same divine nature. Therefore, treating anyone made in this divine image unjustly is like treating everyone, including Jesus, unjustly. This is because of our unity with God, realized or unrealized. We are all, in our deepest essence, divine spiritual beings. It is this divine self we are relating to, either in respect and honor, or disrespect and dishonor. There is no other basis for Jesus to have claimed that the way we treat one another is the way we treat him.

Jesus was like us and we are like him

The writer of Hebrews says, "He was like us in every respect."[16] The writer is emphasizing that Jesus was human, exactly as we are human. If we rob Jesus of his humanity, then we rob ourselves of our divinity. If Jesus was not human, then we cannot be divine. If we take this sentence seriously, it is repeating the same theme that we see throughout the New Testament—Jesus was fully human and fully divine, and we are fully human and fully divine. Jesus was like us in every respect.

Being One with God

> Jesus prayed, "As you, Father-Mother, are in me and I am in you, may they also be in us . . . so that they may be one, as we are one, I am in them and you are in me."[17]

Here was Jesus' fervent prayer that we would realize our divinity —our oneness with God is exactly like he was one with God.

Historian Elaine Pagels says that the kingdom "symbolizes a state of transformed consciousness."[18]

Agreeing with Pagels, mystic Jim Marion further states that the Kingdom of Heaven is the highest level of human consciousness. He defines it as the vision that Jesus held of this world that sees no separation (duality) between God and humans, and no separation between human beings. Jesus' love for us "was based on this vision of our inner substantial union with God and each other."[19]

This is something of the understanding of the Eastern Orthodox Church, sometimes called the Greek Orthodox Church. There are 240 million Eastern Orthodox Christians around the world, and in many European countries it is the largest group of Christians.[20] This ancient Christian tradition boldly names the idea of the future realization of the divine self as divinization, deification, *theosis*, becoming a god, or transforming union. The Holy Thursday litany confesses, "In my kingdom, said Christ, I shall be God with you as gods."[21]

Two early theologians, highly revered by the Orthodox Church, are Athanasius of Alexandria (293–373 c.e.) and Maximus the Confessor (580–662 c.e.).

Athanasius wrote, "God became man so that man might become god."[22]

Maximus wrote, "A sure warrant for looking forward with hope to deification of human nature is provided by the incarnation of God, which makes man god to the same degree as God himself became man."[23]

Thomas Aquinas (1225-1274 c.e.) wrote, "Every creature participates in some way in the likeness of the Divine Essence."[24] He further stated, "The Incarnation accomplished the following: That

God became human and that humans became God and sharers in the divine nature."[25]

Gods Я Us

Jesus, teaching the crowds, said, "The Father-Mother and I are one."[26] Upon hearing that, the religious leaders took up stones to stone him. Jesus responded with, "I have shown you many good works from God. For which of these are you going to stone me?" They answered, "It is not for good works that we are going to stone you, but for blasphemy, because you, though only a human being, are making yourself God." These religious leaders correctly understood that Jesus' claim to being one with God meant he was claiming to be divine. Then Jesus says an amazing thing.

> Is it not written in your law, "I said, you are gods"? If those to whom the word of God came were called "gods"—and the scripture cannot be annulled—can you say that the one whom God has sanctified and sent into the world is blaspheming because I said, "I am the Child of God"?[27]

He reminds them, "And the scripture cannot be annulled." Notice that Jesus uses their *belief* in their scriptures to argue *against* their *understanding* of their scriptures. I love to quote the Bible to those who take it seriously in order to invite them to change their minds about the Bible itself. This is what Jesus did, as the verse he quoted was from their book of Psalms, "I say, 'You are gods, children of the Most High, all of you.'"[28]

That passage was referring to the corrupt judges of the day who were like the corrupt religious leaders of Jesus' day. Jesus said that, as confused, ignorant, and opposed to God as the leaders were, incredibly, they were divine also. His reasoning was that if they were divine, as bad as they were, how could they say he was not divine, as good as he was? Jesus was saying in effect, "If you are considered gods, then look at the way I live. You shouldn't have any trouble at all believing I am divine." Jesus' reply that we all are gods was lost on the crowd and on subsequent generations of Christians also.

How many sermons have you heard on the passage "You are all gods"? How many hymns contain the thought "You are gods"? What I am stating is difficult for many Christians to believe. It is so difficult that it may even sound dangerous. It used to sound that way to me. We have been deeply conditioned by a distorted form of Christianity.

Some say that the word "gods" in Psalms 82:6 refers not to divinity but to "judges." Or, it is pointed out that God said to Moses, "See, I have made you (like) God to the Pharaoh."[29] This points to the idea of God's representative on earth. However, Jesus' own interpretation of that passage makes it clear it is about divinity since the context in the Gospel of John is Jesus' own divinity. The Pharisees had accused Jesus, saying, "You, though only a human being, are making yourself God." Both the Pharisees' accusation and Jesus' response only makes sense if he is talking about divinity.[30]

C. S. Lewis comments on this same passage this way: "The command 'Be ye perfect' is not idealistic gas. Nor is it a command to do the impossible. He is going to make us into creatures that can obey that command. He said that we were 'gods' and He is going to make good His words."[31]

In quoting the Old Testament, "You are gods, children of the Most High, all of you," Jesus was not saying we are the Big God. Remember, in Chapter 14 of John, Jesus said that if they had seen him, they had seen God, but that God was greater than he was. The first time I saw the Pacific Ocean in California I said to a friend, "Is this really the ocean?" He replied, "Of course it is." Did he mean that what I was seeing was the entire ocean? No, because I couldn't see the entire ocean from my viewpoint. I was seeing all of the ocean that I could see from my present altitude. If I could rise up higher, I would see more of the ocean. If I got high enough (literally here, metaphorically in spiritual terms) I could see the entire Pacific Ocean! But the tiny part of it that I was looking at was still the ocean. The higher our viewpoint and awareness, the more we can see of God.

When I hold a handful of ocean water in my hands, I am holding real ocean water that is as much ocean water as any ocean water. Likewise, when I say that I am God, I am as much God as God is God. You are as much God as God is God.

Dame Julian of Norwich, in the ecstasy of her experienced union with God exclaimed, "See! I am God; see! I am all things; see! How should anything be amiss?"[32]

Jesus frames our shared divinity with him in its most daring way —"You are gods." Most Western Christians are afraid to use Jesus' language. I've decided I will not be afraid of using his words. Do we not know that we are all gods? Yes, we are.

We will be like him

The first letter of John continues with the truth that we are gods like Jesus: "When Jesus is revealed, we will be like him, for we will see him as he is."[33] Will we be "a little" like him? Or will we be exactly like him? I believe we will be exactly like him. This means that we are like him in terms of divine essence now, and then we will be like him in terms of awareness and manifestation. God has given us all the time we need to get to awareness and manifestation of the essence of who and what we really are. If we don't get it done in this lifetime, and most of us don't, then we have the next. But the end is assured. We shall be like Jesus. Exactly like Jesus.

The divine mix-up

Paul talks about the same thing in the "divine mix-up." "I live, yet not I but Christ lives in me."[34] This is Paul, the Christ mystic, speaking of his own divinity. He expresses this with his graphic "being in Christ" terminology. His dazzling claim has been diluted into the idea of Jesus coming into our hearts to live as an invited guest. That's a beautiful metaphor that has helped many people to invite Jesus into their lives. However, Paul was not saying that. He was saying that if you look inside to see who *really* lives there, it is not the I of the ego which you find, but rather the I of the Universal Christ. Who is that inside of me at the deepest level? It is Christ. Who *is* Me at the deepest level? I am Christ, the divine daughter/son of God.

Participants in the divine nature

Second Peter says that we participate in the very nature of God: "Thus he has given us through these things, his precious and very great promises, so that through them you may escape from the corruption that is in this world because of lust, and become participants of the divine nature."[35] It is clear from the context this is available as a present reality ("escape from the corruption that is in *this* world"), not something waiting for us in the next life.

This profound statement is a central tenet of the Eastern Orthodox Church and a neglected and often rejected element of the Western Christianity. However, both sides of the Church go to great lengths to make a distinction between God and our participation in the divine nature. The Eastern Church speaks about the difference between the "image" of God and "likeness" of God. Adam and Eve were made in the image of God but were to grow into the divine likeness. The Catholic and Protestant traditions make clear that we can be "like" God in *some* ways but we can never be actually like God who is "uncreated" since we are "created." Traditional theology says we can be similar to God but never really like God in our very essence. I disagree with all of these ideas.

The simple problem with all of this is that it is a theological assumption about what the Bible is saying with no biblical basis. It is read into the texts because traditional Christianity cannot tolerate the real divinity of humankind. Only Jesus can "really" be God —never us.

Jesus simplified it all for us in his three, perfectly balanced statements as understood in the evolved Christology of John: (1) "If you have seen me, you have seen God." (2) "God is greater than I." (3) "You (we) are all gods."[36] If you want to understand how Jesus saw himself and us, this is it! If you want Christology, theology, and anthropology from Jesus, this is it! Jesus was God (god) in the flesh. However, Jesus was not "all there is" of God. We are God (god) in the flesh also. The difference between us and Jesus is that we have not realized, embraced, and manifested our participation in the divine nature as fully as Jesus did.

Changed into God

Paul says, "We all, with unveiled faces, beholding the glory of the Lord, are being changed into that same image from glory to glory."[37] Do you believe that you are being changed into the same image as the Lord? This is not New Age, new theology, or anything new at all. It is original Christianity.

The word "image" here in Greek is εἰκών, or in English trans-literation, *eikōn*. We get our word "icon" from it. It is the same word used in Colossians: "Christ is the *image* (εἰκών) of the invisible God."[38] We are literally becoming "icons" or "images of the invisible God."

Sons and daughters of God

Many times in the New Testament we are called "sons (and daughters) of God." Traditional Christianity would say, "Of course that doesn't mean a 'son of God' like Jesus." Do we believe we will always be just imitations at best? If we are all sons and daughters of God, how can Jesus be the only son of God? Indeed, Jesus called himself the son of "man" ("humankind" in Greek—male and female) as in "folks just like us." Why did he do that? Because he knew what we would do with him. We would put him up high and ourselves down low—so out of reach that we wouldn't even begin to think we are supposed to be like him and will be like him. The early writers of the Gospels and interpreters of Jesus, instead of calling him the son of "man" (humankind) as Jesus himself did, began to exclusively call Jesus the son of God. More than that, they began calling him the *only* son of God. Jesus emphasized his humanity, but we have emphasized his divinity to the exclusion of the rest of us.

The children of people are people. The son or daughter of a horse is a horse. The offspring of a dog is a dog. The daughters and sons of an elephant are elephants. Why then, would not the children of God be gods!

Joint heirs

Paul says, "We are joint heirs with Christ."[39] A "joint" heir means that all the heirs get the same thing. It means that what Christ gets we get. Everything will be divided up between all of us, and Jesus' share is no bigger than ours! We say, "Oh no, not joint heirs. Jesus gets the whole estate and all the fortune, and all that we get is to be with him, and maybe a small monthly allowance!"

However, we are now and have always been divine. All that the creeds say about Jesus is also true about us. We are truly joint heirs. Jesus is what we are even though we have yet fully to realize it or express it. The goal of the spiritual path is to consciously realize and express our divinity.

I saw someone wearing a T-shirt that said, "I found it!" When I asked what that meant, the man said that it meant he had found God. I want a T-shirt that says, "I never lost it! But I do keep forgetting where I put it."

We say, "I don't feel divine!" Just how does that feel? Like Jesus in the wilderness, hungry and tempted? Like Jesus in the Garden of Gethsemane, sweating blood? That sounds like what I feel a lot. Maybe I do feel divine!

The Gospel of Thomas

The previous passages also reflect a major theme in the Gospel of Thomas. Thomas was quite likely the earliest gospel to be written, with parts written around 50 C.E. Jesus said, "Whoever drinks from my mouth will become like me. I myself shall become that person, and the hidden things will be revealed to him."[40]

Jesus, speaking as the Universal Christ Consciousness, said that whoever drinks from his mouth will become like him, which means to know, embrace, and live one's own humanity *and* divinity. We will experience Jesus' True Self, his Christ consciousness, as ours, also. Then we shall see things that were hidden from us before. The ego-driven think they are God. The Jesus-infused know they are God!

Fractals of God

I find a helpful illustration of Jesus' words about the image of God in and as us in the idea of fractals. A fractal is a rough or fragmented geometric shape that can be split into parts, each of which is, at least approximately, a reduced-size copy of the whole. This property is called self-similarity. There are exact fractals and approximate ones. The cover of this book is a chambered nautilus which is an approximate fractal found in nature. Others found in nature are clouds, snow flakes, crystals, mountain ranges, lightning, river networks, cauliflower or broccoli, and systems of blood vessels and pulmonary vessels. You can Google "fractals" and see colorful, dazzling images of transcendently beautiful fractals. Here is a black and white computer fractal image:

Petigen and Saupe (Springer-Verlag, 1988) The Science of Fractal Images, 168. Used by permission.

Putting Jesus' words into fractal terminology, Jesus says: "I am an exact fractal of God. I am a reduced-size copy of the whole. God is the whole. I am the fractal. You, also, are all fractals of God." The more humankind manifests its divinity, the more awesomely gorgeous we appear.

Why was this suppressed in the church?

Our divine identity began to be suppressed by the leaders of the emerging institutional church for two reasons. First, it was difficult for them to comprehend, much less teach, because their stage of spiritual development was nowhere near the level of Jesus. Secondly, Christians who were manifesting their own divinity would weaken the priests' authority as guardians of the true faith. After all, if the church is going to maintain its power over people, you just can't have everyone running around thinking they're god. The church hierarchy easily came to believe they were the only ones God had appointed to transmit the path to God.

Other early church leaders

However, Christian teachers down through the ages taught that our goal was to recognize and express our own divinity. St. Basil the Great (330-379 c.e.) speaks of "the highest of all desires, becoming God."[41] St. Irenaeus (second century—202 c.e.) wrote, "God the Logos became what we are, in order that we may become what he himself is."[42] Athanasius of Alexandria (c. 293–373 c.e.), declared that "God became Man so that Man could become God."[43]

Cyril of Alexandria (370–444 c.e.) wrote that deification was the supreme goal of created beings.[44]

We turn to the poet Hafiz, again, to tunnel around the religious conditioning that pretends we are separate from God, in his poem "We Might Have To Medicate You":

> Resist your temptation to lie
> By speaking of separation from God,

Otherwise,
We might have to medicate
You.

In the ocean
A lot goes on beneath your eyes.
Listen,
They have clinics there too
For the insane
Who persist in saying things like:
"I am independent from the
Sea,
God is not always around
Gently
Pressing against
My body."

Resist your temptation to lie
By speaking of separation from God,
Otherwise,
We might have to medicate
You.[45]

As I am writing today, I am reminded that this week is my birthday. At least, it is my birthday into this body and dimension. My deepest, highest, truest Self was never born and will never die. I can say with Jesus, "Before Abraham was, I am." Before my parents were born, I am. The same "I Am" that was in Jesus is also in me. The same mind of Christ that was in Jesus is also in me. It is a truly happy birthday realization.

I insist upon the theme of Jesus' divinity and ours because that is the only path that Christians can follow to the ultimate goal of the nonduality which Jesus called "the Kingdom of God"—identification and union with God.

The traditional church believes in original sin. The postmodern church believes in original goodness. The integral church believes in original divinity!

CHAPTER 14

Religion on the Escalator
Movin' on Up

What do you do when you have outgrown your religion? Some become agnostics and atheists. Others keep going to temple, mosque, or church by checking their minds at the door and getting some nostalgia and comfort inside. An increasing number search out other religions or try a cafeteria-style, "I'm spiritual, not religious" assortment. Many leave their religion but hang on to God. However, there is another option. Move to a higher stage of your own religion! This is what integral and beyond Christianity and church are all about for Christians—recognizing that wherever you are on the spiral of life, there is a way to follow Jesus at ever-higher levels. The call of the Spirit is always to "build thee more stately mansions."

This is the escalator potential of all spiritual traditions.

Escalators

When I am into movin' on up in the mall, I love to ride the escalator. I ride them in department stores, shopping malls, airports, convention centers, hotels, and public buildings. They seem better to me than elevators or endless stairs. On the escalator I can look around and see everything from an increasingly higher view. I can look down, see where I've been, and look up to see where I'm going. Elevators are usually closed in and besides they can get stuck—not good for a claustrophobic like me! In addition, if you want to go faster on an escalator, you can simply walk up the escalator, even two steps at a time, running if you are really in a hurry to get there.

However, it's not always easy. First, you have to find the escalator. In a big department store the up and down entrances to the escalators seem to get hidden behind columns and counters. Even if you know where the "up" escalator is, you still have to take steps to get there. Then there is that particularly crucial step which requires extra attention—stepping on that first moving tread. Miss it and you can take a nasty fall. Then you must keep your balance. Finally, you must know how and when to get off to shop. Then there is the all-important getting back on to continue to the next floor. All of this applies to the religious escalator, too. It takes awareness, diligence, and effort to find and navigate the religious or spiritual escalator when you want to start movin' on up.

In Part I of this book, Stages, I wrote about stages as floors in the big building of spiritual life. There is an escalator to each of these floors and they are all connected to one another sequentially. As humankind evolves, new floors (or in nautilus terminology, more chambers, or in the poet's terminology, "more stately mansions") are always being added.

As I have pointed out, Jesus served as an escalator between the previous floor of traditional Judaism and a new one that incorporated parts of the previous floor and transcended other parts to make up a new level. He also introduced a number of new floors which are still unfolding.

All the great religions of the world themselves can serve this escalator function if higher floors are currently available and participants in the journey can find the escalator entrances. In this chapter and the next, we take up the level(s) after the postmodern floor, the integral consciousness level and beyond.

Integral Consciousness and beyond

The integral stage is just beginning to emerge as individuals seek greater personal growth, global challenges grow more serious, and the previous stages fail to offer real solutions. The problems of one stage can only be solved from the next stage. Integral and beyond offers new paths to higher levels of the interior life without the emotional and intellectual barriers of the previous stages. Integral and beyond changes the world from the inside out. It champions psychospiritual practices that lead to healing of our emotional wounds and the awakening of our spirits.

Valuing all stages

If you want to reach the top floor from the bottom floor by taking the escalator, you have to pass through all the other floors. That is true in the spiritual life also. Each floor is necessary in order to get to the next floor. The foundation of the integral lens is the understanding of floors (stages), along with the awareness we carry with us at each floor (state development). Natural hierarchies return from their bad reputation at the postmodern level to being understood as normal stages of growth. The goal of the integral stage is the health of every floor, not just its own. Integral-level individuals and organizations work for the health of each stage and the building of the next one. The integral worldview anticipates further evolutionary growth.

It celebrates each one of the previous stages as having an important role to play in our spiritual development. Each level is of value in itself. Every baby born into the world progresses though its own stages at least up to the edge of whatever culture it is living in. Each culture is at a stage that demands understanding and honoring. Each unfolding floor reveals important facets of healthy living. The tribal level gives us family/kinship ties and loyalty. The warrior lens provides world-changing action, and the traditional altitude offers us loyalty and stability. Modernism expands our world with scientific exploration and discovery, and postmodernism gives us respect for all. Integral altitude champions each stage as appropriate for both individuals and cultures and encourages the next natural stage as a way to progress.

There is always a better view

Each floor before integral believes the "real truth" can only be found at its level. Even in postmodernism, the tendency is to say there are many views and none of them are better than the others, except that the postmodern view is really the best and only correct view. Extreme postmodernism insists upon it. Integral sees that there is always a better view.

Integral pulls these "truths" together and integrates them without trying to force change where it is not wanted and without resorting to the relativism that thinks everything is equal. However, the integral altitude does more than just see all points of view which is what the postmodern worldview does. The integral lens both honors them and critically evaluates them. This move from postmodernism to integral consciousness is so momentous and life-changing that it is sometimes referred to as moving from the first-tier station in life to the second-tier worldview.

The integral inner world of the self is not just based on traditional religious dogma and stories, even though it has a place for them, partaking of the best of them and transcending the worst. Rather, the integral lens embraces 1st-person subjective interior exploration, 2nd-person global wisdom, and 3rd-person objective scientific investigation.

Hallmarks of the integral lens

Integral ends the battle between science and religion, taking both science and spirituality seriously. It is the healthy self in an evolving community of others seeking to move toward the visionary and the prophetic. Selfless service is a hallmark of the integral level with such models as Jesus, Mahatma Gandhi, Mother Teresa of Calcutta, and the Buddha. World peace comes from people having spiritual experience at the integral and beyond levels. Authentic joy is also a hallmark of the integral floor.

Steve McIntosh insightfully asks, "What does it feel like to have integral consciousness? He describes "amused anticipation" and a sense of confidence that this is the way forward:

But perhaps the most significant feeling associated with integral consciousness is the way it makes you feel about other people. The practice of integral consciousness definitely results in an increased sense of compassion, sympathy, and respect for those about whom you previously felt consternated. However, accompanying this enlarged feeling of compassion is also a new sense of realism about the inherent limitations of those who dwell in these older worldviews. . . . As integral practitioners we have to see ourselves as ambassadors of the future. . . . It's an exciting time to be alive![1]

An estimated less than 1 percent of the world's population lives at this level. For developed areas such as the United States and Europe, the number might be 5 percent or more, and it is increasing significantly.

Outgrowing your religion

Bishop Spong has remarked that the fastest-growing denomination in America is the church alumni association. Others call them the ABC people—Anything But Church. As comedian Lenny Bruce used to say, "Everyday people are leaving the church and finding God." With more people in this country leaving their churches, a large number of Americans identify themselves as "spiritual but not religious." That phrase now even has a recognized acronym— SBNR! Approximately one in every five persons, roughly half of all the unchurched, could describe themselves in this way. And half of the SBNR say they left traditional Christianity because they felt abused by it.[2] They are often influenced by the postmodern openness to religious pluralism and Eastern religions in particular. Also contributing to leaving the church is the postmodern rejection of church hierarchies that tell people what they should believe and do, and frustration with the rigid dogmas of traditional religion. Integral church moves to a Christ-like inclusiveness which overcomes the exclusiveness of the traditional stage.

Integral Church and the Escalator

Integral church understands that the purpose of the church is to create a community which accelerates our growth in stages of understanding God and states of experiencing God. To these ends, it sees Christianity as a part of the great escalator function that all the great religious traditions of the world can serve. In *Integral Spirituality* Wilber outlines what he calls "a startling new task for religion in the modern and postmodern world." He holds out the possibility that all the world's great religions can provide an evolving spiritual path for those at each of the various stations in life. This would include "*higher levels and stages of their spirituality*, stages that have kept pace with Spirit's own unfolding into the modern and postmodern and integral ages. . . ."[3]

Wilber says that "religion alone, of all of humanity's endeavors, can serve as a great conveyor belt for humanity and its stages of growth."[4] All of the developmental stages of growth will always be with us since every individual personally passes through these stages, beginning with the lowest stage and moving upward as far as their situation allows them to develop.

It appears there will always be fundamentalism, because we all go through that stage between the ages of seven and adolescence, and some people stay there. Tribal, warrior, traditional, modern, and postmodern cultures also all exist today and will for the foreseeable future. Churches for those at these levels exist all over the world. Integral spirituality and beyond exists primarily at present in the form of newly emerging networks. All of these stages of spiritual development are sacred and legitimate worldviews. Every person has the right to be at whatever stage they find themselves and to practice their religious tradition at that stage. Every level has its gifts and strengths to offer which can be included and built upon in the next altitude. Every stage also has weaknesses that must be transcended in order to move up to the next level. Every level has its dignities and its disasters. The dignities of each worldview can be built upon and the disasters of each level can be transcended.

Six different altitudes

Six men, each from a different stage of consciousness, look at a glass half filled with water:

- The tribalist is fearful that the remaining water will disappear. He prays to appease the spirits who protect this water.

- The warrior is ready to fight his neighbors in order to fill his glass. He prays for courage to kill the enemy of his water.

- The traditionalist may be either the optimist who sees this as the best of all possible glasses of water, or the pessimist who is afraid that it is. He prays with thanksgiving or dread.

- The modernist is sure that the glass is twice as big as it needs to be. He doesn't pray.

- The postmodernist is concerned about the elegance of the glass, the quality of the water, how it feels drinking it, and does everyone have enough. He meditates on all of that.

- The integralist ponders the strengths and weaknesses of all these viewpoints, while being grateful to the Great Creative Process that transpired to evolve the water, water systems, the glass, and their nourishing presence here. He is looking for what comes next after that particular glass of water.

Why stay with your religion?

Only the world's great religious traditions can offer the unique stability, history, and legitimacy required for this escalator function. One can attempt to start a new religion or spiritual path, but that might be like reinventing the wheel. In addition, the stability and legitimacy of the new religion would need to be tested over a long period of time. It would have to go through the same learning curve rather than simply building on the historic values of an existing tradition.

Of course, while including the strengths of an existing tradition, its weaknesses must be transcended. That is the task of each new level of development.

The reality is that most of the world's people are already connected in some way to an historic religious tradition. Most will not change that connection to their religion in their lifetime, although they may not actively pursue that religion. *But if that religious tradition offers a version that has kept up with the Spirit's movement, then that move of the Spirit would be more readily available to those people than an entirely new religion would be!* Every world religion that offers more than a traditional level can act as a moving path which provides spiritual nourishment for individuals and groups at ever-higher stages. It can also invitingly hold out the possibility of moving to future stages in accelerated spiritual development.

An individual or group at the warrior stage can navigate moving to the traditional stage without having to change traditions. As I have said before, I am grateful for the traditional level of Christianity which provides a way to follow Jesus at that stage of understanding. Let's say that someone at the warrior level is ready to give up their angry warrior practices and move to the next level. That would be traditional Christianity with its more loving approach that would offer a higher path. Postmodern church would probably not be accessible to that person right now. It would require a leap over the modern rational stage, and stages cannot be skipped—only lived in and worked through. If the next higher interpretation of Christianity is available, then the escalator function allows them to move on to the next level when they are ready to do so. Only a Christian escalator can offer this to Christians. Only a Buddhist one can offer this to Buddhists, and so on. The world's religions are now moving to include versions of each religion that encompass the higher stages of human development such as integral.

A new spiritual explorer in our church recently said, "I have tried Eastern religions and found some help. But I found that I didn't know their stories. I know the Christian stories. So I decided to come back to my roots and see if anything new has developed." She found out that, indeed, something new had developed!

The brilliance of the escalator understanding is that spiritual seekers do not need to change their religion to move along from floor to floor. If you are a Christian at the modern level longing for deeper spiritual experiences, you don't need another religion. You just need the next version of Christianity—the postmodern one. Or the really daring can move more rapidly than the several years it usually takes to embrace a new stage and go for integral and beyond. It is now entirely possible to stay with the tradition which brought you to the dance and continue to deepen in far-reaching ways. The dance of evolutionary awakening is being celebrated with new steps now by practitioners in all of the world's great traditions.

Jesus modeled the religious escalator

Jesus demonstrated the escalator model of remaining with your religious tradition while moving it along by both transcending and including parts of it. He began his life as a Jew and ended his life on earth as a Jew. Judaism, not Christiainty, was and remained his religion. Christianity was a later development, sparked by his pushing his own religious tradition to a new stage. He was a good first century Palestinian Jew who loved and embraced his religious tradition. However, he was not attached to the structures and belief systems of the Judaism of his day. He was not satisfied with the traditional forms of his religion. He included the best of its past and transcended the worst of its present. He serves as a model for us, whatever our religion's heritage may be, of how to transcend and include. It also got him killed, so we probably should only lead a reform movement if we are both thoughtful and brave.

Steve McIntosh says,

> But while the rise of integral consciousness will definitely result in the evolution of spiritual culture, it is more likely that most of this evolution will involve the refinement, integration, and improvement of existing spiritual forms rather than the creation of entirely new kinds of spirituality. The spiritual evolution produced by the rise of the integral worldview will come about as postmodernism's spiritual

excesses and immaturities are overcome, and as the enduring contributions of traditional spirituality are reintegrated into our culture at a higher level.[5]

The Dalai Lama has said, "In order to have genuine faith, you need to have one truth, one religion. But that does not mean you lose respect for those of other traditions."[6]

I believe the preferred new spiritual path is not the blending of all the religions of the world into one new one. They are much too rich and diverse for that. However, all the evolving traditions of the world, including the contemporary "spiritual but not religious" movement, can be resources. We don't need to substitute other paths or invent totally new ones for our own growth. Rather, we can learn from all paths as they illumine our own chosen path.

The problem with the religious cafeteria

If a Christian church attempts to make other paths a major part of its center of gravity, it has then moved from being a church to a cafeteria. The spiritual cafeteria can be an authentic path but it is much more difficult. It takes more time and energy than most of us have in this lifetime to explore in depth many different paths and come up with a combination that is truly authentic.

However, the greatest difficulty with cafeteria religion is that *our egos will always keep us from the healthiest food.* Ego just loves the comfort food that does nothing for our bodies except stuff them. We will choose comfort over challenge every time. We will choose comforting the self rather than dying to the self every time. That is, unless we have a tradition which pushes us to ego death. All authentic traditions do that. Jesus said that we must lose our lives to save them. We must lose our ego self to find our True Self. Cafeterias can offer us "dissolved ego," but we tend not to order it because it doesn't look or smell good, and nobody is telling us we need it. The major traditions of the world will lead us to ego death and resurrection if we let them. Wilber says,

For authentic transformation is not a matter of belief but of the death of the believer; not a matter of translating the world but of transforming the world; not a matter of finding solace but of finding infinity on the other side of death. The self is not made content; the self is made toast.[7]

We cannot individually engineer our own enlightenment or salvation. We really do need each other—the communion of the saints from the past and present—to help us transcend ourselves.

Pick a path

My encouragement is to pick a path. The wisdom of Zen puts it this way: "Chase two rabbits, catch neither." Most of us don't have enough time and energy in this lifetime to pursue more than one rabbit. There is only one river, God, that runs underneath everything. We can dig one well deep and tap into the River. Or we can dig 20 different shallow ones that may or may not get us there. Some drill many wells a few feet deep and then complain they could never find water. What they have not tried is digging deeply in a tried and true path.

If a person is already familiar with a Hindu well, or a Christian well, or a Buddhist well, why not keep digging deeper in that well! All the great religious traditions of the world now are beginning to offer "deeper" wells. What a great opportunity for everyone! This is what integral church offers the Christian path. This is why it is so important and exciting.

Jesus predicted new levels

Jesus not only modeled the escalator function, but he predicted its future function in his daringly integral statement, "I still have many things to say to you, but you cannot bear them, now. When the Spirit of truth comes, that Spirit will guide you into all the truth."[8] *The various emerging versions of Christianity and church are the current fulfillment of Jesus' prophetic statement that he had much more to teach his followers!* With deep wisdom, he told his followers they could not learn then, even from him, all there was to know and experience at their present level of consciousnesses. He assured them that in the future, the Spirit would continue to move us to new stages—if we would listen to the Spirit's call to evolve more stately mansions.

Integral church is crucial

The formation of a Christian path whose dominant center of gravity is integral and beyond is crucial to the ongoing work of the Spirit today in moving Christians and the Christian tradition along toward the dream of Jesus and the mind of Christ. Integral and beyond church can function as the frontier end of the escalator so that Christians do not have to step off the Christian path in order to continue to grow spiritually.

Religion in four modes

Religion comes, broadly, in four forms, or modes. I call them the four "m's"—magical, mythical, mental, and mystical. They move from less love to more love, and from less like Jesus to more like Jesus.

(1) There is the *magical* religion of the tribal and warrior stages. It is filled with fantasy.

(2) There is the *mythical* religion of the traditional state. This stage paints its heroes, such as Moses, Jesus, Krishna, and Buddha, with sometimes mythical language and legends that enhance the founders in ways that reveal the sincere devotion and awe of their followers.

(3) There is the *mental* religion of the modern stage. The modern mode focuses on the rational mind. It uses modern methods of critical thinking in an attempt to distinguish between the mythical elements that framed the written stories of its Scripture and the deeper truth in them. In its mental approach, the modern level may leave the religious path altogether and opt for a more philosophical path. The Unitarian Universalist movement is an example of this. Or

it may incorporate some of the postmodern, as in Science of the Mind churches, in an attempt to find meaning behind the traditional mythic stage.

(4) Just emerging now is the *mystical* religion of the integral and beyond stages. Some initial forms of integral may not embrace the mystical as fully as Wilber and others like myself do, so that is why I always include the "beyond." Integral and beyond has transcended magic and myth to reach the meaning of the mental stage. Then it transcends the resistance of this rational stage to anything not rational (prerational or postrational) and moves into the authentically mystical. The mystical allows us to connect with spiritual realities and, ultimately, to the divine reality that we are all a part of God and one another.

For Christianity to fully serve its escalator function of the evolving work of the Spirit, it must begin to offer the integral altitude and beyond. All religions are called to move to multiple stage understandings and multiple state experiences. This is the future of all religions that wish to hear the Spirit's call to evolve.

CHAPTER 15

Integral Church
The New Frontier

The oldest thing you can say about God is that God is always doing something new. I hope this book will show again that the Spirit is truly doing something new, especially today. I believe one of the new things God is doing now is inviting the church to move on up to what I am calling integral and beyond.

The integral and postintegral levels of faith appear, at present, to be the center of gravity in very few churches. Since we have so few models of this kind of church, my description is primarily my own experience at the courageous church where I have been a pastor since 1963—for (at this writing) the last 48 years. I am sure many other expressions of integral church will develop that will differ from the one that I describe here.

Many traditional-stage church beliefs come from the creeds of the fourth and fifth centuries. In the first three centuries, the church found itself in a hostile environment. When Constantine won control of the Roman Empire in 312 c.e. he elevated Christianity to high status with his motto "One God, one Lord, one faith, one church, one empire, one emperor." But his one faith and one church were severely divided by disputes about Christianity. Elaine Pagels says,

> Constantine declared amnesty for Christians and became their imperial patron. But this practical military leader chose to recognize only those who belong to what may have

233

become, by this time, the best-organized and largest group, which he called the "lawful and most holy catholic church." Constantine's recognition carried with it, of course, enormous benefits . . . Eventually the Nicene Creed, approved by the bishops and endorsed by Constantine himself would become the official doctrine that all Christians henceforth must accept in order to participate in the only church recognized by the emperor—the "catholic church." The emperor ordered all "heretics and schismatics" [about half the Christians in the empire according to Pagels] to stop meeting, even in private houses, and to surrender their churches and whatever property they owned to the catholic church.[1]

In the continuing fifth-century battles over "right belief," Philip Jenkins, in *Jesus Wars*, argues that orthodox beliefs were a product of political maneuvers by "four patriarchs, three queens, and two emperors."[2]

However it came about, being a Christian came to be defined entirely by what specific creeds you believed, rather than by your relationship to and experience of God. Equally disastrous was that what you needed to believe was a series of statements *about* Jesus, rather than primarily believing what Jesus himself lived and taught. The two primary historic Christian creeds, the Nicene and the Apostles creeds of the fourth century, say that Jesus was "born of the Virgin Mary, suffered under Pontius Pilate." Incredibly, in these creeds, the entire life and teaching of Jesus was reduced to a comma in between his birth and death! What was left was primarily beliefs about Jesus fashioned in terms of fourth- and fifth-century Greek and Roman philosophy.

Paraphrasing what has sometimes been attributed to the American scholar Sam Pascoe,

Christianity began in Palestine as an experience;
It moved to Greece and became a philosophy;
It moved to Italy and became an institution;
It moved to Europe and became a culture;
It moved to America and became a business!

Integral Christianity and church attempt to extricate themselves from these developments by including the best of them and transcending the worst. Rather than rejecting or avoiding beliefs, integral church is at home with beliefs, especially if they are integral. Here are my snapshots of what might be some of the beliefs of Christians at the integral stage and how they differ from previous levels.

The Bible

The tribal lens sees the Bible as powerful magic. The warrior lens sees the Bible as the story of the battle between good and evil. The traditional lens sees the Bible as the totally true Word of God containing all we need to know about our relationship to God. The modern lens sees the Bible as a blend of fact, myth, legend, fantasy, and wisdom. The postmodern lens sees the Bible as one of many Scriptures from around the world that teach spiritual wisdom.

The integral level church has found itself with respect to the Bible. The battle about whether it will be traditional and cling to rigid, literal interpretations is over. Most of its members now accept the place of modern rational inquiry in the writing and preservation of biblical documents while also discerning the more radical elements of this approach. The battle about whether the church will, as in some modern fashions, discard the Bible as unusable is also over. Instead, the Bible is studied, referred to, and valued as an indispensable resource. Of course, there are still varying viewpoints about the Bible, but no one is angry about them. The little boy asked his mother what was the difference between pagans and Christians. She replied, "Christians are the ones who fight about the Bible." Integral Christianity has given up fighting over the Bible.

The Bible is now seen as a fascinating account of the evolutionary progress of the spiritual path. Understanding it in terms of stages of spiritual development provides a way to appreciate and value the Bible in all of its aspects. In addition to this kind of developmental history, the Old Testament provides the context for Jesus' life and teaching. The New Testament gospels are indispensable because they describe much of what we currently know of Jesus' life and teaching. The rest of the New Testament is important because it is the interpretation of Jesus' life and teaching that came to dominance in the three centuries after Jesus. Jesus lived and taught from the highest levels. The integral church realizes that the New Testament, including the record of Jesus' life and teaching, was written by those at lower levels, primarily the traditional stage. Although many of the early Christians made a breakthrough into new *states* of consciousness, they had yet to move into new *stages* of understanding. The New Testament was collected and canonized by those often at even lower levels and is interpreted and read by the majority of people at those levels today. We cannot see what our worldview will not allow. What is amazing is that so much of Jesus' higher mode of consciousness and understanding came through so strongly in the gospels and in Paul's authentic letters.[3]

Integral church weaves together all the parts of the Bible into an understandable account that does not dilute or distort the teaching of Jesus. It is Jesus himself who points us away from previous lower stages of development and releases us to more evolved levels of spiritual growth.

At the integral level, the concerns of science and the Bible find a complementary exploration of Spirit which resides in all things. The concerns of the creationist and the evolutionist can find a comfortable peace. Creative design, while not science to be taught in schools, is becoming a favorite version of some thoughtful scientists. They are aware that, when you push back behind the Big Bang, it seems impossible not to have a creative force involved at all.[4]

The integral church also embraces the postmodern value of going beyond the Bible and has opened its heart and mind to other Christian writings such as the ancient Gospel of Thomas. Thomas was collected around the same time as the four New Testament gospels. Most Thomas scholars believe that parts of it were written as one of the first accounts of Jesus' sayings, along with a hypothetical document named "Q." Jesus scholar Marcus Borg places the first edition of the Gospel of Thomas at around 50 C.E. and the canonical gospels from 70 C.E. to 100 C.E.[5]

The integral church also embraces wisdom from across the world's religious traditions. It welcomes the truths of the scriptures of other traditions, the illuminating experiences of the mystics of every path both ancient and modern, and other ancient and contemporary teachers.[6] It wisely discerns the highest truths from all of these resources.

The Bible is best discerned through the life and teaching of Jesus. His treatment of his own Jewish scriptures is a model for us with our scriptures. The scriptures of his Jewish religion were still being compiled in Jesus' day, but they included most of what we now call the Old Testament. A reasonable reading of the four gospels shows that Jesus embraced, ignored, and rejected parts of his scriptures. Or in integral terminology, he both transcended and included parts of his "bible."

We must do the same with ours. When some parts of the Bible portray God as violent and angry toward enemies, and Jesus portrays God as only loving toward enemies, simple reason demands that both cannot be true. The integral approach chooses to follow Jesus and transcend the other less than Christ-like parts.

The Reformation used the Bible *(sola scriptura)* to wrestle Christianity from the hands of the Roman Catholic hierarchy. It was a brilliant and stage-appropriate move which lead to the traditional Protestant church. As with all movements, it did not go far enough. Integral church finds that Jesus now wrestles Christianity from the hands of the traditional church. The Bible then emerges in its most accessible, reasonable, and spiritual light.

God

Looking through the tribal-church lens, God is the heavenly super being who is in charge of the world. At the warrior level God is not only all-powerful but eternally in a bad mood, using divine power to coerce and punish people. The traditional-church lens sees God as both a compassionate and, at times, vengeful super being up in heaven who insists that people can come to "him" only through the historical person called Jesus. The "God up there in the heavens" of the traditional stage is what I call an "in between God," not close enough to be the intimate Father/Mother of Jesus and not big enough to be the infinite God "in whom we live and move and have our being."

The modern stage looks through its physical-reality-only lens and sometimes does not see a God of any kind. The postmodern-church lens sees God everywhere. The integral and beyond sees that God is powerful—but it is a different kind of God with a different kind of power, the power of creative intelligence, evolutionary impulse, all-encompassing love, healing energy, and transforming compassion.

In my ministry I have spent very little time trying to get agnostics and atheists to believe in God. I have used most of my time suggesting that Christians might try believing in a different God. Or in integral terms, to see God through a different lens.

Integral Christianity has given up the traditional idea of protecting God. Barbara Brown Taylor, Episcopal priest and teacher, says, "As a general rule, I would say that human beings never behave more badly toward one another than when they believe they are protecting God. In the words of Arun Gandhi, grandson of Mohandas, 'People of the Book risk putting the book above people.'"[7]

Postmodern people often have trouble defining their spirituality. Philosophical developments have resulted in a postmodern spirituality in which people may believe in God but are left unable to speak about God. When they are asked what they believe about God, they are unable to articulate anything specific. Their non-creedal spirituality leaves them unable to talk about God in meaningful ways.

Integral Christianity recognizes that the word "God" can be both wonderful and weird. The word "God" may be the most beautiful word in the English language. It is a unique linguistic and theological treasure. On the other hand, the word "God" has been so locked into traditional belief systems that it sometimes seems dangerous to use. In my vision of integral spirituality, we have reclaimed the word "God." We have come into the freedom to speak about God without meaning the traditional God. We can also freely use other names and metaphors for God such as Universal Wisdom, Ultimate Mystery, Infinite Being, Higher Power, Sacred Mystery, Being Itself, The Sacred, Maker of Heaven and Earth, Spirit, "I am that I am" (God's reply when asked for a name), Creator, Self-existent One, The Divine Beloved, the Cosmic Christ, the Ground of All Being, Dearest Friend, or The Great I Am.

I believe that panentheism is presently the most expansive way of thinking about the Infinite Face of God. As Michael Brierley says, "The naming of panentheism assists the world's redemption."[8]

The integral Christian and church have also moved past seeing only one or two faces of God. They now see that the fullest possible relationship to God in this life is found in the three perspectives in which Jesus knew God—contemplation *about* God who was greater than he was, communion *with* God who was his beloved Abba, and union *as* God who was Jesus' own True Self.

They have reconciled the Infinite Face of God (3rd-person standpoint) explored in scientific research with the Inner Face of God (1st-person standpoint) explored in interior prayer. They have reconciled the Inner Face of God emphasized in Eastern religious practice of inner divinity with the Intimate Face of God (2nd-person standpoint) found in Western practices of worship, adoration, and surrender to God.

Integral and beyond church members are at home with honoring their own 1st-person inner divinity and beginning to experience it in elevated states of consciousness. They do not hesitate to embrace the intimate 2nd-person face of God in Jesus whom they passionately worship and sing about. They love to adore and contemplate God in infinite 3rd-person viewpoint. This three-standpoint view differs from the postmodern one represented by Marcus Borg. He stops short of all three perspectives of God with his exclusion of the Inner Divine, dealing with only Intimate Divine and Infinite Divine.[9]

At the integral worldview we step back and see the progression from understanding God in tribal worship of nature spirits in shamanism to warrior worship personified in superhero gods. Next comes the traditional worship of the one God who is the mythic father figure in the sky. This evolves into the modern/postmodern panentheistic God who is both in and beyond everything. With integral, and especially post-integral, comes the mystical God of Jesus who is the I Am, the Transcendent Oneness who is not separate from our own Divine Self.

The question of the traditional level is, "Do you believe in God?" This usually means, "Do you believe in a God who sits in heaven and gives out rewards and punishments to us? And some day, if we have believed or done the right things, God will let us come and be with 'him.'"Those beliefs have been put to rest. At the integral level the questions are probably more like, "Do you experience God?" Or, "How do you think about God?" Or, "How do you get in touch with Spirit deep within yourself?"

Jesus

The tribal lens sees a magical wonder worker Jesus. The warrior lens perceives a vengeful Jesus. The traditional lens sees a suffering Jesus who died in our place on the cross to save us from God's wrath. The modern lens sees a human (only human) Jesus who is a wise teacher. The postmodern lens sees an inclusive Jesus who embraces everyone, along with all of their various spiritual paths. The integral and beyond lens sees a mystical, reformer, prophetic Jesus who fully realized and manifested his divine identity. He includes the best of the preceding Jewish paths and transcends the no-longer-adequate elements.

What makes integral Church different from integral Temple (Jewish or Hindu), or integral Mosque, or integral Buddhist Center? The Christian tradition is inextricably tied to the Jesus path, just as Buddha is intrinsic to Buddhism. Jesus is the personification of the Christ consciousness. The Christ consciousness that filled Jesus is within all of us whether we call it Krishna consciousness, the Buddha mind, the Universal Principle, being one with Spirit, Cosmic Mind, or one of the many other names for Spirit awareness. Christians access this consciousness following the model of Jesus. This is the vast God consciousness that envelops us all. It was the deepest part of Jesus. It is the True Self of every person. While Jesus never *confines* God to his religion, he *defines* God for our religion as Christians. As our primary prototype and guide in the spiritual journey, he leads us beyond himself to embrace the divine consciousness of the Cosmic Christ.

Sometimes Christians begin to see the validity of other spiritual paths and how people at the traditional ethnocentric level hold beliefs about Jesus that exclude most of the human race from authentic spirituality. They may then move to "Jesus lite" because they don't want to be mistaken for those who believe that Jesus excludes so many from God's love. I heard about a pastor in a progressive, postmodern denomination who wanted to be very inclusive. The denomination seemed to be embarrassed about Jesus because of the misunderstanding of Jesus at an ethnocentric level. He was in a ministerial meeting where they were asked to share what was important to them. They talked about things like God, love, spirituality, and world peace. When it came this pastor's turn he said, "What is important to me is Jesus." An awkward embarrassed silence followed. He recounted the scene with tears in his eyes. For him, it was *because* of Jesus that he believed in universal love and acceptance, not in spite of him.

The postmodern church dead-ends when it tries to be all things to all people in all spiritual paths. Integral church and Christianity have no trouble identifying themselves as following Jesus. Integral church takes its place on the Christian escalator, seeking to release that tradition into the ever-higher realms of transcendence. *It leaves it to other traditions to do the same.*

The Christian integral path transcends a modern and merely reasoned approach to the spiritual life and re-embraces the passion found in the Bible in relating to God. This church, like the postmodern, rejects dominator hierarchies in the Bible and in the world. However, instead of seeing everything as being of equal value, as in the postmodern Christian life, it now has a place for natural hierarchies. Some viewpoints really are more loving and more Christ-like than others, and integral church is comfortable with rejecting those things that are less than loving and less than Christ-like.

Jesus is the prototype for the new humanity

The first question those in the traditional stage usually ask me as we talk about these things is, "Do you believe Jesus is divine?" This is often the ultimate test of true Christianity as interpreted by the traditional stage. They are relieved when I say, "Of course Jesus is divine." However, their relief goes away when I say, "Not only is Jesus divine, so are you!" I explain that the biblical, orthodox viewpoint is that we are partakers of the divine nature and, therefore, are not only like Jesus in our humanity but also in our divinity.

Christian integralists see that Jesus is the name of the Man from Galilee, a person full of God, whose wisdom teaching subverted the traditional thinking of his day. He was a Spirit person who transmitted God's presence and power to all who were open to receive. He was a healer who transfused healing energy to those in need. He was radically inclusive, welcoming all to his table. He fully realized and manifested his humanity and divinity. As Jesus, the Christ, he is the prototype for the new humanity, modeling what it looks like for a person to embrace and express their own inherent humanity and divinity. And now, more on the relationship of Jesus and Christ.

The Three Faces of Christ

In Chapter 12 I unfolded the Three Faces of God. These three Sacred Faces can provide what is presently the fullest and most complete framework for all religious/spiritual traditions in contemplation, communion, and union with the Divine, however that Mystery is named.

Every event, moment, person, and object in our lives can be seen in its fullest expression from the standpoints of 1st-, 2nd-, and 3rd-person. Looking at God in this way gives us what I call the Infinite Face of God of 3rd-person, the Intimate Face God in 2nd-person, and the Inner Face of God in 1st-person.

I am excited that now in this chapter we can frame the Three Faces God in specifically Christian terms—the Three Faces of Christ. The Three Faces of Christ emerged into my awareness in deep zone prayer only recently. Whole new dimensions of cognitive, devotional, and inner awakening have bloomed into my life with this way of seeing Christ. Let me unfold it for you as it has come to me in 3rd-, 2nd-, and 1st-person perspectives.

The Infinite Face of Christ—the Cosmic Christ (3rd-person standpoint)

As I have previously pointed out, Christians often do not know, as scholars do, that "Christ" is not Jesus' last name. "Christ" is a title, a description of Jesus. The word "Christ" in Greek means "anointed one." At the level of prerational, mythic society, kings were anointed, conferring God's spirit upon them and recognizing their sacredness. Jesus was one anointed by God in this historical sense.

I have always been moved by the words in Colossians, where Paul moves beyond this anointed man, Jesus, as only an historical person, and paints a picture of Christ in the most transcendent colors possible. Paul describes what some, like Matthew Fox and Richard Rohr, have rightly called the "Cosmic Christ." Listen to these consecutive, cascading, cosmic phrases:

> Christ is the image of the invisible God . . .
> The firstborn of all creation . . .
> In Christ all things in heaven and on earth were created, things
> visible and invisible . . .
> All things have been created through Christ and for Christ . . .
> Christ is before all things . . .
> In Christ all things hold together . . .
> For in Christ all the fullness of God was pleased to dwell . . .
> Through Christ God was pleased to reconcile all things . . . .[10]

In the Gospel of John, when Jesus speaks *as* the "Christ" he is speaking as the Cosmic Christ. When he declares, "I am the good shepherd. I am the way. I am the bread of life. I am the door. I am the vine. I am the light of the world. I am the resurrection," he is not speaking as the historical person Jesus, but as the Cosmic Christ. This gospel is quite different from the other three in the New Testament. We can follow Marcus Borg and Eugene Boring and say that in John's gospel Jesus is speaking through the church after his resurrection as the Risen Christ. John is the continuing voice of Jesus through the church. Or, we can follow Stevan Davies and see Jesus speaking in the great tradition of Jewish prophets from an altered state of consciousness as God.[11] Either way, we hear the Cosmic Christ.

In the Gospel of John, Jesus proclaims, "I am the way, the truth, and the life. No one comes to God but through me."[12]

This statement has traditionally been understood as limiting the path to God to the human person Jesus. It is seen as a unique claim by the human Jesus about himself, as one person living in first-century Palestine. When understood that way, only those who know about Jesus in some belief-centered way may come to know God. This moves us back to ethnocentric levels. But Jesus taught a theology of oneness, not a theology of separation. So how are we to understand these words of Jesus?

At the integral level we see that Jesus was speaking as the Cosmic Christ, the Universal Mind of God. This passage is not about the human Jesus but about Jesus' vast God consciousness. Jesus revealed the Cosmic Christ at a particular time and place in history. However, the Cosmic Christ is not limited to Jesus.

The Cosmic Christ is the Universal Presence of God. Christ is the pattern that connects all things for "in Christ all things hold together."[13] The Cosmic Christ holds all of creation and history together. Alex Grey images these complex ideas in his profound painting *Cosmic Christ,* a copy of which hangs in our Faces of Jesus church gallery of 240 images of Jesus from around the world. The golden rope that is Christ surrounds one hundred small inset images of the major events of history from the Big Bang to space explora-tion, the Holocaust and slavery, and the transfiguration and ascen-sion of Christ. The heart of the Cosmic Christ is the crucifixion in the form of the round ball of Earth with everyone nailed together. The Christ child is in the center, crying in the difficulty of the birth of planetary consciousness. It is a vivid image of "in Christ all things hold together."[14]

The Intimate Face of Christ—Jesus (2nd-person standpoint)

The Intimate Face of Christ is simply Jesus, the historic Jesus who is with us now in his always and ever-present Spirit body. The Cosmic Christ is anchored in the historical person Jesus.

In the past some theologians have called the Cosmic Christ the Christ of faith as opposed to the Jesus of history. By whatever names, these two are different, yet intimately connected. The Cosmic Christ was realized and manifested in Jesus. If we have only the person in history named Jesus, we have severely limited our spiritual quest. If we have only the Cosmic Christ without the human Jesus, we have left the intimate connection to humankind found in the historical Jesus. Then we are left without the anchor of Jesus' teaching and life. We are without a concrete model, a prototype of the new humanity.

When we understand Jesus' statement of "I am the way" in terms of the Infinite Face of God as the Cosmic Christ and the Intimate Face of God as Jesus, then we see that the Christ Consciousness, or Universal Mind of God, or Spirit by whatever name, really *is* the only way to God. The Cosmic Christ Spirit is available to everyone and anyone in any authentic, loving, spiritual path. It is the Universal Mind of God, the Mind of the Cosmic Christ present but hidden, in everyone—and which blazed out through Jesus in a breakthrough way. As Steve McIntosh states, "The degree of our transcendence is determined by the scope of our inclusion."[15]

The Inner Face of Christ—"Christ in you, the hope of glory." (1st-person standpoint)

In Paul's wondrous words, "Christ in you, the hope of glory,"[16] we have the Inner Face of Christ, which is our own Original Face, the Very Image of God, our Christ Self.

This echoes the single sentence of Paul that defines the gospel in the clearest and most concise way, "I live, yet not I, but Christ lives within me."

Jesus leads us within to our own Christ consciousness when he says that the Kingdom of God is within. Paul amplifies this with his often repeated "in Christ" and "Christ in you." Christians are literally "little Christs." We become conscious of the Universal Cosmic Christ as our True Self in 1st-person perspective through the awakening of our minds and hearts in Christ. The goal is not to be a Christian but to be a Christ!

The Integral Christ

At the integral level we can embrace the most expansive and biblical understanding of Jesus Christ—the Three Faces of Christ:

(1)   *Christ the Cosmic One* who holds all things together.

(2)   *Christ Jesus* of Nazareth, who is present with us always.

(3)   *Christ in you*, the hope of glory.

Looking at Christ through these three lenses lets us see what we could not see before:

(1)   The 3rd-person objective perspective which embraces the Infinite One, the Cosmic Christ as the Universal Mind of God.

(2)   The 2nd-person intersubjective standpoint which adores the Intimate One, Jesus Christ who was revealed in history as the Man from Galilee.

(3)   The 1st-person subjective awareness which awakens us to the Inner One, the Christ who shines forth as "Christ in you, the hope of glory."

Is it okay to worship Jesus?

Those who have passed through the modern and postmodern stages often wrestle with the question, "Is it okay to worship Jesus?" Once we take Jesus off the narrow ethnocentric pedestal of being the world's only savior and remove him from the responsibility of having saved us from hell by dying for our sins, what is left for him to do? Or be? Why all the fuss about worshipping him? Isn't this idolatry, Jesus-olatry?

No, it is not. We worship Jesus because we are so grateful for his life back then and his presence with us now.

We worship Jesus because we know that we become like that which we adore. We want to become like him. We experience his love, his healing energy, and his guidance as we honor and bow before him.

Technically, when I worship Jesus, I am worshipping God incarnate in Jesus—the God in and as Jesus and the God beyond

Jesus.[17] Theologically, it is okay to worship any divine image that represents God to us in 2nd-person communion. The icon reverence in the Orthodox Church approaches this although they would make a sharp distinction between "honorable reverence" and worship. They say that icons serve "to lift us up to the prototypes which they symbolize, to a higher level of thought and feeling."[18] Yes, indeed they do. The beautiful term "Namaste" reminds us to honor the divine in everyone we meet. I have a growing sense of this in my own life every time I see another person.

I have always thought that a beautiful line in the older Book of Common Prayer wedding ceremony was quite profound. The groom says to the bride, "With my body I thee worship." Perhaps this was a glimpse of the future when we honor, adore, and yes, even worship the image of God in all.

However, I am not personally comfortable, as a Christian, worshiping or surrendering my life in an ultimate sense to any guru, saint, or incarnation of the divine in this life except Jesus. I suspect in heaven, when we are all "transformed into the same image from one degree of glory to another,"[19] we may feel right at home recognizing and honoring one another as icons of God.

C.S. Lewis put it in these words: "It is a serious thing to live in a society of possible gods and goddesses, to remember that the dullest and most uninteresting person you talk to may one day be a creature which, if you saw it now, you would be strongly tempted to worship..."[20]

For now, I believe that Jesus alone is worthy of my *ultimate* devotion in incarnational terms. In terms of passionate devotion to Jesus, I am adoring and giving myself to the One I love and seek to emulate, the living, risen Jesus Christ.

It is good to worship Jesus, *but it is even important to become like him.* Once again, the goal in authentic Christianity is not to be a Christian. The goal is to be a Christ. Since we really do become like that which we worship, worshipping Jesus helps us become more Christ-like. If our theology says that we really cannot be like him, then all we are left with is projecting our own divinity onto Jesus. That doesn't do either one of us any good! This is the great obstacle of previous theological-stage understandings. That must be changed so we can be released to be who we really are—daughters and sons of God, made in God's image, partakers of the divine nature, the light of the world, and in Jesus' words, gods!

My co-pastor at Broadway Church, Marcia Fleischman, enrolled in a self-defense course taught by an expert. She was ready and willing to be taught by the instructor and follow his example. She faithfully attended the classes and did the exercises. At final exam time she succeeded in punching out and knocking down several pretend attackers. She said, "Wow, I felt powerful!"

As she excitedly recounted her experience, I thought of another scenario. What if the classes consisted of repeated introductions of the expert instructor, long histories of his accomplishments, many testimonies and admiration of him and his accomplishments, and little talks on being like him. Part of the talks would include how great he was and how inadequate we are. Then everyone would go home at the end of each class with new admiration for the instructor. What would happen at the final exam where you defend yourself against an attacker? Disaster! That's because everyone knows you can't learn self-defense that way. The idea is not to simply admire the instructor. That is the *first step*, because you would need to know and respect the trainer in order to learn from that person. The crucial *second step* is to learn how to *be like* the instructor—to know you have the potential to know what the teacher knows and also eventually do what the expert does, manifesting it in reality.

The church has settled for only the first step. People go to church and admire the instructor, Jesus. They learn all they can about him. They hear about how he operated and hear little talks about how they should be like him. Then they go home and try to take on an attacker. Ouch. That hurts! No wonder we don't feel powerful as Christians. Honoring and learning about the teacher is only the first step.

The next crucial step is to personally learn what the instructor knows and feels. We want to practice and experience what the instructor practices and experiences. Then we can *do what the teacher does* because we have moved from our *potential* to the reality of being like our instructor. And the result is that we feel powerful! This is the path of embracing our divinity.

One river, many wells

Using Matthew Fox's analogy of "one river, many wells,"[21] here are seven pegs on which to hang our thinking about Jesus, the Christ.

(1) God is like an incredible underground River flowing throughout the world.

(2) Jesus is like a well that taps into the underground River.

(3) Jesus is not the Water. He is a well.

(4) Christ IS the Water. Christ is the anointing Spirit of God.

(5) Any well that taps into the River (God) is a real well.

(6) All wells that tap into the River tap into Christ, the water, whether they call God's Spirit by that name or not.

(7) Jesus is the decisive well for Christians, who may also visit and drink from other wells.

Following Jesus

In review, remember that I usually talk about integral Christianity and integral church together because I believe one without the other is incomplete. We need a new vision of Christianity that includes a new vision of the church. Although integral Christianity/church focuses on following Jesus, it has given up the idea of Jesus' uniqueness in two ways. He is not the only person who has revealed God to us in extraordinary ways, as other religious traditions testify. Even more importantly, he is not one of a kind compared to you and me. He came to teach us that we are all, at heart, just like him and can realize that potential. He offered us a prototype and pattern which showed us that we could *become* like him because he knew we *are* like him in our deepest selves. He told us we are the light of the world, just as he is the light of the world.

I love my spiritual roots in Christianity even as I see the contributions of other religious paths as different flavors of the Universal Spirit of God. It delights me to see Eastern traditions that have long been at home with the recognition of the divinity of every person. Some Western postmodern spiritual traditions, such as the Spiritual But Not Religious and New Thought movements recognize the inherent divinity of every person. However, most versions of Christianity do not. Integral Christianity can and should.

E. Stanley Jones was a missionologist of an earlier generation whom I admired greatly. He spoke about a traveler who got lost in the jungle. The lost traveler came upon a village in the middle of the forest. He asked a tribal member to lead him out. The local agreed, and for an hour he walked ahead of the lost traveler, clearing a way through the jungle thick with trees and vines and plants with a machete. Eventually the traveler asked, "Are you sure we are going the right way. Isn't there a path somewhere?" The villager smiled, "My friend, I am the path."

Jesus is our path. That's *what* I mean by following Jesus.

Buckminster Fuller said, "Never change things by fighting the existing reality. To change something, build a new model that makes the existing model obsolete." That is *why* I follow Jesus. Jesus is the new model of humanity.

Healing, Helping Prayer

The tribal lens sees prayer as persuading an all-powerful heavenly being to protect, heal, and guide whoever they are praying for.

The warrior lens sees prayer as doing battle with evil.

The traditional lens sees prayer as a conversation with God (or Jesus), that includes petitioning God up in heaven to intervene down here on Earth.

The modern lens sees prayer, at the most, as something like uplifting thoughts.

The postmodern lens sees prayer as many things.

The integral-mystic lens sees prayer as inspired states of consciousness where we experience God in both relationship and identification. Prayer, including communal worship, is central in integral and beyond church. Healing prayer is sending the healing energy of the Spirit from within us to others.

At the integral and beyond level, prayer in 3rd-person practice is reflection, contemplation, and meditation *about* the Infinite Face of God. Prayer in 2nd-person practice is communion *with* the Spirit in a personal way, sitting next to you as the Intimate Face of God. It is connecting with the non-physical world of Spirit beings and spiritual guidance. In 1st-person practice, prayer is the release of sacred energy from deep *within* ourselves into the world. Don't ask God to do it for you—you're divine like Jesus, so do it yourself! This is owning the Inner Face of God within us. This is not the traditional mythic God out there who intervenes in human history, but a God who resides within and as every person and from there shapes human history. We are co-creators with and as God.

However, I want to point out that the Spirit also responds to all levels of prayer and seeking. This includes yelling "Help" to God. God doesn't wait until we get the words or ideas just right before the world of Spirit responds to us. The integral journey of faith includes a 2nd-person relationship of gratitude, worship, prayer, and surrender to God. Good relationships are responsive to all the various levels and parts of us.

While the integral level appreciates many forms of praying for others, it tends to move from "interventionist" prayers, to "transmission" prayers. The interventionist prayer is based on the traditional level model that God is absent and needs to be reminded to come "down" from heaven and intervene in a situation. Jesus did not operate this way. He never asked God to heal anyone. Rather, he owned his own divine healing energy from within and released it to others with remarkable results. The transmission model sees that God already desires to heal and simply needs an incarnate divine vehicle to do so. That vehicle is you and me.

In transmission prayer we see ourselves as the vehicles for releasing the manifestation of God's desire to heal and redeem. We, rather than a God up there and out there, are the voice and hands of the Spirit. Our refusal to own our inherent divinity and to pray as Jesus did keeps us asking God to do what Jesus said we can do.

In addition, 1st-person prayer which focuses on the Inner Face of God can be practiced by making affirmations that point to our inner divinity such as the biblical passages quoted in Chapter 13.

Integral and beyond worship can now include all Three Faces of God as the fullest expression of personal and corporate worship:

- 3rd-person contemplation and reflection *about* God's Infinite Face in everything as we seek to be open to the Spirit while we read, reflect, study, sing, and talk;

- 2nd-person surrender and adoration directed *to* God's Intimate Face near to us in personal and corporate times of thanksgiving, praise, surrender, and divine conversation; and

- 1st-person interior consenting to God's Inner Face within and *as* us in deep affirmation of our own sacred divinity. This is the compassionate heart of God that expresses itself in the world in liberating service through our spiritual gifts.

Sin and Salvation

The tribal-, warrior-, and traditional-church lenses see sin as disobeying God and salvation as being saved from the penalty of that disobedience which is available only through faith in Jesus Christ. This is reflected quite strongly in traditional church creeds, doctrine, and leadership. However, I am gratified to note that the people in the pews are beginning to think differently. A recent Pew survey shows that well over half of the people in traditional churches believe that other religions can lead to eternal life.[22]

The modern-church viewpoint sees sin as anything that harms others or us. Salvation is the release of healing and justice into the world. The postmodern church sees sin (probably without using the word) as alienation and salvation as that which connects us to all others in the spiritual realm.

The integral and beyond perspective has taken the word sin back to its original meaning; the Greek word "sin" simply means "missing the mark." However, integral church probably does not use the actual word "sin" at all. "Sin" has become loaded with two millennia of abusive religious baggage that often invites self-loathing, a focus on sexuality, and unhealthy introspection.[23] The word "sin" may be replaced by the idea of identifying with our ego in reference to the interior life. In reference to the exterior culture, sin might be called "oppression." Sin is manifesting a wrong identity in unloving attitudes and actions. *Sin is not being true to our Divine Self.*

In thinking about "salvation," integral church has left sin/sacrifice/atonement theologies behind because they are seen as punitive, vengeful, and less than Christ-like. Instead, salvation is coming home to the spiritual reality of the universe—we are all the beloved children of God.

The traditional church teaches that we are to love others as Jesus did and, in general, act as Jesus did. However, the traditional church makes it clear that, in fact, we are not at all like Jesus, and so it becomes an impossible and oppressive goal. In integral church we come to see that we are intrinsically like Jesus in our truest self. Our Authentic Self is already a Christ. From this basis, then, it actually becomes possible to be like Jesus, to act like him, because we *are* like him at our deepest level. *Integral salvation is simply being liberated into who we really are.*

Heaven and Hell

According to Jesus, hell is "garbage dump existence." It is real. And it has nothing to do with traditional ideas about eternal punishment when we die. The word "hell" is the English translation of the biblical word *Gehenna*. It was the name of a garbage dump located just south of Jerusalem. It had an ugly history of child sacrifice and, in Jesus' day, fires were kept going to consume the refuse dumped there.

The Linns, in one of their many beautiful books, write:

> Perhaps one reason Jesus used Gehenna or hell as an image of what happens to us when we behave in an unloving way was to remind us of what psychosomatic medicine has recently discovered. If we act in unloving ways, not only will we feel like garbage, but we will also find our physical body and our whole self deteriorating just as did Gehenna's garbage."[24]

Jesus talked about hell (Gehenna) more that anyone else in the Bible (11 of the 12 times). However, we have changed from Jesus' use of the word to outlandish and oppressive meanings. Note the following facts about hell in Jesus' viewpoint as recorded in the New Testament gospels:

(1) Jesus never, not once, connected hell with whether one was a Christian or not. He never connected it with anyone's religion.

(2) In every instance, Jesus connected hell with being unloving, not with being unbelieving.

(3) Hell was Jesus' radical commentary on those who oppress others in the world here and now.

(4) There are over 30 passages in the New Testament that say no one will be left behind in any kind of eternal hell because everyone will be ultimately brought into eternity with God.[25]

We have twisted Jesus' eternal words about being unloving into unloving words about eternal destiny. The garbage of hell is alienation from our True Self and manifests in all those things that are not love.

At the integral and beyond level, heaven may be understood as existence, now and later, in the realization and manifestation of our identification with God. Therefore, heaven has a present dimension and ever-evolving future. What I have called the three standpoints, Plato classically called the Beautiful, the Good, and the True. That provides an eloquent and expansive framework to think about integral-and-beyond heaven. *Most simply, heaven is ever-expanding beauty, goodness, and truth, wherever they are found.*

The Kingdom of Heaven

The tribal, warrior, and traditional churches see the Kingdom of Heaven (or Kingdom of God, which is identical in meaning in the gospels) as primarily a place where Christians go after death. The modern-church lens sees the Kingdom of Heaven as primarily healing and justice in the here and now. The postmodern church probably does not use the term Kingdom of Heaven because the word "Kingdom" is quite patriarchal. I have used it in this book because it is so familiar, and the alternatives such as "dominion of God" or "realm of God" don't seem to do it justice either. The postmodern Christian probably sees the Kingdom of God or Heaven as living in the reality that we are all spiritual beings on a human journey.

At the integral level, the Kingdom of Heaven, for the first time, is now understood as the great nondual vision of Jesus, that there is no separation between us and God, or between us and one another. Jesus did not come preaching Christianity was at hand. Instead, he preached the Kingdom of God was at hand. The traditional church believes that the goal of the spiritual life is to get us into heaven. *Integral church believes that the goal is to get heaven into us!*

To put an even finer point on it, in my understanding of the good news of Jesus the Christ, the goal is to realize that heaven is *already* and *always present* within us—and our goal is to realize, embrace, and manifest that reality in the world here and now.

Under the guidance of a few early church leaders who came to prominence, traditional Christianity evolved as one of the brilliant, stage-appropriate ways for the earliest Christians to understand Jesus. It was then shaped by Greek and Roman thought into the creeds of the fourth century. The institutional church took it from there and we pretty much have what we call Christianity today. What is better than Christianity? The Kingdom of God is better than Christianity! When Jesus talked about the Kingdom of Heaven, he was talking about *God consciousness*—living life in, with, and as God!

Luke records Jesus saying that the Kingdom of Heaven is within us.[26] The Gospel of Thomas records Jesus saying,

> If those who lead you say to you, 'See, the Kingdom is in the sky,' then the birds of the sky will precede you. If they say to you, 'It is in the sea,' then the fish will precede you. Rather, the Kingdom is inside of you, and it is outside of you. When you come to know yourselves, then you will become known,

and you will realize that it is you who are the sons of the living Father. But if you will not know yourselves, you dwell in poverty and it is you who are that poverty.[27]

If we "will not know" our deepest self, then we will not know God, for they are one and the same. The Kingdom of God is first an inside job. Then it flows outwardly to a needy world.

The Mystical

Tribal mysticism may be a mixture of both authentic union with nature and fear-based superstition. Warrior mysticism is filled with power fantasies of winners and losers. Traditional mysticism is the one we study about in the Bible, but it is believed to have ceased with the Bible's completion. To the modern eye, mysticism doesn't exist. Postmodern mysticism includes everything that isn't rational, from prerational fantasy to authentic psychic experience. Integral and beyond mysticism distinguishes between the superstitious and the spiritual, while embracing both the scientists' exploration of the universe as well as the mystics' exploration of that same universe.

The idea of the supernatural of the traditional church is replaced by the idea of the mystical in the integral church. Supernatural suggests that God intervenes from the outside. Mystical suggests that God is already present and we become aware of that ever present reality.

A mystic is someone who experiences God. God is an experienced reality. One may have all kinds of beliefs about God, and that is quite different from experiencing God.

Jesus was first a mystic. His life and teaching eventually morphed into what became Christianity. Traditional Christianity today is a doctrine-based, fear-based faith which warns against the mystical. There are relatively few mystics left in churches today because they have had to seek a more welcoming home in the spiritual-but-not-religious movement or in Eastern religions.

Integral and beyond Christianity welcomes mystics. Mystics believe there is a deeper state of existence beyond the ordinary world which we see in our daily life. The integral and beyond church is at home with the altered state experiences of the New Testament and the mystics of many traditions down through the centuries.

The most crucial weakness at this point in the larger world of integral philosophy and practice is that mysticism is currently almost entirely an individual consciousness. Most integral practitioners seem to be without a collective. I do see hopeful signs of that changing.[28] The most progressive integral mysticism is communal as well as private. For Christian integralists, elevated spiritual state experiences must become a regularly occurring and normal part of corporate worship and small group gatherings.

Strengths and Limitations

This chapter has basically been an exploration of the strengths of my version of the integral stage of Christianity. Hopefully there will be other interpretations, too.

When it comes to integral's limitations, it is still too early to see the most important ones. Of course, there will be criticisms of any new ways of thinking, some of which will turn out to be true, and some not. However, the really important limitations of any stage only become visible when enough people inhabit a stage long enough to begin to see beyond it. The only thing we can be sure of is that integral, like all stages, has limitations that will need to be transcended if we are to continue to answer the Spirit's call to evolve.

Religious, social, and political activism

My readers may notice that I seldom mention the important areas of social and political action in the world. Jesus framed his own just action in light of his mission statement in his inaugural sermon in Luke 4:

> The Spirit of the Lord is upon me, who has anointed me to bring good news to those who are poor, who has sent me to proclaim release to those who are captive and recovery of sight to the blind, to let those who are oppressed go free, to proclaim the year of the Lord's favor.[29]

Jesus identified with that quote from the Old Testament which itself points out that being "anointed" by the Spirit must *precede* our work of liberation in the world. I understand that *Jesus' redemptive action stemmed from his relationship to his Abba.* This is how he knew what to say and do—and where to say and do it.

This book's focus is on that communion and union with God. I leave it to another book to focus on the great themes of healing the world. Much sincere and well-meaning action in the world comes from inner shadow and not inner Source. These results are often do-goodism and burn out.

In my own life I have experienced trying to minister coming from my shadow rather than Source. As I have moved to more directly operating from communion and guidance from the Spirit Source within, let me tell you—that's the only way to go!

Communion and union with the extroverted Abba God of Jesus always results in the loving flow of redemptive action in the world that is consistent with one's spiritual gifts.

Including and transcending the previous stages

Integral spirituality represents a major breakthrough in its awareness of including and transcending other religious and spiritual altitudes.

The sense of wonder of the tribal level is included in a return to the mystical. However the magical level projection of our own divinity outward onto a super being or beings is transcended. We give up believing in a superhuman-like God who can be controlled by incantations, sacrificial offerings, and prayerful pleading. In the authentic mystical we take back our projections and own our divinity. We experience the mystical union and identification with God that allows us to interact with the spiritual world as Jesus did.

Some of my most deeply ingrained images are from the traditional mythic level. I can't ignore that part of me. Every part of us needs to be "fulfilled." The traditional part of me often needs traditional level images to convey the Spirit. In integral church I can value the traditional church, knowing that just because it is mythic doesn't mean it can't be meaningful. Just because it is literal doesn't mean it can't be living.

When I begin to sense too much tension between the traditional parts of myself and other growing parts, then I am ready to make a change. I need each level until I have "fulfilled" it. Don't try to take anything away from me if I am not ready for it.

Integral Christianity learns from all levels of churches. It learns from tribal church to settle into the church community with ferocious commitment and loyalty. It learns from warrior church to be passionate about the spiritual life. It learns from traditional church about working together in faithfulness. It learns from modern church to keep thinking. It learns from postmodern church to be sensitive to where each person finds themself, and to be as inclusive as possible.

How is integral Christianity different from postmodern, progressive, emergent churches, New Thought, and the Spiritual But Not Religious?

I have a deep appreciation for all of these movements. They each have valuable things to contribute to the evolving church. If traditional and modern churches would move a little toward any of these, everything would be much better in churchland.

Progressive Christianity

The term "progressive Christianity" began to come into wider use around the 1990s. In part, it came about as Protestants, who were frustrated by the conservative surge, began to form outside of churches in parachurch organizations. One stream focuses on freeing Christians from traditional theology. Another stream focuses on a concern for justice growing out of the social gospel of the early twentieth century. Process theology forms another current of some progressive thought.[30]

The Emerging Church

The emerging or emergent church movement is a recent and lively movement that attempts to engage postmodern people, especially the unchurched. It remains to be seen if it is actually postmodern or a more traditional level that seeks to engage postmodern persons. It has great potential.

The emerging church movement contains a great diversity in beliefs and practices. Some have focused on ancient rituals, art, drama, and social activism. It is a fluid network of churches with little organization, but that may be changing as the movement grows. Perhaps the one thing emergent churches have in common is their disillusionment with all the varieties of traditional church. They want to move beyond the traditional.

I am grateful for the growing emergent church movement and find myself cheerleading for them. They seem to offer a somewhat small, and therefore accessible, next step in spiritual evolution for those in the traditional church. It seems currently like a launching pad for the great hunger for something more. I guess that's why it's called emerging.

How can the emerging churches and movement keep from becoming just like the "liberal" mainline churches? That can be accomplished by making the life, teaching, and presence of Jesus central, encouraging authentic spiritual experience, and continuing to take the Bible seriously within an overall framework such as the one I am proposing.

Brian McLaren, prominent emergent spokesperson, is charting an excellent, evolving course for those who will follow his lead.[31] At this writing it remains to be seen how many will.

I would like to dangle integral church in front of them as an enticing natural next step for those free enough to dive in.

Postmodern Church

This is a larger, more general category that sometimes includes both ancient forms of worship such as Taize and contemporary, multisensory worship. Churches have replaced the song leader with the worship team, traded the organ for a band, and said goodbye to the choir. They seek to minister to the whole person, both saving souls and sharing concern for social involvement. They reflect multiculturalism and value diversity. The focus is on relationships in the community and spirituality. They embrace the arts as a way to communicate.

For the sake of clarity and visioning, here are some differences between these church movements and integral church and beyond.

Three concerns with progressive, emergent, and postmodern church movements

(1) These churches may try to make a few changes without really addressing deeply held traditional theology. Progressive, emergent, and postmodern churches often seem to avoid defining their thinking. It actually appears at this point to be intentional, perhaps because they want to be accessible to Evangelicals. Perhaps another factor is that previous theological definitions have been so confining, excluding, and rigid. They want their theology to include a diversity of beliefs and to focus on experience and relationships. Therefore, they avoid any definition that would directly challenge the traditional stage of Christian beliefs in general. The primary belief seems to be, "If you are willing to relate, talk, and not be angry about others' beliefs, then come on in." The Unitarian Universalist church is one end product of such an endeavor with its rich inclusivity and breadth. However, it no longer identifies itself as a Christian church. Eventually, any church, including integral and beyond, must define what it believes if it is to survive as a church that seeks to be Christian and contribute its path of love to the world mix.

One goal is to have a world, a neighborhood, a workplace that is truly open to all and does not promote one religion or non-religion over another. This kind of world is a goal of the integral church also. However, the gift of each tradition at the integral level, including Christianity, is how that tradition promotes such a world. Giving up the uniqueness of your given tradition then robs it of its power to move the world to a totally loving community. I desire such a world *because* of following Jesus, not in spite of it.

(2) These movements, at present, seem to discount the value of experiencing God in transcendent states of consciousness. While not rejected as in the traditional church, the Spirit zone is often not intentionally taught and sought.

(3) These groups usually embrace an expanded 3rd-person Infinite Face of God in study and reflection. They are usually at home with the 2nd-person Intimate Face of God in worship and prayer. However, they continue to neglect the 1st-person Inner Face of God which comes from the experience of our own inner divinity. The idea of directly experiencing our own divinity is usually out of their comfort zone.

The New Thought Movement

New Thought emerged in the late nineteenth century and is a loosely allied group of organizations, authors, philosophies, and individuals who share a set of metaphysical beliefs concerning healing, life force, creative visualization, and personal power. They promote the idea that God is all powerful and ever-present, only Spirit is real, true human selfhood is divine, divine thought is a force for good, most sickness originates in the mind, and "right thinking" has a healing effect.

Unity churches are the largest New Thought group and generally maintain their Christian identity. Religious Science, also referred to as United Centers for Spiritual Living, focuses on the powers of the mind rather than any distinct Christian identity. Interestingly, its founder, Ernest Holmes, based his *Science of the Mind* primarily on Jesus' teachings.

The difference between integral and beyond church and New Thought is that integral church is firmly anchored in the life, teachings, and presence of Jesus.

New Thought has enriched spiritual practice and thinking in many ways. I value their contributions within my more distinctly Christian tradition.

Spiritual But Not Religious

The Spiritual But Not Religious (SBNR) movement is a primary spiritual path for many at the postmodern mode of consciousness. About one in five Americans consider themselves spiritual but not religious.[32] This movement was formerly called New Age, but most no longer want to be called that. Typical beliefs may include both pantheism and panentheism, reincarnation, karma, existence of energy fields that can be seen by some and contain information about the world, personal transformation, and ecological values. There is a fairly consistent view that all paths lead to God by whatever name one calls that Mystery. In general, SBNR people feel free to shop around for any belief or practice that fits for them.

The SBNR movement has great strengths

Most of those involved with the Spiritual But Not Religious movement are, or have been, Christians. They wanted more than their traditional church was giving them, so they began exploring New Age-type spirituality. *This movement represents a genuine attempt at finding a new path that builds on some aspects of traditional religion and attempts to transcend its limitations.*

The SBNR have reminded thirsty Christians of the refreshing water of the Spirit zone. I doubt that the New Age movement would have ever existed if churches had taken altered states and Spirit zone experiences seriously. Christians who have disparaged and made fun of New Age beliefs need to check out their Bibles again. Yes, there are warnings in the Old Testament about contacting the dead. However, Jesus himself is the foremost model of doing that very thing with Moses and Elijah in the Transfiguration event.

Christians decry trances and channeling. Yet the book of Acts specifically refers to both Peter and Paul as falling into trances. Any close examination of prophecy will show it is what New Agers call channeling—although, hopefully at the highest level. Christians may, and should, question the source of the communication, as whether it is from high-level spiritual beings or lesser beings or even from the influence of spiritual beings who have lost their way. But the phenomenon is the same.

The churches' rejection of the detailed and frequent spiritual experiences of the New Testament hardly seems much different from their rejection of Spiritual But Not Religious-type spiritual experiences. We need less rejection of what really exists in the New Testament that is similar to New Age/SBNR phenomena and more discernment about the quality and source of what is being channeled or prophesied.

SBNR has great weaknesses

Beliefs here can be all over the developmental map with a blend of magic, narcissism, fairy tales, self-help, traditional wisdom, psychic phenomena, and genuine spiritual exploration. It is a postmodern attempt to get in touch with authentic spiritual energy and phenomena. It is also postmodern in its embracing any experience, whether prerational or postrational without discernment.

Its foundational belief is "You create your own reality." This is held with fundamentalist fervor. The truth of this belief is that we do have an amazing ability to change our lives and "attract" those things we want. Changing your thinking can help you change your response to life. That is a great truth which can help you stop being a victim. It is also a partial truth.

Thoughts influence reality but do not create it. The part that is not true is not understanding that our lives are also affected by the reality of the physical world and other people.[33] Anytime we take only one of the Big Three as all of reality, we have created a partial truth. "I create my own reality" is a powerful 1st-person subjective truth. However, when someone says, "Consciousness creates reality," the question is, "Whose consciousness? Yours or the other 7 billion people alive right now?" Creating our own reality must be balanced with the 2nd-person truth that other people are also creating their own realities which affect our lives dramatically. You probably did not "attract" the drunk driver who totaled your car.

We must also embrace the 3rd-person truth that part of our reality is created by the nature of the material world around us.

Tornadoes and giant tidal waves are not created by our thinking but by the natural world.

"I create my own reality" is subjective truth, and without the balance of 2nd-person and 3rd-person truths it looks a lot like the magical thinking of the tribal/magic stage. To the integral mind, much New Age mysticism appears to be nonsense. Yet, the openness to mystical realities is welcomed by the integralist.

SBNR ideology may contain some forms of the egocentricity of the warrior stage. What is termed "prosperity" thinking appears to be merely spirituality in service of the ego.

SBNR beliefs about the divinity of all get confused with inflating the ego when the ego self and the True Self are not differentiated. Our ego loves to hear that we are God. Our True Self already knows that and aims to keep the ego from clouding it over.

Integral church transcends the postmodern practice of what Trungpa Rinpoche calls "idiot compassion."[34] Idiot compassion believes that no viewpoint is better than any other viewpoint. All viewpoints are wonderful. Therefore, it ends up affirming what is pathological and harmful. There is no discernment about viewpoints because that looks like the old judgmentalism and absolutes of the traditional mythic level. Integral church recognizes that genuine love and compassion require wisdom to discern whether one is helping or harming others.

Beyond Integral

The phrase "integral and beyond" is often used in this book. This is because there are levels beyond integral that are still being explored, and any fuller description of them is not the purpose of this book. Therefore, I have just called them "beyond." They are sometimes called self-transcendence, illumined mind, meta-mind, transpersonal, and unity consciousness. Jim Marion calls them by their state names, psychic, subtle, causal, and nondual stages, considering them stage-states.

When the connecting (subtle) stage first becomes a permanently accessible state, there is a turning within. One becomes inward directed. The self is understood as the inner witness, the observer.

As the connecting state progresses, there is a basic completion of the healing of inner wounds. There is little ego left, which leads to a new level of inner freedom. There are deeper understandings of spiritual truth and constant realization of them.

I long to be that kind of Christian in a church that is longing for that, too.

PART IV
SHADOW

Our shadow is composed of the weaknesses, strengths, shortcomings, and instincts that we have found unacceptable and have disowned and buried deeply inside ourselves. We then tend to project this out onto others as their parts, not ours. Our deficiency becomes another person's weakness, certainly not ours. We are sure we are seeing things as they really are. However, our shadow causes confusion in perceiving reality because we do not distinguish what belongs to us from what belongs to others.

Shadow work is representative of all emotional and inner healing and the multitude of approaches that bring greater emotional wholeness.

CHAPTER 16

"The Shadow Knows"
Inner healing

I am a wounded healer. All of us who attempt to lead and minister are, in Henri Nouwen's liberating phrase, "wounded healers." This wounding is deep inside of us and does not easily lend itself to healing.

I grew up an only child in a dysfunctional home. That means all the neurosis was dumped on me. My mother was stuck in an unhappy marriage and periodically had hebephrenic schizoid episodes. Under stress she would move into an unreal state of laughter, out of touch with reality. I would come home to find her hiding on the floor in a closet. She would sometimes literally bang her head against a wall. My father escaped into his photography hobby, hiding out in his darkroom in the basement, developing pictures. Mom stressed out over dad's many affairs, and sometimes he would leave home when the arguments about them got to be too much. As a seven-year-old, I would call my aunt and uncle when mom was in the closet or dad left home. They would call the doctor for mom and go with me to get dad back.

The church saved my life in all of this. My Sunday School leaders were sane and wonderful, at least while they were at church. I was at church several times each week as a teenager. In St. Louis I had to take two streetcars and a bus to get to church by myself. The one or two hours waiting for streetcars and buses at age 12 at 10:00 P.M. at night was safe back in the 1940s. It was the price I didn't mind paying in order to be around some kind of happiness and peace. I loved church and it was there I first learned about God loving me.

I came to my current church in 1963, while finishing seminary. In a few years the church attendance doubled, then tripled, and the budget grew more than that. I say this not to brag but to make the point that in the midst of all of that outward success I was still a much-wounded healer. I was anxious, panic-ridden, incredibly lonely, and so out of touch with my feelings that I could not even identify them. If you would have asked me about the last time I was sad or angry, I would have replied, "I don't get sad or angry." Ha! Sure!

I remember sitting in the back of our sanctuary during a packed Sunday evening service feeling like I didn't know who I was or what I was doing there. I was a lonely stranger to myself.

When I left my home in St. Louis for seminary in Kansas City, my panic attacks increased and I was often unable to sit through classes. My doctor put me on something for anxiety and, at age 22, I started seeing a counselor. I am 73 now and I still go to therapy. I'm a real tough case! I had always been rather independent and shut down, so only the pain of panic moved me to seek help in psychotherapy those many years ago. The other side of that is I am smart enough to get all the help I can.

I share all of this to point out that I never recommend to others something I have not done myself. This is why I encourage everyone to get some kind of inner healing in whatever form fits for them. Shadow work has been a staple of my own journey for years. The art has developed over the years and is now in its most accessible form.

The Shadow in radio-land

After school, for all eight years of grade school in the 1940s, I would rush home to listen to *The Shadow* on the radio. Lamont Cranston was the Shadow who had "the power to cloud men's minds" and become completely invisible. From the opening line, "Who knows what evil lurks in the hearts of men? The Shadow knows!," to the always-victorious ending, I was entranced. Little did I know that this was an amazingly accurate description of what Carl Jung had been talking about and Fritz Perls was soon to enshrine in his two-chair

Gestalt technique. *The shadow does have the power to cloud our minds and is invisible to the ordinary mind.* It takes work, sometimes called shadow work, to make it visible, and make friends with it so that it loses its power over us.

Jesus and the Shadow

Jesus asked, "Why do you see the speck in your neighbor's eye but do not notice the log in your own eye? . . . First take the log out of your own eye, and then you will see clearly to take the speck out of your neighbor's eye."[1]

Most of us think that this admonition was simply about not being critical of other people. Keep your eyes on your own faults, not on others. But now I see it is much more profound. Why did Jesus connect the speck we see in another's eye with the log in our own eye? Because they *are* connected! When something bothers you about another person or situation, it is most often about you, not them!

Think of the person who annoys you the most. Think about how frustrating they are. This is a good description of your own shadow. Psychologists call it projection. We take parts of ourselves that we cannot own and project them out onto other people or situations. We take the qualities that we find unacceptable in ourselves and put them out onto others. It is not *if* we project, it is *when* we project, because we all do it. Our projections give us a blurred view of reality. We are unable to tell what is real about others and what are the disowned parts of ourselves that we project onto them. The more defensive we are about how accurately we see a situation, the more likely it is all about our log and not their speck.

Jesus connected our criticizing others with looking at ourselves because understanding that is one of the most powerful ways to grow emotionally and spiritually. Look around and see who and what you feel critical of. What produces strong feelings in you? That's the clue that you are dealing with your shadow, your projections, not reality. The term "projection" had not yet been invented, but Jesus saw it working all the time.

Angrily observing a speck in another's eye is always a grand opportunity to rid that inside ourselves and discover long-repressed parts within us. We can literally learn to make friends with those parts of us, instead of seeing them as enemies. Jesus told us to love our enemies and one way to begin is with what seems like our closest enemy—the shadows hiding within us. Shadow work has been around for a long time, sometimes referred to as "projection," "transference," or "gestalt two-chair work." In two-chair work with the guidance of a therapist, I would sit in one chair and in my imagination put the disturbing person or situation in the other chair and face them. Next I would *talk* to them, saying whatever I was thinking and feeling. Then I would literally trade places, go sit in the other chair, and *be* the other person or situation. Playing the role of that person, I would share back to my self—the self which I would imagine still sitting in the first chair. I would sometimes go back or forth several times between the chairs, one time being myself and the next time being the other person or situation.

The insight and revelation that would come to me would be amazing. I would begin to hear and see a more realistic picture and own my projection. My strong feelings would begin to subside and dissolve.

A simple, transforming practice

Two-chair work has now been efficiently compressed into an amazingly simple practice that does not necessarily require seeing a therapist. It is a powerful way of doing shadow work based on the Big Three of 1st-, 2nd-, and 3rd-person. In the book *Integral Life Practices* it is called the 3-2-1 technique, or face it, talk to it, and be it. Here it is.

You begin by *facing* the person or situation in your mind. This is seeing it in 3rd-person awareness in your imagination. Next, in 2nd-person mode, *talk* to it, him, her, or them, saying what you are feeling and don't like. Finally, *be* it, becoming the other person or situation in 1st-person mode. You take the place of that person or situation in your mind. You then express how you feel and what you think *as* that person or situation. Shorthand for this three step process is Face, Talk, and Be.

Let's say that you believe your boss is angry with you and so you feel fearful. You decide to try this technique out. In your imagination, you *face* your boss. Then you *talk* to him, saying something like, "You are always mad at me. I don't understand why you have it in for me. You are such an angry person. I don't like you."

Then you *become* the boss. As the boss, you might find yourself saying, "You know, I am hard to get along with sometimes. People tell me that. But I am not angry with you. I think you are a good worker."

You then become yourself again and perhaps say, "You act just like my father. Come to think of it, you do remind me of him. He was always on my case. Hmm. So you really aren't mad at me? Maybe I am mad at you. Or, more accurately, I am still mad at Dad." You then begin to do some work on your anger with your father, since that is where the real problem is. Your anger at Dad is taken off of your boss where you had been projecting it. (At this point you also can do a Face-Talk-Be with Dad and find out more of what was going on there.)

You have gotten rid of the speck you were seeing in your boss's eye into yourself and have seen the log in your eye. Now you can take steps to own it, deal with it, and let go of it. As long as it looked like something big in your boss's eye, you had no way to actually deal with the real problem which was ancient anger with your Dad. So you just kept thinking and feeling that your boss was mad at you. Now you can separate your boss from your dad and you can handle them as two different situations. You end up a lot happier this way.

You may ask, "But what if your boss really is mad at you?" First of all, you may not know that until you try the exercise. The smart, intuitive, but hidden part of you on the inside probably knows all about the boss. Only then can you uncover your own feelings about the situation you may be disowning and projecting out on your boss. After you have made friends with your own rejected feelings, you can now deal with what is real about the situation, not about your projections. Let's say that you discover your boss really is angry with you. Only this time you are not as afraid because your feelings are not contaminated with old feelings from the past. The anger from the past comes from when you were a vulnerable kid and these strong feelings were difficult to handle. However, your current feelings come from the here and now situation. You can handle those.

Jesus said that we shouldn't get stuck worrying about the past or future, just live in the present, one day at a time. That we can always handle.[2] If you are only dealing with here and now feelings, you will find you don't clinch up in frustration like you did as a vulnerable youngster with your parents or other significant people in your life. You will be much more likely to be able to address the true situation when you have eliminated any confusion with your own shadow.

What about when you find yourself angry about the real oppression and unfair treatment of someone? The first thing is to do a "face, talk, and be" process to take care of your own projections. Then you will be free to see the real injustice, not just your shadow reaction to it. You will actually now be in the best situation to see what is actually going on and how to be redemptive. That is exactly what Jesus was talking about when he said, "First take the log out of your own eye, and then *you will see clearly to take the speck out of your neighbor's eye.*" We can often be very helpful with real infections in another's eye as long as we take care of our own log stuff first.

I have now learned to do the whole thing in my mind in just a minute and on the spot in any situation that I have negative feelings about. I do it at night before I go to bed as I reflect on the day. When I wake up from an upsetting dream, I do the Face-Talk-Be right away before I go back to sleep. It only takes a minute or so.

How Jesus handled his own shadow

Jesus was motivated by his anger at the oppressive treatment of his people. He spent enough time alone in prayer and reflection that he could keep his own stuff separate from his Spirit-given outrage at the oppression of the vulnerable. He tended to any logs in himself so he could freely bring insight and action into the situation.

An extraordinary example of this is his temptation experience in the wilderness. He was dealing with his own "log" projected out onto a Satan personification. "Satan" was tempting him to misuse his power. But it was his own inner temptation that he was projecting out onto the figure named "Satan." The log was his own ego which needed to be identified, wrestled with, and put into place before he could give himself in authentic selflessness. When he settled his inner ego projections, he could then see the real evil and speak up and act against the institutionalized religious, political, and social oppression of his day in a selfless, egoless way. He courageously spoke up and stood up for the vulnerable from his own place of wholeness.

Healing happens inside of us when we begin to own the feelings which we have placed on another person or situation. Doing your own shadow work can move you through both stages and states in an accelerated way because it removes emotional blocks to your own evolution.

My Shadow

While writing this chapter I wrote down one of my many on-going shadow work sessions. In a dream one night, I found myself paralyzed, unable to move, but trying to. I was frightened and full of anxiety. When I finally woke up, I was afraid to go back to sleep lest I get back into that nightmarish dream. So, lying in bed, in my mind I faced the situation of being paralyzed. I talked to it. "I am scared and panicky. Why can't I move? What is happening? Why are you doing this to me?" Then I became the "paralysis" which was holding me down. "I am holding you down. I am going to keep you from doing all the things that you want to do. I am going to make you afraid and you won't even be able to get out of bed. Ha, ha!"

Then I moved back to being myself and didn't know what to say or do next. So I took another stab at being the "paralysis." This time I realized how powerful I felt as the "paralysis." Wow, I had lots of power to hold myself—Paul—down. I liked being powerful. What if this power was a part of me I was projecting out? What would happen if I owned how powerful I am? At that point I decided to take the disowned power back into myself. I said, "I am powerful." Oh, that felt so good. I felt powerful! I went back to sleep with no fear.

Resistance

Attempts to confront our shadow will be met with great resistance by our ego. Our ego defines who we are, usually as a composite of various traits we find acceptable to have. Our other traits which we do not find acceptable are pushed down into us by our ego and become our shadow. We see these traits of our shadow in other people as the source of what's wrong in the world. When we try to make contact with our shadow, our ego quickly tells us that is bad and to be avoided at all costs.

Wilber says, in his pointed way, "You might be happy not to work on neurotic crap, but everybody around you can see that you are a neurotic jerk, and, therefore, when you announce you are really in One Taste [a deeply spiritual state of consciousness], all they will remember is to avoid that state at all costs."[3]

On the positive side

This whole shadow process also works on positive feelings. Our shadow represents all of the qualities that we find unacceptable and have repressed in ourselves. These qualities may be negative, such as lust, greed, dishonesty, avarice, or hatred. But they may also be positive ones such as speaking ability, leadership, a strong personality, philanthropy, spirituality, or the good feelings we desire but which we believe we can never have.

If we are overly enamored of someone, we are probably projecting our own positive feelings on that person. When we don't own our positive qualities and power we suffer from bad self image which is ultimately unrealistic.

One night, Friday, November 2, 2007, according to my journal, I had a dream about getting acquainted with some new folks I didn't know. They invited me to a special meeting around a table. I felt very intimidated when they showed up in immense black robes looking very powerful and Nazi-like. I felt afraid of these powerful figures. Then I woke up, still feeling afraid. The strong feelings were the signal to do shadow work. I thought back to the scene in the dream and *faced* the black robed "bad" guys. I *talked* to them. I said, "You look evil. You look really mean, like Nazis. I am terrified of you. What's going on here?"

Then I *became* them. I found myself saying, "Oh, we are not evil. We are just strong and powerful. You think everyone who is powerful is evil. We are powerful but not evil."

As I heard myself say that, the fear dissolved. But even more, I decided to take these powerful figures back into myself. They were part of me. No wonder I felt intimidated. I was disowning my very own power and giving it away to them!

An often-repeated scenario in my life then suddenly opened out in a new way. I have often considered myself a little nobody. I don't have any power. I play weak because I don't want to be intimidating. I don't want to be seen as powerful. I don't like being a leader because leaders become convenient screens for somebody else's home movies. They get "projected" on me quite often. Leaders get blamed for others people's logs all the time. I don't want to be powerful because I don't like being misunderstood. I will just disown my power and be intimidated. Marianne Williamson's words came to me. "Your playing small doesn't serve the world."[4] I felt a sudden shift. An "aha" moment. I began to feel powerful in a good way. I have always wanted to use my influence for good, not evil. And that's the point. If I don't own my power, I cannot use it for God. Sometimes perceptive people look at me and sense that my protestations of not being powerful don't fit. In the dream where I was intimidated by others, I was simply disowning my power.

When I first came across Ken Wilber's writings and talks ten years ago, I found myself overwhelmed and enamored with his vision and insight. That motivated me to wade through all of his books, including the totally dense parts which still elude me. My own spiritual growth leaped forward because of his wisdom which I quickly embraced. I knew it was right and true. In addition, the spiritual practices which I had been doing for many years now intensified because he encouraged them. Because of his attention to state experiences, I saw that my own spiritual experiences were more valid and valuable than I had thought.

However, at one point I realized I seemed *too* captivated, infatuated, smitten, charmed, or "something" by his teaching and practice. So I did a Face-Talk-Be and sure enough, I was projecting some of my own power onto him. I found, when I "became" him in the "be," 1st-person part, of the process that "he" (that is my own inner knowing) told me I was projecting on him. He (my own intuitive, really smart self) told me that I was more powerful than I thought and I should get over putting him on a pedestal. After I did that, I immediately felt the difference. I was still incredibly grateful for his help in my own spiritual growth, but I no longer "worshipped" him. I could feel and sense the difference. I could take him or leave him now, depending on what I found valuable. I could even see where he missed it at times. Egad, I was really owning my own understanding and wisdom!

Taking back our spiritual projections

At tribal consciousness we project our power out onto nature. It is the spirits who are everywhere in trees, the mountains, rivers, and animals that have power over our lives. When we take back our power, then nature is full of both beauty and terror, but it is not a "spirit" that is out to get us.

At the warrior consciousness we project our anger out onto the God up there in heaven. God is angry and punishes us. As Ann Lamott says, "You can safely assume that you've created God in your own image when it turns out that God hates all the same people you do."[5] When we take back our anger and get it off God, we can see that Jesus lived and taught about a God that is not fear-based fantasy but love-based reality.

At the traditional level we project our own capricious moods of sometimes anger, sometimes love, sometimes pleasure, sometimes displeasure onto God. When we take back our various unacceptable moods, we find that God is not our up and down moodiness but rather the pulsing, constant, creative drive to greater love in the universe.

Our most devastating projection

We especially project what is most unacceptable to us out onto authority figures. Knowing this and doing constant shadow work can help us recover these disowned parts of us. But this is more than just emotional healing. We can learn from shadow work about welcoming back our disowned spiritual identity.

From the integral level it seems apparent that in previous levels of faith and church we have projected our own divinity onto Jesus. It is easy to do because he was so obviously an incarnation of the Big Mind Big Heart of God. In disowning the image of God in and as us, we do what we always do with disowned parts of ourselves— we see those parts in someone else, namely Jesus, for Christians. In doing our own spiritual shadow work we can take back the projection of our divinity onto Jesus and become aware that we, too, are divine. *This does not make Jesus any less divine.* Jesus has all the divinity that he needs. He not only doesn't need ours, he came to help us recognize our own. Jesus insisted that we are gods, too. The Spirit is insisting now that we take back the divinity that belongs to us instead of projecting it all on Jesus. We can honor and adore him for his advanced consciousness of his own divinity while we become aware of our own Sacred Self.

I had a powerful, life-changing, vision experience of this one day as I sat down for my prayer/meditation time. I saw Jesus in front of me. I saw him in my mind, not with my physical eyes—but it was very real. Suddenly, he looked at me, held his hands together in prayer-like fashion in front of his heart, bowed his head, and said, "Namaste." I knew what "namaste" meant —"I recognize and honor the divine in you." I quickly protested. "No, no. You're the Lord, not me." He quietly gazed into my eyes. I quickly realized that he was giving me a visual and felt experience of his honoring of my divinity as I honored his. As I reflected on this, I decided to do a Face-Talk-Be with Jesus. I *faced* him in my mind. I *talked* to him and asked, "Jesus, am I projecting my own divinity onto you? Then I *became* him. He (my own inner Divine Self of infinite wisdom) easily and quickly answered, "Sure, but you're getting over it. Namaste." And the vision ended. Wow!

The great contribution of Western psychological practice to spiritual and emotional development is the recognition of shadow and how to deal with it. Prayer cannot take care of the shadow. Worship cannot. Reading and study cannot. Meditation cannot. Serving others cannot. Only some form of shadow work can reveal the logs in our eyes. It is an incredible, accessible, and life-changing practice for emotional and spiritual healing. Start doing it! Don't wait. Do it right now!

PART V
STEPS

Steps are those practices we undertake that move us incrementally toward our goals. Every journey begins with the first step, and then many, many more. Each step gets us closer to where we want to be. There may be some leaps and bounds in our journey, but most of it is in the multitude of tiny steps we take again and again to get us to where we are going.

CHAPTER 17

Taking Care of Your Self
Becoming a practicing Christian

My friend and worship pastor at Broadway Church, David Hunker, shared with me two recent elevated state experiences that impacted his life in a wonderful way. He often has had these transforming experiences, and you will see why when you know some things about his lifestyle. Here it is in his words.

> This past week, I had two extraordinary encounters with Jesus. At the end of her Sunday morning teaching, Marcia [one of the two co-pastors at Broadway Church] asked each of us in the congregation to listen for the answer to this question: "How much does God love you?" After a brief time of quiet, she asked for people's responses. From their answers, I knew that most folks had *heard* something. At that point, I realized that I hadn't heard anything; rather, I had *seen* something.
>
> What I saw was an image of Jesus, standing in front of me and looking down at me. We were close enough that he was grasping my shoulders, and then cupping my face with his hands. The scene was brief, but powerful. I sensed very strongly that Jesus was completely engaged with me and in our interaction; nothing else mattered to him at that moment but me. He was completely involved with me!

I continued to think about the experience after the picture had faded. While the image was important, it was the accompanying feeling that struck me deeply. I felt a very intense sense of connection; again, the word that keeps coming to mind is "engaged." At that particular moment, Jesus was engaged with me to the exclusion of all else. I was important to him and he wanted me to know that at the core of my being.

On Tuesday, I shared my encounter with Marcia and Paul. As I described it to them, I once again felt the intensity of that sense of engagement, of Jesus' interest in me. It wasn't that I was interested in him; it was that he was interested in me. It wasn't a feeling of love or caring; it was how very sincerely Jesus wanted to *be* with me.

Paul was excited by my "vision" and characterized it as a mystical experience. Internally, I discounted Paul's enthusiasm; he had taken a brief mental image and raised it to unwarranted heights. At the same time, the experience seemed valid and important. For most of my life, I've not been able to connect with Jesus on an emotional level. I've felt a sense of connection with the Spirit, and through the Spirit to God. But, I didn't have a deeply felt, emotional bond with Jesus. The idea of a personal relationship with Jesus didn't resonate.

On Wednesday, I shared this experience with Patricia, my counselor and mentor. As I recounted my story, I began to weep. Once again, the sense that Jesus had been totally focused on me seemed very powerful. I was keenly aware of how difficult it is for me to believe that I'm worthy of such attention.

Patricia then asked me to close my physical eyes and to open my inner, spiritual eyes. She invited me to envision an intense white ball of light, much like the sun, in the near distance. As I did so, she asked me what or who came out of that light. Once again, I began weeping. Jesus came running out of the light toward me, grabbing me under my arms and swinging me around. It was as if we were playing. Jesus gazed at me with great fervor and said, "I've been waiting for this moment for so long."

I continued to cry and to feel the presence of Jesus' spirit in the room. As the image faded, I realized that Patricia was weeping also. She, too, was strongly aware of Jesus being there.

In retrospect, I think Paul was correct—I did have a mystical experience that extended over several days. In addition to the vivid images, I was also left with a confidence that Jesus would now be accessible to me. My spiritual life would be enriched by the addition of Jesus as older brother and guide to my more familiar experiences with the Spirit.

Great experiences, right? It would be wonderful if we could all have these things just happen to us. Right? Some people just have all the luck when it comes to cool spiritual experiences. Right? Wrong! Here's why:

Notice all the practices, *12 of them*, that David used to help him drink in more of the intoxicating wine of the Spirit. (1) He regularly practices going to church. (2) He had previously worked to find a church that nourishes him and encourages transcendent experiences. (3) He actually listened to the sermon! (4) He participated in the suggested transformative exercise. (5) He continued to reflect on his experience. (6) He has developed a network of friends he shares with on a regular basis. (7) He shared this experience with them. (8) He thought about their feedback. (9) He sees a counselor/mentor regularly. (10) He shared his experience with her. (11) He practiced sharing his feelings on the spot by crying. (12) He did the visualization that she suggested. And *Voila*! He ended up with even more of the new wine of transcendent state experience!

Change is not easy

A recent medical study showed that even when doctors told their seriously at-risk heart patients they would literally die if they did not make changes such as improving their diet, exercising more, and quitting smoking, only one in seven patients actually made any change! The other six probably wanted to live but they just could not do what it took to change.[1]

New wineskins

"You must put new wine in new wineskins," said Jesus. Why? Because new wine will split apart old brittle wineskins and leak out. The wine of the Spirit does not come to us from the past in dull repetition. The Spirit's nectar comes to us from the future in creative allure, enticing us into ever-new dimensions. Only flexible and elastic wineskins can contain and direct the soul-stirring experiences of higher spiritual consciousness. Without good wineskins the new wine just spills out and evaporates. "Do not get drunk with wine but be filled with the Spirit," says Paul as he connects the heady effects of wine and Spirit. These wineskins include the *practices* which one uses to consciously hold the intoxicating Spirit in our lives.

Body, Mind, Heart, and Spirit

More and more people are becoming familiar with broader levels of understanding such as integral philosophy. But not as many are actually moving into the integral and beyond levels of experience. This is because they confuse reading about an integral worldview with living it. Reading a book on weight training will not give you strong muscles, unless, of course, the book weighs a hundred pounds and you pick it up to read 30 times a day. Living it requires practice—body and mind practices, soul-healing practices, and interior practices. These are the four areas of the Jewish ideal in this incredibly integral statement that Jesus quoted when asked what was most important in life: "You shall love the Lord your God with all your heart, and with all your soul, and with all your mind, and with all your strength." Practice involves loving God with your body ("all your strength"), mind ("all your understanding"), emotions ("all your heart"), and spirit ("all your soul").[2]

With a few practices, we can rapidly accelerate our spiritual growth. Practice does not make perfect, but it does make one perceptive, peaceful, passionate, and potent.

We do not have to become masters of any step. Just do a few exercise steps on a regular basis. Doing more than one kind of practice dramatically increases our development. Pick a physical one, a mental one, an inner healing one, and a spiritual one, and any others that might fit for you. This is integrating body, mind, heart, and spirit.

Temple Maintenance: Taking care of your physical self

Our bodies are temples, a physical home for the Divine Self. Temple maintenance faces two challenges in today's world that premodern society did not have—cars and fast food. Jesus walked everywhere he went and ate the original Mediterranean diet! Of course, the marvels of medical science keep us living longer, but exercise and eating well are where it all begins. I will not dwell on this except to encourage it as a spiritual practice to take up in whatever way works best for you. As I have gotten older, I have changed from racquetball to power-walking two miles most days. I take loads of supplements recommended by a doctor who keeps me up with the latest in testing and preventive medicine. I eat lots of organic vegetables and watch my weight. The better I feel, the better I pray. As Walt Whitman pens in "I Sing the Body Electric," "If any thing is sacred, the human body is sacred."[3]

A mental map: Taking care of your cognitive self

Embracing a comprehensive mental map is central to moving to the integral worldview. The integral approach is, among several things, a cognitive map of human potential created by taking all the stage studies of human cultures and making a composite. The new map includes all the areas that might be left out in any of the other maps. This then becomes a framework for our own awareness, organizing everything that comes to us as it arises. It is a map of the territory of your awareness. It is a fuller map that replaces the less complete maps.

Wilber says:

Without a cohesive and comprehensive mental framework, things fall apart faster than you can sing "Feelings." Over the past three decades, one fact has surfaced time and time again: without a mental framework to actually hold spiritual experiences, those experiences just don't stick.[4]

This is especially true with spiritual experience. Theology is loving God with your mind. Having the best theological map possible gives one a framework for what experiences are available and how to understand them. However, spiritual seekers do not need to be scholars or even like to read. There are other ways to broaden your mental map besides intensive study. It can look like *talking* with others in a regular and intentional way. One can *listen* to good teachers who help us explore the higher levels at church, seminars, and on CDs. It can look like exploring brief articles, websites, and blogs on the internet. Never before in history have we had research and insights from around the world and from so many centuries and traditions so available to us. It's a feast for the mind.

Heart Healing: Taking care of your emotional self

Damaged emotional receptors can keep us from receiving the experience of God's presence and from fully engaging in loving and being loved. In my early twenties I began with talk therapy, moved to intensive gestalt therapy, then to marriage counseling, and now to energy healing from an advanced spiritual practitioner. But it is still therapy, and it is still healing me. Somewhere along the way, I received enough emotional healing to begin experiencing God in beautiful, life-giving ways. However you do your shadow work, DO IT! You deserve to be emotionally healed and whole.

Interior practice: Taking care of your inner Self

Who am I? What am I? Why am I here? Those are the most profound questions that life is all about answering. For most of my life I have believed that I was a human being on a spiritual journey. I not only believed that, I acted upon it, deeply pursuing spiritual matters. That served me well for a period of time and I am grateful for that stage. Now I believe that I was wrong. I was not only wrong, but I was 180 degrees wrong. When I came to that conclusion, I changed my mind—or, in biblical terms, I repented. Now I believe that *I am a spiritual being on a human journey.*[5] Those words have become a familiar and often overused slogan for many in the "spiritual but not religious" movements. However, for many churchgoers like me, it was a new discovery. *It was an enormous and amazing awakening for me when I saw that it was the model and message of Jesus!* Before, I thought that Jesus was the only person who was actually a spiritual being on a human journey. I believed that Jesus had always existed ("before Abraham was, I am"[6]). I believed he would never die because he was a truly spiritual being who came from heaven to become human for a while. Since Jesus knew where he had come from and where he was going, he was able to express what it looks like to be a spiritual being in incredible ways in the midst of his human journey.[7]

I believed that I was quite different from Jesus because I was a sinful human being who was born, would die, and might possibly go to heaven, whatever that was. I was a human being working like crazy to become a spiritual being. Now I have stopped trying to become a spiritual being. I stopped trying because I *realized I am already a spiritual being*—and always have been! I realized I am already like Jesus in terms of my true identity and inner self. Before Abraham was (in history), I am, also.

The vast difference between Jesus and me is that he *knew* he was a spiritual being and manifested that knowing in all of his life. I have not known this for most of my life. Even now that I know this, I still keep forgetting it. What helps me to remember most is my prayer life. The goal of prayer is to know your Self as a divine spiritual being. The Spirit and our deepest Self are ultimately one and the same.

Here is a little ritual that helps me connect with my body, thoughts, and feelings as a spiritual being:

I have a body, but I am not my body. I am grateful for my body. It is a gift from God. I am not my body. I am the spiritual being who is aware of my body.

I have thoughts, but I am not my thoughts. I am grateful for my thinking. It is a gift from God. I am not my thoughts. I am the spiritual being who observes my thoughts.

I have feelings, but I am not my feelings. I am grateful for my feelings. They are a gift from God. I am not my feelings. I am the spiritual being who is conscious of my feelings.

What I truly am, have always been, and will always be is a *spiritual being*. I don't just have a spirit—I am Spirit!

The "I" of our True Self is Spirit. Taking care of our spirit or our Authentic Self, our "I" of the Real Self, is an inner practice. Jesus said the Kingdom of God was within us and he meant it. Therefore, to find my True Self I must go inside. Prayer is an inside job!

I will devote the major portion of this chapter to the interior practice of prayer, the most neglected and misunderstood dimension of spirituality. Nearly six in ten adult Americans pray every day. One in four pray at least once a week. Four in ten adults meditate at least once a week.[8] That's a fair degree of praying and meditating. The question is, "What is this praying and meditating all about?" What level of spiritually does it reflect and what is it reaching for? Is it, as my praying was for years, an exercise in anxiety? Is it a rote ritual? Is it magical? Or is it contemplation, communion, and union with Spirit?

If you don't go within, you go without!

Spiritual practice which leads to awakening is fundamentally the same as preparation and practice for death. Death is the dissolution of the physical so the spiritual can shine forth in its eternal journey. Once our fear of death is eliminated, then our way of being in the world is transformed.[9]

Spiritual practice for Christians centers on going within in prayer. Deeper reflection and prayer is the royal path to move from any one stage to the next. The sublime poet Hafiz fashions it in our terms of moving from the warrior stage to the traditional stage.

You could become a great horseman
And help to free yourself and this world
Though only if you and prayer become sweet
Lovers.
It is a naïve man who thinks we are not
Engaged in a fierce battle,
For I see and hear brave foot soldiers
All around me going mad,
Falling on the ground in excruciating pain.

You could become a victorious horseman
And carry your heart through this world
Like a life-giving sun
Though only if you and God become sweet
Lovers![10]

"Build thee a more stately mansion, O my soul" happens when God and I become sweet lovers. What do lovers do? They spend time together, talking back and forth, sharing their hearts, and becoming one in love-making. That's a great description of prayer. Most Christians think of prayer as just saying something to God. That is good—and quite limiting. I understand prayer as the larger turning of our attention inward to spiritual matters which may or may not involve talking *to* God. For instance, I believe a major element in prayer is *listening* to God talk to us. As we have seen, hearing directly from God was a central feature of the New Testament church and can be today once again. Full-orbed prayer includes gratitude, worship, devotion, inner listening, awareness of other deeply intuitive energies, and connecting to spiritual realities. These realities may, in addition to Jesus, include visions, words from the Spirit, other spiritual guides, and angels. The deepest dimension of prayer is in uniting with God in the love-making of Oneness. These are all accessed from within our deepest Self. *Not to go within* in these ways of prayer *is to go without* our primary resources for life in the flow of the Spirit.

Learning to pray

No one taught me how to pray as a young person, either at church or seminary. Rather, I learned to pray by listening to the sincere but long-winded orations in church services, Sunday School classes, and seminary. I learned from the obligatory "opening" and "closing" prayer which asked God to "lead, guide, and bless us." I suppose at least some of my leaders had deep prayer lives, but they never talked about it or tried to pass it on. Later on I learned to lead in prayer publically by sometimes using the beautiful written prayers from various sources. It took me many years to unlearn that way of praying, or more accurately, to see that those were often appropriate, public, spoken prayers and quite different from actual interior prayer.

The problem with the Lord's Prayer

I was taught that the prayer we should all pray is the Lord's Prayer. To be honest, it never seemed to help my prayer life much. As a young person I did not know why. Now I do.

First of all, it wasn't the Lord's prayer. The gospels never record Jesus praying that way. I suppose he, or his gospel editors, may have offered this beginners' prayer as an example of a prayer that his Jewish listeners could relate to. It was very similar to the Kiddush prayer of Jesus' day. Jesus' own stunningly deep prayer life was revealed to us in his wilderness vision quest of 40 days, in his healing ministry, his nightlong prayer times, and his struggle in Gethsemane. None of these looked like the Lord's Prayer. It would seem incongruous to think that at any of these profound times Jesus would recite the "Lord's prayer."

Secondly, I eventually discovered that no one else in the entire Bible was recorded as praying the Lord's Prayer either. So here was the great prayer that Christians have prayed all over the world in many languages for centuries that no one in the Bible, including Jesus, is recorded as ever praying.

A third problem with the "Lord's" prayer as the model for what prayer looks like is that it is a one-way monologue directed to God. It is not a conversation or a dialogue. There is no listening for a response involved. There is no centering or movement within. While many sincere believers use it and seem to get good out of it, it does not teach us what we need to know about what Jesus recommended and practiced concerning prayer.

The Lord's Prayer itself has more than one version in the gospels. Matthew probably has the most original in terms of forgiving debts. This is a reminder of the plight of the world's poor who are literally in debt. Luke changes it with the church's growing focus on sin by making it about forgiveness of sins.

The Lord's Prayer is filled with wonderful images and magnificent principles of the spiritual life. *But it is a prayer for teaching, not a prayer for praying.* It is more like a creed for reciting than a way to enter deeply into God's mystical presence. It is a problem if we see it as the model for interior prayer.

Here is what Jesus taught and practiced about prayer: "Whenever you pray, go into your room and shut the door and pray to your Father-Mother who is in secret; and your Father-Mother who sees in secret will reward you."[11] I hear that as, "When you pray, go inside to your inner room, keep away all outward distractions, and time there will cause you to blossom in all of your life."

Rather than the Lord's Prayer, I wish someone had taught me in church or seminary how to go inside my inner sanctum through something like centering prayer. Father Thomas Keating says,

> Centering prayer is a method of refining one's intuitive faculties so that one can enter more easily into contemplative prayer. It is not the only path to contemplation, but it is a good one. As a method, it is a kind of extract of monastic spirituality . . . you have to keep up a certain level of silence in the psyche and nervous system if you want to obtain the benefits of contemplative prayer.[12]

Cynthia Bourgeault, in her beautiful book *Centering Prayer*, says:

> Virtually every spiritual tradition that holds a vision of human transformation at its heart also claims that a practice

of intentional silence is a non-negotiable. Period. You just have to do it. Whether it be the meditation of the yogic and Buddhist traditions, the *zikir* of the Sufis, the *devkut* of mystical Judaism, or the contemplative prayer of the Christians, there is a universal affirmation that this form of spiritual practice is essential to spiritual awakening.[13]

We learn to pray authentically in two ways. First, we learn from those who connect deeply with the Spirit by listening to what they write and/or say. Secondly, we learn to pray by praying. We keep seeking God's face in prayer until, in words of the Gospel of Thomas, we are disturbed and amazed.[14]

The two major modes of prayer: connecting prayer and being prayer

As outlined previously, it seems to me there are two major realms of prayer. The first is what I have called *connecting prayer*. This is where we relate to spiritual realties in the world of forms such as thoughts, images, and ideas. We connect to Jesus as the Risen Lord and talk to him. We may relate to spirit guides such as Moses and Elijah who guided Jesus. We may sense the presence of angelic beings. We may have visions and hear messages from the Spirit. These were normal experiences in the New Testament and are normal today, too. They are wonderful.

There is an even deeper level of prayer which I have called *being prayer*. In being prayer we move away from the dualism of relationship and into the unity consciousness that Jesus had. He lived in his Oneness with God. Of course, he also freely moved in connecting prayer. But his deepest experience was of being one with God. He was not only relating to God, he was identifying as God. In being prayer I experience myself as Jesus experienced himself—as an infinite, divine being.

This is the goal of the spiritual life. This is the Kingdom of God. Some call this the causal or nondual level. Jim Marion calls it the Christ consciousness. It is here we know and embrace the "I" of our True Self as divine infinite being. We know that we have come from God and are going to God. We know we are spiritual beings on a human journey. We know that we, like Jesus are divine sons and daughters of God. We are one with All That Is.

The deepest experience of God is not only a relationship but an identification. The connecting level of prayer is crucial to our lives and will be a major element of praying for most of us. However, it also remains a duality. Forms always contain duality because they have boundaries. The being level heads us toward *Oneness*—nonduality.

Getting started in interior prayer

Prayer begins with a focused intention. "God, I want to become aware of you. I want to know you, hear you, see you." You check your old baggage at the door, release the busy thoughts, and leave your worries behind. It takes time, energy, and practice to get to that focused place.

The focused state of praying means we have to become still, inside and out. This is difficult for most of us to do. Much of my life has been spent trying to calm my busy mind. I would begin to sit down and pray and suddenly I would be in another room on the telephone. How did I get there? I had left my quiet place because I thought of someone I wanted to call and, without thinking, I just hopped up and started dialing!

Our egos hate silence. When we are quiet for very long, our ego begins to reveal itself. Ego loves to hide and hates to be exposed. Exposing our ego means it loses its power. The ego hates the absence of forms even more than silence. In being prayer, the ego simply has no place for itself. It dissolves.

This is not to imply that we cannot pray while walking or enjoying the delights of nature, or going about our day. One may have deep transcendent states at times in these situations. However, we also need, on a frequent basis, times of deep stillness.

Breathing

The Greek word for "spirit" is πνεῦμα or "pneuma" in English transliteration. We get our English words like pneumonia and pneumatic from it. It is a critically important word for Christians. The word can be translated as "breath," "wind," or "spirit," depending on the context. In the New Testament it is usually translated as "spirit." This connection between spirit, breath, and wind is of both mystical and practical importance. It is no coincidence that many spiritual practices of the world's religious traditions involve paying attention to the breath. Often, the way to begin praying is to go inside of our ourselves by turning our attention to our breathing. We may even count our breaths as a way of centering down. This gets us in touch not only with our bodies, but with our inside self.

Wandering thoughts

At some point while beginning to pray we become aware of the many busy thoughts in our minds. It is then we begin to gently let go of whatever thoughts come up, letting them pass. We should expect to have wandering thoughts. That is totally normal and absolutely unavoidable unless somebody knocks you out. What we do with the thoughts is the important part. When a drifting thought comes into our minds in prayer we can do one of three things. We can shame or criticize ourselves for wandering. That's not only a waste of time, it is harmful. Another thing we can do is "entertain" the thought: "Oh, what a nice thought. Why don't you come in and stay awhile. Let's sit down and discuss this." You may even serve refreshments! However, entertaining a thought moves us away from our intention.

Rather than "entertaining" our drifting, wandering thoughts, we can do the third thing, which is to gently say goodbye to them and let them pass on by. Even when we find that we have been entertaining a thought for a while, as soon as we realize this, we do not condemn ourselves, but return to letting go. We decide not to attach ourselves to the distracting thoughts and images that come into our minds. This can be done by repeating a sacred word that brings us back to our intention.

As we deepen our focus, these thoughts and images at times may actually become whispers of the Spirit to us. Words, pictures, sensations, and images from the Spirit are a primary way God has of guiding and encouraging us. That brings us to the connecting level of prayer.

Connecting prayer

Now we begin to consciously connect to spiritual realities. That is why I call it "connecting" prayer. This state of consciousness is also called the subtle state, communion with God, and, at its most basic level, it is what we usually think of when we hear the word "prayer." It is talking to God in the most popular understanding. We may often talk to God, or Jesus, or the Spirit, or other spiritual beings whom we invite to be present with us.

For the past year I have primarily addressed God in 2nd-person connecting prayer as "Daddy." I pray this way, using Jesus' own model, because after reading the gospels, I became convinced it was a powerful way for me to pray, also. If Jesus prayed that way, maybe I can, too. Whenever I just say the word "Daddy" in prayer, a blanket of warm heavenly peace comes over me. I feel safe and cared for. I experienced my earthly father as remote, angry, and mostly absent. But I experience my heavenly father much differently. He is always there in tender nurture and felt reality as he wraps his arms around me in affectionate closeness. In that warm embrace I share my heart with him. (Others may experience this in praying to God as "Mommy" or numerous other names.)

But connecting prayer includes more than talking to God. If we will listen, Jesus, Abba, or whoever we address will talk back to us by bringing words, images, feelings, or inner knowing to our minds and hearts. We should take these responses very seriously. This is what the New Testament calls "prophecy" or visions, and what some today call "channeling." Not everything we "channel" or hear is necessarily from God. We know from contemporary ideas and practices of channeling that what we receive can run from the silly and weird, to the dangerous and manipulative, or to the insightful and authentic. That is why we must discern what we hear, feel, or see. As we get used to this we begin to easily sense when something is coming rather directly from the Spirit. If we have questions about it, it is time to share with others to help us discern what we are hearing. This is precisely the advice Paul gives, saying that others should "weigh what is said."[15] In general, if it's from the Spirit, it will feel loving and freeing, not coercive and condemning.

We may also write, draw, or paint what we hear and see while in this state as we listen for words, images, sensations, or an inner knowing from the Spirit.

Eddie Ensley says,

> Visions are natural. They are not miracles—inexplicable interventions of the supernatural into our workaday natural world. They are natural manifestations of the fullness of reality.
>
> Visions are human. They come from our humanity just as much as they come from God.
>
> Visions can transform, heal, and brighten our lives.
>
> Visions are a bridge between God's splendor and our natural, tangible world. They are not "extra" in our spiritual journey. They are essential.[16]

We can also communicate with body language such as kneeling, hands uplifted or held together, dancing, turning around and around in Sufi style, bowing, or lying prostrate on the floor.

A wonderful way to express ourselves to God is with our personal language of prayer and praise. This moves us out of our minds and into our hearts and spirits while still using transrational verbal expression. We can also "sing with our spirits" by toning, chanting, or singing in our prayer language.[17]

Being prayer

"Being" type prayer is also called meditation, centering prayer, and union or identification with God. Here we move beyond all thoughts and feelings and come into a state of simple presence. We enter into "nothing," which is "no thing." Where there are "no things" there is only Spirit without distraction. We are just "being there." This is different from prayer which uses "things" such as imagery, imagination, feelings, and thoughts to help us connect with spiritual realities. These are wonderful and indispensable parts of following Jesus.

However, in "being" prayer we let go of all thoughts, feelings, and images—even ones about God. We become present to our True Self, which means we are becoming present to the Spirit of God. We sink down into the void of our own center. It is empty of all thoughts, images, and forms. There is nothing but God there. This kind of praying usually requires a clear intention to enter into it and much practice.

Hafiz eloquently describes formless "being" prayer in "I Have Learned So Much."[18]

I
Have learned
So much from God
That I can no longer
Call Myself
A Christian, a Hindu, a Muslim,
A Buddhist, a Jew.

The Truth has shared so much of Itself
With me
That I can no longer call myself
A man, a woman, an angel,
Or even pure
Soul.

Love has
Befriended Hafiz so completely
It has turned to ash
And freed
Me
Of every concept and image
My mind has ever known.

Jesus recommended praying in secret

Jesus offered this profound practice about prayer: "Whenever you pray, go into your room and shut the door and pray to your

Father-Mother who is in secret."[19] Why did he say this? Because this is the way he prayed! He went off by himself and found the quiet center within.

We can commune with God briefly and many times during the day. However, "shut the door to pray" requires that we quite literally get away from our daily activity and enter into another state of consciousness. We are all different when it comes to how often and how long we do this. I have found that most who pray deeply recommend at least 20 minutes daily or at least several times a week as a good beginning. However, five minutes once a day or even once a week can introduce us to this kind of prayer. One can come to a lightly centered place in just a minute or two at the beginning of each day, or in the midst of the day.

It appears that Jesus was so in tune with his spirit that he knew when he needed to withdraw from daily activities and from others to have an extended time of prayer. Sometimes he would spend an entire night in this kind of prayer. We see examples of *connecting* prayer as when Jesus was in the wilderness being tempted and in Gethsemane talking with his Abba. Although not specially described as such, I am certain he experienced *being* prayer often, as have his followers and others down through the ages.

My prayer practices

I found new openness to spiritual experience in the charismatic movement of the 1960s. However, I did not find much in the way of instruction in cultivating my interior life of prayer. I share my prayer practices here because I wished others had shared theirs with me earlier in my life. I offer them only as what I have found helpful for myself. Each person in their own exploration will find what fits for them at their particular time of life and it will look differently for each of us.

The word for today is . . .

Some years ago I realized how helpful the Unity movement's "word for the day" was. One day it occurred to me that it would be even better if I could hear a word from the Spirit specifically for me. What was the word I needed most during that particular day or time in my life? Then I remembered Jesus said that we do not live by bread alone but by every *word* that comes from the mouth of God.[20] I decided that I would like to have at least one word each day that came from the mouth of God. I don't think God has a mouth but that's an excellent picture of what I experience: God whispers something in the ear of my mind when I ask for a word for the day.

For 40 years now, on most mornings, I have taken just a few seconds upon awakening to listen for a word to guide my day. For the first five years the word was usually "trust." When I complained that it was always the same old word, I heard, "When you don't need the word 'trust' any more, then you won't hear it any more. You asked for what you needed, not what was interesting. I'm not in the entertainment business." Since my primary emotional wound is fear and anxiety, trust was definitely what I needed. I stopped complaining, and some years ago I was finally released from the "trust" focus to begin hearing other words.

Yesterday the word was "flow." Several times I thought of this word again during the day and intentionally moved to a deeper Spirit zone. This morning, while writing, for the first time ever, I heard the word "contentment." My attention was drawn to the fact that, at least for a brief time, I felt incredibly content. This listening for a word takes only a few seconds.

Zone Prayer

I have a prayer/listening/worship/meditation time most days of the week, taking from ten minutes to an hour or more. I call it "zone prayer" because my goal is to enter the Spirit zone. I "close the door" by turning off my house phone and cell phone and anything else that might interrupt me. I always sit in the same chair. Often I play a CD which uses brainwave entrainment technology to help me into a deeper state of consciousness.[21] I have been using this technology for ten years now and find it helpful along with other practices of zone prayer. I usually keep my eyes closed and often will wear a eye cover called a Mind Fold to keep out distracting light.[22] I sit quietly in the silence or listen with stereo headphones to a brainwave entrainment CD with its various sounds such as singing bowls and rainfall.

Sometimes I begin by anchoring myself in the 3rd-person contemplation of God by reading. I love to read, and it excites me to read a spiritually stimulating book. Sometimes I read from the Bible, often the four New Testament gospels or the Gospel of Thomas. Sometimes I read from contemporary mystical writers, including Eckhart Tolle, Andrew Harvey, and Jim Marion. I read until I find something that connects with me.

Then I become even more deeply quiet by paying attention to my breathing and moving from "out there" to "in here." When I feel centered, I state my intention. This is something like, "Lord, I turn my attention to you and ask you to help me focus and hear you." I often then simply listen. I take the Apostle Paul's challenge about the importance of "prophecy" quite seriously. I want to hear what God is saying to and through me. The beginning of an altered state is usually signaled almost immediately with a feeling of a flow of energy rising up from my heart to my throat.

Professor of psychology at the University of California, Berkeley Dacher Keltner, who studies the emotions of "uplift," writes: "When we experience transcendence, it stimulates our vagus nerve, causing a feeling of spreading, liquid warmth in the chest, and a lump in the throat."[23]

This rings true for me as it is a clear and identifiable "sensation" which is most easily released and expressed in my own language of prayer and praise. Praying this way seems to complete the sense of flow. I do this from a few seconds to five or ten minutes.

I usually pray and listen with pen and paper nearby. I often hear words or sentences which give me guidance and encouragement about various parts of my life. Sometimes I will pose a question to focus my listening. "God, what do you want to say to me today?" Or, "God, I am wrestling with this situation. Is there anything you want to tell me about it?" I write down the word or brief sentences that I hear. Sometimes I write down, using one word for each, the names of situations and people I am concerned with. Then I go back over the list in my listening mode and hear how I am to handle the situation or what I may be supposed to do, if anything.

Several times a week my sitting prayer time involves moving into a more "being" state of awareness by quietly sinking down into my own deepest Self. I may begin with the connecting mode as described above and then move into a being mode that does not contain words or images. This is a quiet, still time when I leave behind the forms of the subtle connecting state and simply let my own "spiritual being-ness" arise in my inner awareness. When all thoughts cease, all that is left is the pure awareness of God, who is always present but hidden under our busy minds.

My guides

A vital part of the experience of Jesus that we call the Transfiguration was centered on Jesus connecting with his spiritual guides, Moses and Elijah. I have taken his model seriously. At one point some years ago I decided to explore a similar kind of guidance for myself, which I described in Chapter 11. Often in my extended prayer times I become aware of my spiritual guides. Jesus appears, in my mind, directly in front of me as the Risen Lord. Michael, a wise scholar and ancient monk from around the time of Constantine, is to the right of Jesus. John, the beloved disciple of Jesus, reveals himself by placing his hand on my shoulder from behind me on my right side. I experience this in a physical way as a clear and comforting sensation on my shoulder. Mary, the mother of Jesus, is to my left, and rarely says anything. She is just present. I enjoy the company and communion of these gracious saints and may ask questions or just listen for anything they may have to say to me. They are part of my cloud of witnesses.[24]

Following these times in connecting state awareness I am usually refreshed and armed with new focus and motivation to live that day more fully and to follow the vision and longings of my heart for the Spirit's call today.

A Big Three "prayer break"

As a ritual of invocation I sometimes begin with a liturgy or exercise framed with the Three Faces of God that I have discussed previously.

This can take from a few minutes to an hour or so, and anyone can do this anytime during the day as a "prayer break." It can look like saying or reading something like one of the following.

Speaking about the Infinite God

- All creation declares the glory of God. The heavens reveal the majesty of God, the oceans disclose divine power, the earth tells of sacred handiwork. I see God wherever I look and in all that is arising within me. It is the very energy of the Divine, the Great Web of Life, that holds all things together. The life of the Spirit flows in everyone and everywhere.

Speaking to the Intimate God

- Beloved, I give myself to you in surrender and adoration. I gladly lay down my life for you. Help me be open to all that you have for me. Master and Lord, teach me your ways in all that I do. Thank you for your gracious presence with me every minute of every day and night. I let myself sink down into your all-encompassing love and ever-flowing blessings.

Speaking as the Inner God

- I rest in God as my own Self, my deepest I. I am open to the Mind of Christ within. I am the Witness within. I am the Light of the world. I and the Mother-Father are One. I live, yet not I but the consciousness of Christ lives within me and as me. I am Infinite Spirit who was never born and shall never die. I am fashioned in the very likeness and image of God. I am part of the Big Mind and Big Heart of God. I AM. In this ever-present awareness, I go about my day.

A list from the Bible

Because the Bible is an important part of my life, I keep this list of affirmations from biblical passages in the front of my Bible and sometimes meditate on them as a part of affirming my identification and union with God.

> "I am made in the image of God." (Genesis 3:22)
> "I am like God." (Genesis 3:22)
> "I am the light of the world." (Matthew 5:14)
> "I am a participant in the divine nature." (2 Peter 1:4)
> "I am one with God." (John 17:20, 22)
> "I am a joint heir with Jesus of all that is God." (Romans 8:17)
> "I am like Jesus in every respect." (Hebrews 2:17)
> "Before Abraham was, I am." (John 8:58)
> "I am one of the gods right now!" (John 10:34)
> "I am filled with the fullness of God." (Ephesians 3:17)

A simple sentence from the Psalms of endless depth

Recently I have been quietly repeating this transcendent verse from the Psalms in my quiet sitting times:

> Be still and know that I am God.[25]

The context of this beautiful sentence in Psalm 46 is the waves of terror which spread over the earth and within our lives—the changing earth, roaring waters, trembling mountains, tottering kingdoms, and uproar in the nations. In the midst of all troubles we are invited to be quiet and know God.

The meaning of these words depends entirely upon who you understand and experience God to be. Is God a supernatural being out there somewhere who has good moods and bad moods? Is God up there, rather than right here? Is God not only here present with me, but also in me? Jesus said the Kingdom was both without and within.[26] Since my fullest experience of God is found in Jesus' model of speaking *about* God, *to* God, and *as* God, I pray this beautiful sentence from the Psalms in the Big Three framework. In 3rd-person reflection, I contemplate the stillness in which God is known. In 2nd-person communion I hear God speaking these word to me: "Paul, be still and know that I am God." Then, I let the words become 1st-person mystical reality where the "I Am" of my True Self is the "I Am" that is God. I say this slowly, as a "baby divinity"—a divine spiritual being who partakes of the very nature of God.[27]

I speak *from* my eternal spirit body, *to* my physical, emotional, and mental bodies. As I speak these words to my often tense material body, my often up-and-down feelings, and my busy thoughts, I become quiet and still.

> Be still and know that I [meaning me] am God.
> Be still and know that I am.
> Be still and know.
> Be still.
> Be.

As I end with the simple "Be" I sink down into my deepest Self, the Inner Face of God that is my own True Face.

Praying with others

The next worldwide step in spiritual evolution is the move from individual higher consciousness to shared higher consciousness in community. The self does not evolve in isolation, but with others on the same journey. Genuine spirituality has to have a collective experience. The day of the mystic alone in his cave is over. Contemporary consciousness movements are waning in their attempts to continue to evolve by merely reading books and attending occasional talks and retreats by the latest guru. They are beginning to see that one can only go so far alone. Church people do get together regularly, but, unfortunately, they don't know what to do except have traditional church services. That must change.

Jesus was not a loner. When Jesus wanted to change the world, the first thing he did was get a group of people together who wanted to follow him. He could have just taught the masses. He could have just written a book. He could have passed his teaching on to one other person who would take his place. Instead, he called a small group together to work it all out as a little community of spiritual explorers. Authentic spiritual life has a cognitive (stage) component, a subjective (state) component, and a communal ("we" standpoint) component. The higher "us" is an awakened and shared consciousness *between* people.

Integral church involves a sense of self that is beyond the individual self and encompasses a communal self. Eventually it is destined to become the Cosmic Self that Jesus was in touch with. This was what Jesus was pointing to when he said, "Where two or more are gathered together in my name, I am there." That was not a consolation prize for ministers with small congregations. It was a decisive spiritual principle. We know he is with those same two or more all the time, whether they are together or apart. So what did Jesus mean by "I am there"? Jesus is present in a special way when we gather with the intention of connecting with spiritual realities. Here is how I read his statement: *Two or more together with spiritual purpose and awakened consciousness elevates the level and intensity of the experience of God's presence.*

We may need some times or periods of isolation when we are in the desert as Jesus was, working things out. But normal life on the Jesus Path is also with others. It may, at times, be with another who is a professional therapist if we need special help in healing emotional wounds. It may include a partner or best friend. Most often it will also be a network or company of others on the same journey.

If we want to evolve, we must eventually open ourselves to stages, states, standpoints, shadow, and steps in shared consciousness with a few others as Jesus did. These are the higher truths (stages), transcendent consciousness (states), multiple perspectives (the Big Three standpoints), emotional healing (shadow work), and liberating practices (steps) that awaken compassion for all.

Spiritual growth is eventually about collective evolution, not just individual attainment. This may appear to be more difficult because we must work it all out together, not just in a cave off by ourselves. However, the give and take of rubbing up against one another actually provides a richer context to accelerate our growth rather than hinder it. God comes to us disguised as our life. We are meant to meet God here.

In our narcissistic culture where individualism reigns, who will move us into the next stage, the "together" level? What a great opportunity for real church! Gathering around the story and presence of Jesus brings the Christian community together. Then the presence of God is magnified by "Spirit consciousness" in worship and the community of faith. Being together as the worshipping community is so important that I will devote the entire next chapter to it.

Neuroplasticity—changing your brain

Neuroplasticity (variously referred to as brain plasticity, cortical plasticity, or cortical re-mapping) refers to the changes that occur in the organization of the brain as a result of experience. According to the theory of neuroplasticity, thinking, learning, and acting change both the brain's physical structure and functional organization from top to bottom. Canadian psychiatrist Norman Doidge has described neuroplasticity as one of the most extraordinary discoveries of the twentieth century.[28]

Neuroplasticity means that the right spiritual practices can actually change our brain wiring to help us be more conscious of God. Modern science is confirming the Apostle Paul's words, "Be transformed by the renewing of your minds."[29]

Becoming who you already are

In traditional church we often attempt spiritual practices in some sense by trying to be who and what we are not—and never will be. This is quite different from integral and beyond Christian practice. The deepest understanding of spiritual practice is that it is waking up to who we already are—and have always been! You are a spiritual being, a daughter or son of God who partakes of the divine nature because you are the very image of your heavenly Mother-Father. Spiritual awakening is not about technique. *Technique is just a framework to help us wake up to what is already intrinsically there.* It is not to get us someplace we are not. It's about gently waking us up to where we already are.

What I heard from the Spirit

Here are the words that I heard through a channeled message a few years ago from the Spirit through a collective of spirit beings that I call "The Teachers." (Again, if you are a Christian who continues to think this is weird, turn again to the gospels and read about Jesus' Transfiguration experience. Or, refresh yourself with what the apostle Paul wrote on the value of prophecy in 1 Corinthians.) These were words for me as a teacher, pastor, and church leader as I was "worrying" about how to help others move along:

> It is imperative that you recognize that this is the state where most people are today around personal experience: they cannot take in new experiences that go beyond their small frames of awareness. So they create trauma for themselves in order to stop themselves and still have a great amount of difficulty. The teachers are asking you to take in, embrace, insist that people look inside to their internal space. Insist that they do their work. Insist that, whatever they are looking for, you are not in charge of causing that to happen. You can simply have your joy in their learning what you are talking about. By doing that you can have peace and creativity, and people will have pieces and sections of what you offer. The most important piece that they should hear is that they do *their work.*

In writing about spiritual practices Jim Marion concludes *The Death of the Mythic God* with,

> But I believe that more important than anything else in realizing higher consciousness is not one's practices but one's intent. Jesus promised that those who truly ask will surely find—provided we want God, as Jesus said, with all our heart and soul and mind and strength ... it needs to be a ferocious intent. . . Put God first. Be willing to sacrifice everything else to realize your divinity... Think about it and act upon it every day from the first thing upon waking to the last thing

before going to bed. Seek God, God, God. If you do, you will succeed—and all else will be added.[30]

One last recommendation about spiritual disciplines and practices comes from Jesus himself when he was asked about spiritual disciplines by his disciples.

> His disciples asked him, "Do you want us to fast? How should we pray? Should we give to charity? What diet should we observe?" Jesus said, "Don't lie, and don't do what you hate."[31]

Jesus' two responses were pure wisdom about spiritual practices. (1) Don't kid yourself. Be honest about what fits for you and what does not. (2) If you hate it, don't do it!

He didn't say if it's difficult don't do it. Or if it's new and strange to you don't do it. He didn't say if it takes getting used to don't do it. But he did say that if you actually hate doing it, then don't do it! Doing something we hate won't do us much good. If we find ourselves really hating a particular spiritual practice that we are trying, that's a signal that it doesn't fit for us. So listen to yourself. Don't kid yourself. Stop doing it!

Count on Jesus to be real!

18

The Worshipping Community
Going to Heaven with your eyes open

Today Christians live in the world and go to church. The first Christians lived in the church and went to the world. They were mystics with a community.[1] While I don't want to romanticize their experience of community, I do believe that the communal experience of intense and frequent meetings of the earliest travelers on the Jesus Path made church an all-the-time living reality rather than a weekly meeting to attend. I have tasted some of this "living in the church and going to the world" and found it difficult, challenging, nourishing, and, most often, delicious. This has been the attraction through the centuries of the monastic communities. However, most of us must start somewhere else, and our weekly "going to church" meeting is a great place to begin.

Enlightenment teacher Andrew Cohen makes a great case for real church for Christians even though that is not his tradition. For this chapter's subtitle I have borrowed the title of one of his "quote of the week" brief essays. Here are Cohen's words:

> The goal of Evolutionary Enlightenment is not merely a personal attainment in which the individual has reached a higher stage of development, has access to a higher state of consciousness, and lives in the awareness of a higher perspective. The goal is to transcend the individual and collective ego and attain all the above principally so that one *can connect and interact with others in that same place, in that same*

space, in that same dimension. When we have the powerful and life-transforming experience of not only transcending the ego but interacting with others who have also transcended it, even if only temporarily, a communion of the Authentic Self occurs. In this communion, we experience a revelation as we enter into an ecstatic higher state, where suddenly everything begins to make sense. We recognize in a way that's nothing less than dramatic who we really are, why we are here, and how being the human beings that we *already* are fits perfectly into the stream of the creative process, as it is occurring in the present moment. It's like dying and going to heaven with your eyes open.[2]

Ken Wilber says, "It takes a spiritual path and some sort of involvement with a spiritual community for people to convert this integral theoretical understanding to an integral, embodied, alive, realized understanding."[3]

That spiritual community where the communion of the Authentic Self occurs is the subject of this chapter.

What Would a Regular Weekly Church Service Based on the Principles in this Book Look Like?

The elements of integral philosophy that are most relevant to spiritual growth, are stages, states, standpoints, shadow, and steps. But you say, "Surely all of these cannot be addressed in an hour on Sunday morning." And I say, "Yes, they can!" They may not be fully addressed, but they can be encouraged, illustrated, modeled, and form the intentional framework for why we meet.

The goal of integral level church is to create a community where we can accelerate our spiritual growth in both stages and states. We need the other three (standpoints, shadow, and steps) to help us get there. If one accepts this premise, then corporate worship could move to an entirely new place and purpose. The church worship service is the first place that most Christians could begin to experience elevated states of consciousness. It is also a primary avenue for the kind of teaching/preaching/information that invites others to whatever is the next natural developmental level for them. Until our worship services and other gatherings provide a venue for these five elements, most of our church members will simply have no idea what another state of spiritual awareness or spiritual growth is like. They just "go to church," hoping for a little encouragement, fellowship, and help for their lives. So much more can happen.

Think about it: Buddhists do most of their meditating in private. Hindus focus on personal worship practices such as chanting during their daily activities. Muslims practice daily prayer times as a devout ritual. The Spiritual But Not Religious read lots of books and meet occasionally at big meetings with the latest guru. But Christians already have built into their spiritual path the idea of "going to church" each week. What an incredible opportunity for real growth in spiritual stages and states to take place!

The current situation

Reflect in, hopefully a kindly but pointed way, about the current situation of church services.

Mainline churches have many tiny sections in their hour of worship such as a responsive reading, choral response, pastoral prayer, announcement, special music, and the sermon—all interspersed with a hymn here and there as a pause or break between these other events. If one began to enter an internal worship zone at any point, just wait a minute and you will be jarred back by some activity into thinking about something. You would be asked to listen, or stand, sing a hymn, or whatever. This provides little chance for an altered state to begin or stay alive for very long. It gets killed with worship service paraphernalia! Nor is the worship experience geared to actual invitations to move on up to whatever is the next natural level of awakening. The sermon is often just a few minutes of hopefully inspiring thoughts.

Baptists and other evangelical churches may have rousing singing, but it often is just a prelude to the real thing—the sermon and invitation to become a Christian. Larger evangelical churches may have inspiring musical performances and grand choirs with orchestras to enhance the congregational singing. But the idea sometimes seems to be more about having a spiritual pep rally than moving out of the gross waking state into the connecting state awareness of the Great Mystery! Enough charismatics may infiltrate a large evangelical church to give it some actual awareness-altering flavor with their hands raised and intense devotion during praise songs, but they have only recently been tolerated. The sermons of the larger churches and in African-American churches can be rousing and inspiring but may offer little content that moves one to stage-changing insight.

New Thought churches may have a meditation time but corporate worship is primarily good but heady affirmations, inspiring spiritual entertainment, and a short talk about some interesting topic. One watches, listens, and is inspired, but it may not go much further than that.

Our Catholic and Orthodox sisters and brothers offer the beauty, power, and focus of the Mass and liturgy. If one is already practiced in moving to an elevated inward state of spiritual consciousness, then the Mass can be a great time for that. But if one doesn't have any idea how to do that, Mass itself will probably not get you there. For those at modern and beyond stages, having to translate traditional level religious images and words into a deeper meaning can also be distracting. The typical ten-minute homily probably doesn't provide much either in the way of challenge or practice to move on in stage evolution.

The majority of churches in this country have fewer than one hundred worshippers. Most struggle through a few hymns, long, detailed, and deadening announcements, and a 20-minute sermon by a sincere pastor who may or may not have an active spiritual practice or have developed to another level of spiritual growth in the last 20 years in his/her own life. More likely they are lonely, frustrated, and struggling to know how to move their congregation along to more than just institutional survival.

Have I painted a bleak picture? Yes. But it is also like the two sales representatives of a shoe company assigned to interior Africa. One said, "Oh my God, nobody there wears shoes. I'll never succeed." The other said, "Oh my God, nobody there has shoes. It's a wide open field. We'll clean up!"

The weekly church service already has in place the strong, culturally affirmed idea that one should attend worship services or Mass as often as possible. And we Christians, at least around 40 percent of us, do! So it's a wide open field, ripe for corporate worship to become a hotbed of altered state worship and invitations to move up to the next stage of spiritual development by pointed teaching about these stages.

The integral church gathers for worship around the story and presence of Jesus in order to accelerate our growth in terms of stages, states, standpoints, shadow, and steps.

Let's take these five elements, one at a time, and explore their place in our worship services.

1. Stages

Stage growth in the church service focuses on cognitive knowing about the Sacred. The sermon or teaching time as well as thoughtful words in hymns and songs and readings can invite the congregation to become aware of the next stage appropriate for them. There can also be an invitation to move on to the next stage with a little gentle mind-stretching. I have taught each of the chapters in this book over a two-year time in our services. Of course, I have been doing this for years with our church. We began, years ago, by introducing new directions in classroom and retreat settings. As the congregation became more familiar with an intentional learning focus, I gradually moved from "Sunday morning sermons" to using these precious 20-30 minutes I am given each week to offer new information and direction to the wonderful folk who journey with us in the Jesus Path.

2. States

States refer to the actual experience of God, the Transcendent and Immanent One. Stages refer to the developmental structures that determine how what is experienced in the states will be interpreted and assimilated. When the higher stages and states are combined, they bring forth the life of Spirit in a quite exhilarating way.

States center on the experience of communion and union with the Divine. These times of elevated spiritual awareness can be invited in a church service by silence, meditation, reflection, deep worship, joyful praise, warm fellowship, healing energy, inspiring and compelling truth, and beautiful architecture, symbols, and surroundings.

Marcus Borg calls these states by the metaphor of Celtic Christianity's "thin place." A thin place is where the boundary between the physical world and the spiritual world becomes porous and permeable. We can see God all around us. He says, "If we took seriously that a major purpose of worship is to become a thin place, it would affect how we would conduct our worship services."[4]

One of the primary aims of the early churches' gatherings as elaborated on in Chapter 10 was to provide an opportunity to enter altered states of consciousness. Today this would also include the contemplative states which are not reported to the degree that the more easily described God-intoxicated ones were in the New Testament documents. This is a crucial function of integral church today. In many, if not most, churches there are few opportunities to move into more transcendent consciousness. Since leaders themselves have not been trained and transmitted into these states there is no one to lead congregational members into them. Instead, at best, we aim for a "pleasant" church service or an entertaining Sunday morning "worship" with "nice" meditation, beautiful music, or "inspiring" preaching. Worshippers are not invited to do anything but try to be appreciative spectators who sing and read aloud when asked. Yet corporate worship is the most likely place for most people to begin to experience elevated states.

The most neglected practice among *all* integral practitioners, those of every religious tradition and of none, is the *corporate* experience of the higher states. The next step for mystics of all persuasions is community. The truest transcendence is found

- in the company of the committed,
- with the explorers of enlightenment,
- in the meetings of the mystics,
- in the assembly of the awakening,

- among the people of the prophets,
- in the partnership of the prayerful, and
- with the caravan of the compassionate.

This is the Christianity of the future!

3. Standpoints

We can shape our church services by using the framework of the three Standpoints—the three basic ways of relating to God that Jesus modeled. Here, again, is the nine-word sentence that I suggested be memorized:

Jesus spoke *about* God, *to* God, and *as* God.

In these three approaches, Jesus modeled for us the fullest possible relationship to God in the human journey. These are the three faces of God—Infinite, Intimate, and Inner. They can also form the basis of the most expansive church worship service possible.

(1)   *About* God—Gathering together provides an exciting time to hear good teaching, information, and discussion *about* God and the Spirit's work in the world. There I can learn *about* the spiritual life and practices in ways that help me grow.

(2)   *To* God—In the corporate shared energy field of others on the same journey I can relate *to* God in worship and prayer. I can surrender *to* God in intimate communion, majestic praise, and passionate devotion.

(3)   *As* God—We regularly need to be reminded that our deepest, highest, truest Self is Christ. The same consciousness that was in Jesus is in us. Our task is to become as aware of it as he did. We long for affirmation of our own sacred worth *as* divine spiritual beings. We need to hear Jesus say to us, "You are the Light of the world." Our souls reach out for the words of Jesus, "Do you not know that you are gods?"

When these three standpoints are offered, we are nurtured, trained, and filled up on our way into the coming week of growing in Christ. The experience of Spirit-filled corporate worship goes beyond personal inspiration, individual learning, private ecstasy, and interior knowing. It reaches toward the ultimate in transcendence—the fulfillment of the Jesus prayer that we may all be one—and experiencing that oneness here on Earth.

Let's explore each of these three elements in more detail.

(1) Learning about God

This is probably the most familiar part of most church services. We can grow in our ability to love God and others through good sermons, enlightened teaching,[5] and even the words (hopefully intriguing, pointed, and not too many) of responsive readings, litanies and songs. A primary learning goal in Christian church gatherings is a presentation of Jesus' life and teaching through the lens of the highest stage possible, hopefully integral and beyond. This kind of teaching points to the incredible breakthrough that Jesus modeled in radically higher levels of understanding and experience. It then gives an invitation for us to move on to whatever is the next natural step for us personally.

Stevan Davies argues that Jesus' entire teaching style, including the parables, was directed at producing an altered state of consciousness.[6] Good teaching and "preaching" can move us to altered states at times, shaking up our old notions and inviting us into new life-changing insights.

Traditionalists, in worship, want to hear the comforting words of the past. Modernists want an intellectually satisfying and socially oriented lecture. Postmodernists want everyone to have a voice and participate. Integralists like all the above and also want teaching and worship that invites us to new stages and state of awareness.

(2) Relating To God

Deep communion with the Spirit can happen in the times of praise, prayer, worship, and surrender *to* God. In a small group setting it may look like a time of devotion and quiet. In most church services it usually includes singing hymns and songs of praise. There are prayers and invitations to connect with God. The one word that would describe the most helpful kind of worship is "passionate." There is the old story of the man who became enthused during the singing of a worship hymn and began saying loudly, "Praise God, praise God." An usher moved over to the man and quietly said to him, "Sir, we don't praise God in this service."

Of course, passion does not always have to be loud. Passion can overflow in times of quiet contemplation, also. The hush of deep reflection expands our awareness of spiritual realties if we have been trained in how to "be still and know that I am God."

(3) Being present *as* God

God and Jesus are exalted and honored in most of our churches in song and worship. How can we also wisely, artistically, and impactfully honor the divinity of us all? To honor Jesus as the Christ is the first step in the Jesus Path. The second step is to take Jesus seriously by honoring the True Self within all of us as also the Christ. To refuse to take the second step, as the conventional church has done, is to dishonor Jesus and totally stop further spiritual growth in becoming like Jesus.

This is a great challenge both theologically and practically because we typically don't have songs or worship forms which express the truth of seeing God in ourselves and one another. We await a new generation of song writers and poets to lift this powerful truth. Here are the words to a beautiful new, flowing, contemporary hymn *Namaste* by Mark Hayes, which express this reality.

> Namaste, Namaste, Namaste.
> The divine in me blesses
> 　　and honors the divine in you.
> The beauty of God stands before me,
> 　　expressing uniquely as you.
> The spirit of goodness within you
> 　　shines forth in all that you do.

> Namaste, Namaste, Namaste.
> The divine in me blesses
>   and honors the divine in you.[7]

At our church we sing the beautiful worship song called "Emmanuel" by Bob McGee that uses the meaning of Emmanuel as "God with us." The first verse is *about* God. The second verse is *to* God. But there is no verse *as* God. So we wrote a new verse with the words, "Emmanuel, *our* name is called Emmanuel. God with us, revealed *as* us, *our* name is called Emmanuel."

"Turn Your Eyes Upon Jesus," written in 1922 by Helen Lemmal, is a beautiful devotional hymn sung in many churches. The chorus is:

> Turn your eyes upon Jesus,
> Look full in His wonderful face,
> And the things of earth will grow strangely dim,
> In the light of His glory and grace.[8]

I have written a final chorus which affirms the Inner Face of Christ:

> Turn your eyes upon Christ within,
> Look full in your wonderful face
> In your deepest soul see Christ again,
> In the light of God's glory and grace.

After visiting Broadway Church and hearing our emphasis on the Inner Face of God, songwriter, author, and friend Jann Aldredge-Clanton, wrote this new hymn that both affirms the feminine image of God and the divinity within us all.

Shekhinah* Is Our Dwelling Place

Shekhinah is our dwelling place,
The life Divine within us all;
She gives us power, love, and grace
To open doors and take down walls.

Shekhinah shines within all hearts,
Revealing our divinity;
Her liberating truth imparts
A hope beyond all we can see.

Shekhinah dwells throughout all earth,
Inspiring just and peaceful ways;
She brings abundant life to birth,
And shows the path to glorious days.[10]

Singing these kinds of songs together in congregational worship is an exhilarating move to the consciousness of our shared divinity. We sense that we are truly God's heart, hands, and voice in the world in a deeper way.

Beauty, truth, and goodness

One last thought on the Three Standpoints in worship. Beauty, goodness, and truth are the classical way of naming the Big Three. Beauty deals with the 1st-person self and self-expression. Beauty is in the eye of the beholder. Goodness refers to 2nd-person or the ways we treat each other with respect and kindness. Truth refers to 3rd-person objective truth which is best investigated by reason. Integral worship desires to be beautiful, good, and true. As we plan our worship service each week, we aim for beauty, goodness, and truth.

*Shekhinah is a feminine Hebrew word translated "dwelling" or "settling," and is used to denote the dwelling presence of God and/or the glory of God. (Exodus 29:45; 40:34-38)

4. Shadow

Jesus said that he came to "heal the broken-hearted."[11] Most of us have a broken heart at some time in our lives. Shadow work and other therapeutic practices can bring great healing. They can even be introduced in mini form as a transformative practice in any church service. At an appropriate point in a church service or group setting we can be encouraged to think of some person or situation that annoys us. Then we can be led in a Face-Talk-Be shadow process, taking four or five minutes of guided quiet time to do it. Those that lead and speak can illustrate from their own lives their own inner healing journey. Congregations can be pointed to groups and therapists that enable these things. "I did a Face-Talk-Be last week," can become a common phrase in church. Talking about what we learned in therapy or journaling can be another topic between friends.

5. Steps

The practical steps that move us to conscious spiritual evolution can be illustrated, modeled, and actually experimented with in our church services. Those who teach and preach in the church service can share the steps they take each week to grow in Christ. The various practices such as centering prayer, quiet, formless meditation, or learning to listen to the Spirit can be subjects for sermons. Time in the weekly worship service can be set aside for trying out various practices. We call this the "transformative practice" time in our services. We take a brief time, four or five minutes, to do a spiritual exercise. The exercise moves us out of passive listening or observing to doing something. This may mean inviting the congregation to write down what they hear, draw pictures of what they see, or describe what they sense in a time of listening. It may look like a burning bowl ceremony where we write down the things we want to leave to God and leave behind, place them in a bowl, and light them to burn as an offering to God. It may be a guided mediation or an extended version of the Three Faces of God Invocation that I illustrated earlier. Recently I passed out small mirrors at the end of my teaching, and everyone looked into their own face and eyes as we reflected on "Christ in you, the hope of glory." Could we dare to see the face of God deep down inside of us? Then we sang the new verse to "Turn Your Eyes Upon Jesus" that I had written.

Whatever practices we come up with, they are the steps we take to make real the spiritual journey. They go beyond listening to a sermon or singing hymns. Of course, we must be sensitive to what pushes people beyond their limits. For a brief time, years ago, we tried spontaneously moving to small groups of three or four in the pews to share thoughts and pray for one another during the service. This was great for some and absolutely terrifying for others. We stopped when we realized that more than one person quietly escaped to go get a drink or to the restroom. They did what fit for them while waiting for the leaders to come to their senses.

For a number of years, off and on, our church has practiced healing prayer during the Sunday morning church service. About once each month we invite members of our healing prayer team to come to the front. Those who wish physical healing, emotional healing, or a prayer of blessing come forward and are lightly touched on the head or shoulders, anointed with oil, and briefly prayed for. There may be quiet singing or music in the background. The entire five-minute experience can be very moving for those who remain seated as we visually and energetically experience praying for one another in a here-and-now way.

At other times we may invite those who wish prayer to simply stand while those around them may touch them and quietly pray for them. This is also a powerful time, and it models how we take healing prayer for physical and emotional needs very seriously.

Body language

I use my body as a part of my symbolic language to express myself to God. Psychologists call it body language. I just call it natural. Think about how we naturally use our hands and arms to communicate:

Waving hello, it's a hand up.

Giving up, it's "hands up."

Welcoming someone at the door into your home, it's arms open wide.

Cheering at the football game it's "hands up."

Getting into the zone at the rock concert, it's waving "hands up."

Inviting someone to come with you, it's hands beckoning.

Winning a gold medal at the Olympics it's "hands up."

The police asking you to surrender, it's "Hands up!"

A child wanting you to hold them, it's hands up.

Including the whole world, it's hands outstretched.

Or, when you pray or go to church to worship God, you hold a Bible, a hymnal, or the bulletin in your hands and *sit very, very, very still*. So let me ask, Which is more "natural"?

My favorite body language is holding my hands open in front of me. This says "I am open. I receive." I regularly raise my hands and arms further upward and outward, physically saying, "I surrender," or "I celebrate."

Movement allows us to access a wider range of emotions, including sensing the presence of the Spirit and expressing gratitude in worship and owning our divinity. Haitian Christians say that they go to church to talk about God. They dance to become God.[12]

A Sunday morning at our church

I hesitate to describe the church service of the small congregation of which I am a part. It is not because I don't think it is exceptionally beautiful and wonderful, because I do. But there are, and will increasingly be, many different and evolving expressions of integral and beyond worship. I do not want to suggest in any way that, at Broadway Church, our always-evolving model is the only way or better than others. But we do need models which can help us toward our own best path. So I offer us as one example.

While writing this chapter, I decided to record my thoughts and feelings during a Sunday morning worship service at our church. We have a beautiful pipe organ, grand piano, guitar, flute, and percussion (a trap set, tympani, and conga drums) which accompany our singing in various combinations. Three or four worship leaders stand in front to lead the singing with their presence and voices. Long ago we invested in the finest sound system we could afford since music, singing, and speaking are such primary elements in our times together. Our congregation, founded in 1872, meets in an historic, beautiful, traditional, Gothic-style church building.

We usually have an uninterrupted period of music, hymns, worship songs, quiet, and prayer for the first 20-30 minutes. This is enough time to move into the prayer/worship zone. This is followed by a greeting time where everyone moves about, hugging and briefly greeting one another. The offering is taken while our wonderful pianist plays something classical or religious. This is followed by a teaching/message time from one of our pastors, often ending with a brief transformative practice to apply the teaching, and then a closing hymn or song. We have Communion and healing prayer, each about once each month.

During the singing this particular morning, two women with an interest in Sufi spirituality, who have recently begun attending our service, moved quietly into a large space on the left side of the sanctuary in front of the first pew. They began turning and turning in the beautiful Sufi style of worship, their flowing dresses whirling around them. I stopped singing to watch this incredible expression of worship. As they gently turned in place with hands gracefully outstretched on either side, I felt tears in my eyes. They had tears in their eyes, also.

As we sang the Mark Hayes song "God is All There Is"[13] I felt this welling up from within my heart through my throat as I softly began expressing my adoration and worship in my prayer language.

I did this throughout most of the song. The beauty of the music, instruments, and voices released this sense and expression of worship.

During the teaching time Marcia (Marcia and I alternate months in the teaching time) talked about the passage from the Gospel of John, "I have much more to tell you but you cannot bear it now." It was a powerful word. In spite of having not had enough sleep the night before, I didn't have a moment of tiredness during the entire service.

In the transformative exercise time in the service, Marcia asked us to sit quietly, close our eyes, and imagine Jesus sitting next to us. We turned and asked him, "What do you want to tell me about today," I did this and heard immediately "You're getting the knack of flowing with my Spirit today. It energizes your body and moves you past your fears." That was an encouraging word for where I was.

Churches have differing degrees of freedom to order their worship service. You can squeeze integral-level change into any service even if all you have to work with is the sermon or homily. The more freedom a church has to design its own service as in the free church tradition the easier it is to move to integral church using the service itself. But other gatherings can foster these same things. Every Christian tradition can provide corporate experiences at the integral and beyond level.

Conclusion

I have now shared with you my understanding of Christianity and church. It is following Jesus in the ways I have outlined in this book. I can now introduce another description of integral Christianity, and that is "inclusive Christianity." I have hesitated to use that term previously here because it has often been limited to racial inclusion and more recently about inclusion of all sexual orientations. Jesus-type inclusivity is much bigger than those, important as they are.

I understand integral Christianity to be the most inclusive version of following Jesus yet seen. As I have stated in various ways philosophically, it includes:

- All people—not just Christians, or white, straight males

- All authentic spiritual paths—not just Christianity

- All stages of development

- All states of consciousness

- All of life—not just the "spiritual" part

- All Three Faces of God—not just one or two

- All Three Faces of Christ—not just one or two

- An inclusive Jesus as a blueprint for all of us

Jesus said, "By their fruits you shall know them." What fruits was he talking about? Not having the right religion? No, he made the Samaritans and the Gentiles with their various religions the heroes of his stories. Not having the right rules? No, he discarded the traditional rules that were not compassionate. Not having the right beliefs? No, his message of the Kingdom of God was not about dogmatic creeds and beliefs.

Jesus will have none of that. The only thing Jesus will tell us to move toward is inclusive love. Jesus said God is kind and merciful toward enemies. God is compassionate toward all. Inclusive love comprises the two greatest commandments. Jesus demonstrated that God is love and only love. Only that which leads to more compassion, more liberating justice, more understanding, more respect, and more love for all is that which leads to God.

The reason we push Christians and churches to change is not because we don't love them. It is because we *do* love them. We love Christianity too much to let it alone! Why did Jesus criticize his exclusivist religion so severely? Because he loved it! The only measure of a church is transformation in ever more inclusive love. Which stages and states produce the most liberating compassion for all? What beliefs and practices bathe the greatest portion of the world in the love of God? The thesis of this book is that the higher the stage and the deeper the state, the greater the love. The more in touch with God, the greater the love. Higher *stages*, deeper *states*, all three *standpoints* of relating to God, healed *shadows*, and regular *steps* in spiritual practice all generate more love.

This is my final and ultimate rationale. It is Jesus' argument. It is the goal of reasonable people, of moral people, of spiritual people everywhere. More love.

CHAPTER 19

Jesus' Most Astonishing Statement
"You are the light of the world."

If there is one statement that sums up the core of Jesus' integral view of the spiritual life, it is this: "Jesus said to them, 'You are the light of the world.'"[1] This statement may not seem all that great to us if we have been steeped in traditional theology. But it gets more and more staggering when we look at the context. Who are the "them" to whom Jesus was speaking? Matthew attempts to describe the "them" by writing, "When Jesus saw the crowds, he went up the mountain; and after he sat down, his disciples came to him. Then he began to speak, and taught them saying . . ."[2]

Is the "them" of the "taught them" the crowds or the disciples? It looks like it could go either way according to Matthew. In Luke the setting for this same account goes like this:

> There were a great crowd of his disciples, and a great multitude of people from all Judea, Jerusalem, and the coast of Tyre and Sidon. They had come to hear him and be healed of their diseases . . . Then he looked up at his disciples and said . . .[3]

Luke seemingly inserts a narrative description that Jesus "looked up at his disciples and said . . ." Perhaps this is because Luke also makes the point that there were two kinds of people there—a crowd of Jesus' disciples and a multitude of others. This means that there was a group of those who considered themselves followers of Jesus and a much larger group that were not followers of Jesus. It appears the writers and editors of Matthew and Luke, writing some 40 to 60 years later, either believed or attempted to make it appear that Jesus was speaking only to his followers. *But there is nothing in what Jesus said to indicate this.* Jesus did nothing to distinguish the "crowd" of disciples from the "multitude" of others.

The geographical area where Jesus spoke these words was probably near Capernaum which was built along the edge of the Sea of Galilee. While this has been called the Sermon on the Mount, there are no real mountains there, just hills. One can actually stand on one of these small hills and speak out into the natural amphitheater which is formed there and be heard quite clearly, even by thousands of people who might be gathered there. Other passages indicate that Jesus' crowds were often in the thousands, such as the feeding of the five thousand (which numbering did not include women and children). His disciples (also not counting women and children) were numbered at times from 70 to 120 to over 500.[4] I doubt that there were crowd control guards who marked off the multitudes of thousands from the disciples of possibly hundreds in some way.

Scholars tell us that Jesus most likely spoke these same words many times to many crowds. That was his method of teaching and the way his followers could have drilled into them what he was saying. There were no tape recorders or videos or even scribes there to help them remember, only repetition.

I believe Jesus knew that he was addressing the entire multitude. He did not identify his disciples as being separate from the multitude. He did not point out that he was talking only to his disciples. He did not say, "Although it may appear that I am speaking to all of you, I am really only talking to my followers. The rest of you should know what I am saying is not true for you. You can listen in, but only the people in the front rows are who I am talking to." This is what it appears the writers of the account tried to do, *since by that time they had adopted a belief that only Christians could be "light."* But Jesus himself did not make that distinction. If we had been there it would have been clear to us that Jesus was addressing the entire crowd without distinction.

As we have noted, Luke points out that the thousands in the larger crowd that Jesus drew at this point came from all around, including the notoriously pagan cities of Tyre and Sidon in what we now call Lebanon. Those cities were about 30 miles away from Capernaum. The point is that these were not Jewish cities. They were the historic centers of Canaanite paganism. They were cities with Greek and Roman gods, and wild sexual rituals at the religious temples. Going to church there was not what we mean by going to church today.

Six amazing things about this crowd that Jesus called the light of the world:

1. Nobody there was a Christian, not even the disciples. Not even Jesus!

For years, every time I read this passage I just assumed everyone he was speaking to was a Christian. Now I see that I was wrong—really wrong. There was not one Christian there, not even Jesus. The religion of Jesus was Judaism. Jesus was a Jew, not a Christian. The religion of the first disciples was Judaism. What we now call "Christianity" was shaped by the Apostle Paul and others and had not yet appeared on the scene. Nobody there, even the disciples, held any of the beliefs which we have come to associate with Christianity. The disciples at that point were not sure who Jesus was. They certainly had not made a profession of faith in Jesus as Lord and Savior and been baptized as Christians. They were not remotely aware of any of the classical doctrines of the Christian faith or any of the creeds which were formulated much later. The followers of Jesus were only much later called Christians in Antioch, and that did not include the doctrines and creeds that later defined Christianity.[5] At this time, the disciples were not "Christians." They were simply followers of Jesus.

Can you imagine a television evangelist today addressing a crowd of people, none of whom were Christians. His crowd might be a mixture of some people interested in Jesus, some of other religions, some atheists and agnostics, and some notorious sinners. Would the evangelist begin with, "You are the light of the world"? Of course not, because he would believe that only Christians are the light of the world and, then, probably not even all of them. He would go to great lengths to distinguish the Christians from all the others if he was making any statement about who was the light of the world. Jesus made no such distinction.

2. Most of the crowd were not disciples of Jesus.

There were curious people of many religions and no religion who came to listen. Luke points this out by indicating the great multitude included people from Tyre and Sidon, which were Gentile cities. Some were seeking healing from the newest healer come to town, of whom they had heard amazing stories.

3. Some were the "pagans" and others, the outcasts of society.

We are not talking about nice, meditating Buddhists and beautiful, chanting Hindus. We are talking about people who practiced the wild religions of ancient Greece and Rome. There were the lepers at the back of the crowd, who were not even allowed to enter the Temple at Jerusalem. Instead, they were shuffled off to some far corner of society to fend for themselves. There were prostitutes who sold themselves to other people so that they would have food to eat. There were the poor, the blind, the deaf, the emotionally distressed, and the physically handicapped. There were the so-called "sinners"—Jewish people who did not keep all of the 613 basic Jewish laws. The crowd was filled with the outcasts of Jewish society who did not measure up to the Jewish standards of being acceptable to God.

So we have Jesus addressing a crowd of people in which there were no Christians, and many of whom were "sinners" and "pagans" with strange religions.

These were the people Jesus said were the light of the world. Got that? What would happen if that fact dawned upon the Christian world one day. No more "you're out, I'm in." No more superiority. No more putting down of others for anything—not their religion or lack of it—not their lifestyle—not anything. Because everyone is the light of the world.

4. Jesus did not say, "Some of you are the light of the world."

There were no qualifications for being the light of the world. The only challenge, which Jesus pointed out next, was not to hide it under a bucketful of ego. Whoever we are, each of us is sitting on the hillside and listening to the words of Jesus. Jesus is talking to you and me. We are *all* the light of the world.

5. Jesus did not say, "You must become the light of the world."

He was not telling them that they needed to become the light. He was telling them that they already were the light. He then told them not to hide that fact from themselves or the world. He said, "Let your light shine." He did not say, "First of all, you must become the light before you can let it shine."

If Jesus had said, "Become the light of the world," that would have been a burden too great to bear. They could not do it. Rather, this was a call to realize who they actually were in their deepest self. When we know who we truly are, we are transformed.

Jesus says to every person, "You are the light of the world." Not, "You can become the light of the world." Or, "With the right beliefs and hard work you can achieve being the light of the world." Jesus says, "You are the light of the world right now."

What would have been your response? Perhaps, "You've got to be kidding. I'm not even one of your followers. And even if I was, I don't look very light-like. I am poor, sick, crippled, and ugly. I don't keep all the rules. I have sinful thoughts about sex. Come on. Get real."

What is real is that Jesus said that you are the light of the world and he didn't make you an exception. So what did Jesus mean when he said that we are the light of the world?

6. Jesus meant that we were the light of the world exactly like he was the light of the world!

Later on Jesus was to say, "I am the light of the world."[6] He used the same words when he said that we are the light of the world as when he said that he was the light of the world. We are divine spiritual beings on a human journey just like he was. He said we could do what he did and more. He said we could embrace and become aware of our oneness with God just like he did. All the wisdom and compassion of the Big Mind and Big Heart of God that was available to him is available to us.

The mystical poet Hafiz grasped this and experienced it. Therefore, he could write: "I wish I could show you when you are lonely or in darkness the astonishing light of your own being."[7]

God resides in everyone—Hindus, Christians, Buddhists, atheists, straights, gays, the good, the bad, and the ugly. God wants the light within us to shine. The Spirit wants us to be connected to that light within and transformed by it.

That light is *already* inside of us. It is *always* inside of us. It has never left and will never leave. You don't need to get it. It's already there. You can't earn it. It's already there as the real you. You can't lose it, because it's the real you which is part of God. And God never loses any part of herself anytime or anywhere. This is "the astonishing light of your own being."

Divine light, heavenly lampstands, and baskets of ego

One final word about our being the light of the world and the integral framework of this book. Jesus did not qualify his statement that we are the light of the world. But he did elaborate on it, saying:

> No one after lighting a lamp puts it under a bushel basket, but on a lampstand, and it gives light to all in the house. In the same way, let your light shine before others so that they may see your good works and give glory to your Father-Mother in heaven.[8]

Jesus said that in the physical world no one lights an oil lamp and then puts a basket over it. But he knew that in the spiritual world people find themselves in just that situation. Look around. Does the world look full of seven billion bright lights? So what gives? Maybe we are not each the light of the world. No, Jesus will have none of that. However, he also knew that even though the divine oil lamp within is always radiating light, that light does not always get out to light up the world's house.

Using Jesus' technique of the parable, let's end where we began this book. Let's see how the five points in our Spiritual Positioning System show us how to let the light that is us shine out brightly to the world and give glory to the loving, infinite, intimate, inner God of All.

(1) **Stages.** "No one after lighting a lamp puts it under a bushel basket, but on a lampstand, and it gives light to all in the house." Each of the six stages of evolving illumined consciousness can be seen as accompanied by ever-evolving lampstands. These lampstands hold up the divine light that is each of us blessing the world. As the world around us evolves upward into new stages, the divine light in and as us benefits from a loftier lampstand so it can continue to "give light to all the house." The warrior stage needs a higher lampstand than the tribal stage provides in order to lift the light up to shine. The traditional stage requires a more elevated lampstand than the warrior state. The loftier the stage, the higher the lampstand must be to spread light to the whole house. The larger the stately mansion, the higher the light must stand. It must move ever upward, hopefully always *ahead* of the culture surrounding it to continue to illumine that culture.

(2) **States.** The astonishing light of our own being is deep within us, accessed and released by the *connecting* and *being* states of non-ordinary consciousness. As we become conscious of our own inner light, we are then able to let it radiate out through our lives every day. We press past all of the destructive conditioning from religion and society about how bad we are and how separated from God we are. It is in the depths of prayer, reflection, and worship that we come to glimpse our own Unique Self that is One with the God of All Light.

(3) **Standpoints**. Infinite, Intimate, Inner God. The light of *Infinite* God shines brightly in the beauty of nature,

and in the ever-evolving physical world and beyond. We access it by observation, reflection, and scientific study. For Christians and others who will look, the light of *Intimate* God shines in Jesus, the awesome light of God in first-century sandals. The light of the *Inner* God is that indescribable radiance of our True Self. This inner light is the one most hidden under our inadequate beliefs and lack of awareness. The vast majority of Christians have been taught this light does not exist *as* us, but only, at the most, as a visitor or guest *in* us. We must exchange this less than adequate belief for Jesus' clear word that we *are* the Light. It takes all three standpoints to let the Light shine most fully.

(4)   **Shadow**. "No one after lighting a lamp puts it under a bushel basket . . ." This bushel basket, spiritually speaking, takes the form of our wounded self, our projected false self, our egoic self. Healing our shadow punches liberating holes in our bucket full of ego and drains it dry. The more "holely" the ego basket, the more the light gets out!

(5)   **Steps**. Finally, the journey to letting our light shine is always one step, one practice, one day at a time. Each repeated practice of exercising and nurturing our physical, emotional, mental, and spiritual bodies moves us to releasing more wondrous light into this world.

But don't take my word for it that you are the gleaming light of the world. Don't take the Bible's word for it. Don't take Jesus' word for it. Don't take the word of devout Christians and other spiritual seekers who have shone down through the ages. You can take your own word for it! You can discover it for yourself. It is verifiable in your very own life and inner self. You know how to do it. Move on it now. It is your destiny. For at this very moment, deep within, you are the sublime, dazzling, resplendent light of the world!

Notes

Introduction

1. John 16:12.
2. Visser, *Ken Wilber,* xii.

Chapter 1: A Spiritual Positioning System

1. John 16:12-13.
2. These stages correlate with Beck and Cowen's *Spiral Dynamics stages of Purple: Magical/animistic (tribal); Red: Impulsive/egocentric (warrior); Blue: Purposeful/Authoritarian (traditional); Orange: Achievist/ strategic (modern); Green: Communitarian/egalitarian (postmodern); Yellow: Integrative (integral); and Turquoise: Holistic (beyond integral).*
3. Matthew 7:20.
4. DiPerna, *The Infinite Ladder,* 100-101.
5. Romans 12:2.
6. Luke 18:25.
7. The term "Kingdom of Heaven" is synonymous with the term "Kingdom of God" in the New Testament. There are limitations in using the term "kingdom" because it is patriarchal and has no context in today's world for the way the term was used in Jesus' day. Jesus would certainly not have used the term today. Brain McLaren insightfully suggests that perhaps Dr. King's saying "I have a dream" was one way of stating the idea today. Or, he continues, "we might talk about the dance of God, the community of God, the party of God, the song of God, the school of God, the movement of God, the peaceful revolution of God." John speaks of it as abundant life or the life of the ages. (See *Connecting Like Jesus,* Tony Campolo, 217.)

Chapter 2: Tribal Church

1. Other common superstitions today are fear of a black cat crossing or breaking a mirror. People may cross their fingers to bring good luck or to excuse themselves for telling a lie. Other superstitions include finding a good luck penny, or believing that washing your car causes it to rain, even if it always seems to turn out that way. Knocking on wood comes from the ancient belief that the gods lived in the trees. When a person needed a favor or something good, they would touch the bark, ask their favor, and then knock on the bark as a note of thanks.

    There's nothing wrong with blowing out your birthday cake candles all in one breath and making a wish, but do we really think it contains just a bit of magic to get what we wished for? Do we ever assign good luck to having a rabbit's foot or finding a four-leaf clover? That is thought to have originated with the Druids who believed such a find would help them see evil spirits more easily.

2. Psalms 111:10.

3. Mark 3:33-35.

4. Luke 8:3.

Chapter 3: Warrior Church

1. Romans 12:19.

2. Psalms 19:9.

3. 2 Corinthians 5:11.

4. Revelation 19:11-16.

5. 2 Thessalonians 1:7-9.

6. "A Midnight Service Helps African Immigrants Combat Demons," *New York Times*, December 18, 2007.

7. Armstrong, *The Case for God*, 271.

Chapter 4: Traditional Church

1. Pew Survey on Religion in America, 2008, http://religions.pewforum.org/. (accessed 8/08).

2. Pew Survey on Religion in American, 2008.

3. Ibid.

4. This is in spite of the great majority of passages in the New Testament about eternal destiny which proclaim the universal salvation of all. See my booklet, *Hell? No! A Bible study on why no one will be left behind*. www.paulsmith.com.

5. Matthew 10:21–22.

6. Mark 3:31-35.

7. Luke 9:59-60.

8. Matthew 10: 35–37, *The Message*.

Chapter 5: Modern Church

1. Gospel of Thomas, Saying 2.

2. John Spong, "A Call for A New Reformation," 26 June 2008, http://www.dioceseofnewark.org/voxspong.html.

3. The Jesus Seminar, http://www.religioustolerance.org/chr_jsem.htm

4. See Funk, *The Five Gospels*.

5. See Wright, http//www.ntwrightpage.com/Wright_Five_Gospels.pdf.

6. John 14:9, 28.

7. Acts 17:28.

8. Personal conversation, June 23, 2001.

9. See Stendahl, *Paul Among Jews and Gentiles*, 78.

10. Wilber, *Sex, Ecology, Spirituality*, 29.

Chapter 6: Postmodern Church

1. *Albuquerque Journal*, December 1998.

2. Schwartzentruber, *The Emerging Christian Way*, 10.

3. Borg, *Reading the Bible*, 3.

4. Ibid., 12.

5.   Borg, *The Heart of Christianity*, 6, 13.

6.   Borg, *The God We Never Knew*, 12.

7.   Ibid., 51

8.   Clayton., *In Whom We Live*, 272.

9.   See Herzog, *The Parables*.

10. Borg, *The Heart of Christianity*, 89-91.

11. Borg, *Reading the Bible*, 218.

12. Tolle, *A New Earth*, 56.

13. Johnston, *The Mirror Mind*, 7.

14. Village Presbyterian Church Seminar, Kansas City, MO, April 27, 2007.

Chapter 7: Reading the Bible in a Jesus-Friendly Way

1.   Genesis 6:11.

2.   Exodus 4:24.

3.   Exodus 4:24.

4.   Exodus 9:12.

5.   Isaiah 45:6-7.

6.   Joshua 11:20.

7.   Exodus 23, Deuteronomy 7.

8.   Numbers 15:32-35.

9.   Psalms 104:35.

10. Psalms 137:9.

11. See his books, *Jesus Against Christianity: Reclaiming the Missing Jesus* and *Is Religion Killing Us?*

12. Jeremiah 31:20, Isaiah 46:3-4.

13. Genesis 18:18, Isaiah 42:6.

14. Hosea 6:6.

15.   Matthew 9:13, cf. 12:7.

16.   Matthew 5:21f.

17.   Matthew 5:27f.

18.   Matthew 5:38, from Ex 21:24, Lev. 24:19.

19.   Matthew 5:39f.

20.   Matthew 5:43.

21.   Matthew 5:43-45, Luke 6:35-36. *The New Testament and Psalms: An Inclusive Version.*(Hereafter noted as IV)

      The New Testament and Psalms: An Inclusive version, from Oxford University Press, "has undertaken the effort to replace or rephrase all gender-specific language not referring to particular historical individuals, all pejorative references to race, color, or religions, and all identifications of persons by their physical disability alone, by means of paraphrase, alternative renderings, and other acceptable means of conforming the language of the work to an inclusive idea." (From the General Introduction to this version.)

      I often use the Inclusive Version because I want to reflect the inclusive teaching and actions of Jesus in rendering the Scripture itself into today's world. He broke down gender, racial, economic, and other barriers that exclude and label people as different. Language both reflects and drives those barriers. For instance, using the word "mankind" today reflects a barrier based upon the idea that supposedly men represent the human race, including women, in a way that women do not. This makes women something less than men linguistically. Jesus broke with the tradition of demeaning women.

      A real tension often exists between a modern translation and the Greek text itself, which was written at a time when many of these barriers were still in place. One must choose whether to be very literal, which almost no translation is, or to move to rendering the Greek into English in a way that does not continue to stereotype and exclude.

      An important example is when Jesus called God "Father." Was he trying to say that God was male rather than female? Or was he trying to use the most intimate word for the dominant parent of the day, which was "Abba," meaning papa or daddy, used by both infants and adults. This says that God is like a strong, caring parent in relationship to us. Additionally, in Jesus' time the "father" was the "corporate personality," representing mother and, indeed, the whole family. That is not true today.

Today, the word "Father" clearly means male parent as distinct from female parent. Therefore, the Inclusive Version either translates *pater* (Father) as God or adds the word Mother when *pater* is used to identify God to make clear that the point is not the maleness of God, but rather the close, caring, parenthood of God. If one holds a theological position that God is indeed masculine in a way that God is not feminine, however those terms are defined culturally, then one would have difficulties with that rendering. Another use of the Inclusive Version is an attempt to move the title "Christ" (anointed one) away from an exclusively male meaning. When Jesus as an historical person is spoken of, masculine pronouns are always used. When a passage is speaking of Jesus as the Christ, this translation does not then use male pronouns for the Christ because Christ transcends gender categories.

Most simply put, I use Father/Mother together to remind us in today's language that Jesus was NOT saying that God was male rather than female, but rather God was like a caring parent.

For further explanation see the General Introduction to the Inclusive Version, and also see my book *Is It Okay to Call God Mother? Considering the Feminine Face of God* for a readable and thorough exposition of gender language and God.

22. Matthew 5:17-18.

23. Kittel, *Theological Dictionary*, VI:294.

24. Matthew11:11-12 .

25. Galatians 3:24.

26. John 16:12.

27. Hosea 6:6, cf. Amos 5:22, Micah 6:6.

28. Matthew 9:13, cf. 12:7.

29. Matt 9:2, Mark 2:5, Luke 5:20, 7:48.

30. *Against Marcion, Tertullian,* bk 1, 8 June 2008 <www.newadvent.org/ fathers/o312.htm.>.

31. Romans 12:2.

32. John 16:12-13 IV.

33. 2 Corinthians 3:18.

34. Luke 23:34.

35. Mark 11:17, italics mine.

36. John 3:36.

37. 2 Thessalonians 1:6-9.

38. Revelation 16:1.

Chapter 8: The Spirit Zone

1. For more on ordinary flow experiences, see Csikszenthmihalyi, *Finding Flow.*

2. Young, "The Zone."

3. I would more carefully define the "control" element of the spiritual state as the loss of control by our egoic self and the gaining of control by our True Self.

4. Wilber, *The Integral Vision,* 147.

5. The Baylor Religion Survey.

6. Weil, *The Natural Mind,* 23.

7. Ken Wilber and Jim Marion unfold these at length in their books. Marion speaks of them more in terms of permanently accessing these states so that they become stage-states, rather than temporary, passing modes of consciousness.

8 . In a follow-up to *The Cloud of Unknowing,* called *The Book of Privy Counseling,* the author writes of worshiping God with one's "substance," coming to rest in a "naked blind feeling of being," and ultimately finding thereby that God is one's being. *Wandering Joy: Meister Eckhart's Mystical Philosophy,* The Estate of Reiner Schurmann, 2001. Similarly, Meister Eckhart, the mystic genius, used the word "Isness"

for God. "Isness is so noble. No creature is so tiny that it lacks isness. What is God? God is." *The Cloud of Unknowing and the Book of Privy Counseling.* Ed. William Johnston, Author unknown, Doubleday, 1966, 156.

9.   John 10:30.

10.   Galatians 2:20.

11.   Psalms 34:8.

Chapter 9: Jesus in the Spirit Zone

1.   Luke 2:52.

2.   See my book *Is It Okay to Call God Mother?* for an examination of the meaning and significance of Jesus use of the word Abba and the use of gender-specific names for God.

3.   Kittel, *Theological Dictionary,* VIII;84.

4.   John 1:49.

5.   Mark 2:8.

6.   Luke 6:19.

7.   Mark 5:30, Luke 8:46.

8.   Isbouts, *Young Jesus,* 155.

9.   From the root word of "capacity" or "being able" or that which accomplishes something (Kittel, *Theological Dictionary,* II:284).

10.   Marion, *The Death of the Mythic God,* 133.

11.   Luke 9:1.

12.   Matthew 17:20.

13.   John 11:41-44.

14.   Mark 9:1.

15.   Mark 9:2.

16.   Luke 9:3-10. The word "departure" is *exodus* in Greek. Matthew 17:2.

17.   Deuteronomy 18:11.

18. Luke 4:42, 5:16, 6:12.

19. Borg, *Meeting Jesus, 35.*

20. John 7:38.

21. John 7:39.

22. Acts 2:17.

23. John 1:4. Italics mine.

24. John 6:35; 8:12.

25. Davies, *Jesus the Healer,* 151-152.

26. Gospel of Thomas, Saying 70.

27. Gospel of Thomas, Saying 77.

28. Gospel of Thomas, Saying 3b.

Chapter 10: The Early Church in the Spirit Zone

1. Acts 10:10.

2. Acts 11:5.

3. Thayer, *Greek English Lexicon,* 199.

4. Kittel, *Theological Dictionary,* II:450.

5. Acts 22:17.

6. Dunn, *Jesus and the Spirit,* 84.

7. Acts 10:11-16.

8. Acts 10:46.

9. Acts 4:31.

10. 2 Corinthians 12:2.

11. Acts 22:17-18.

12. Acts 19:6.

13. According to the Pew Forum on Religion and Public Life survey of the religious landscape, released in 2008, 9 percent of Protestant, 9 percent of Catholic, and 12 percent Eastern Orthodox pray weekly or more often in their personal prayer languages.

14. For the Barna survey, this included people who said they were charismatic or Pentecostal Christians, that they had been "filled with the Holy Spirit" and who said they believe that "the charismatic gifts, such as tongues and healing, are still valid and active today."

15. Barna Group, "Is American Christianity Turning Charismatic?"

16. Anderson, *An Introduction to Pentecostalism*, 11-12.

17. Acts 2:4.

18. 1 Corinthians 14:18.

19. *Glossa* is "language used by a particular people in distinction from that of other nations." Thayer, *Greek English Lexicon*, 118.

20. The word "glossolalia" is constructed from the Greek word γλωσσολαλιά, itself a compound of the words γλῶσσα (*glossa*, meaning "tongue" or "language") and λαλεῖν (*lalein*, "to talk").

21. 1 Corinthians 14:18-19.

22. Another reason is sociological—it has sometimes been a mark of spirituality for those in lower economic groups.

23. Stendahl, *Paul Among the Jews and Gentiles*, 120.

24. 1 Thessalonians 5:19-21.

25. 1 Corinthians 14:1, 4.

26. 1 Thessalonians 5:20.

27. I Corinthians 14:31.

28. Boring, *The Continuing Voice of Jesus*, 38, 84.

29. Ibid., 272. (italics his)

30. John 16:12-13.

31. 1 Corinthians 14:1.

32. 1 Corinthians 14:29, 1 John 4:1.

33. 1 Cor 14:3.

34. Acts 10:44-48.

35. Ehrman, *Lost Christianities*, 135-157.

36. Maslow, *Religions, Values, and Peak-Experiences*, 19.

Chapter 11: In the Spirt Zone Today

1. Ephesians 4:18.

2. Gospel of Thomas, Saying 13.

3. James, *The Varieties of Religious Experience*, 338.

4. Krister Stendahl, *Paul Among the Jews and Gentiles*, 122.

5. Wilber, *Integral Spirituality*, 196.

6. The statement is actually, "The devout Christian of the future will either be a 'mystic', one who has 'experienced' something, or [the person] will cease to be anything at all." (*Theological Investigations*. I: 7, p.15).

7. Wilber, *Integral Spirituality*, 5.

8. Wilber, *One Taste*, 21.

9. Wilber, *Grace and Grit*, 234.

10. Movement of Inner Spiritual Awareness.

11. Jim Marion uses the word "mystic" in a more nuanced way, saying, "What is important is that we become what Christian tradition calls *contemplatives*, that is, serious meditators. It is not necessary for us to become *mystics*, which is a contemplative with pronounced psychic abilities." (*Putting on the Mind of Christ*, 78.)

12. Wilber, *Grace and Grit*, 22.

13. Garnett, *Minister Commissioner Report*.

14. Psalms 42:1 NIV.

15. Gospel of Thomas, Saying 44.

16. Wilber, *A Brief History*, 60.

17. Borg, "A Portrait of Jesus."

18. Personal correspondence, May 8, 2008.

19. Wilber, *The Marriage of Sense and Soul*, 163, 166.

20. Borg, "Me & Jesus."

21. Maslow, *Religions, Values, and Peak-Experiences*, viii.

22.   Barrett, World Evangelization Research Center. Barrett projects that by 2020 the number of Pentecostal/charismatic Christians will reach 811 million.

23.   Emily Yoffe blog.

24.   It may be helpful to some to think of spirit guides in terms of the many voices of Self. Dialoguing with the many voices that are part of us, as in Dennis Genpo Merzel's *Big Mind—Big Heart,* can awaken something in us that appears to be similar to connecting with spiritual guides. In these practices one identifies and speaks in Gestalt two-chair fashion to parts of your own Self. One may also speculate that the voices of voice dialogue may, at times, be the spirit beings and guides that are also available to all. Perhaps it is a both/and.

25.   I learned from these dozen or so men and women that they were a part of a fourth-century monastic community. Some lived together in the monastery, while others lived in the nearby town. I did not know there were such groups that early, that they included women, or that some lived outside the community until I researched it later. They were in the throes of debating what to do about the Constantinian edict that required them to ascribe to the Nicene Council's beliefs or lose their property and favored status. Their focus was more Thomasinian and quite egalitarian in terms of women in leadership and affirming the feminine image of God. They saw that all slipping away.

26.   I use an Alex Grey Mindfold which allows you to easily open your eyes while no light comes in.

27.   I began with the Monroe Hemisync series and then moved to listening to the Holosync series. There are a number of different kinds of these CDs.

28.   John 7:38. The Greek word is "belly." This is also the area of the third and fourth energy centers.

29.   Hafiz (1315-1390), a Shi'ite Muslim, was a Persian lyric poet whose poetry today is incredibly popular. He, if not himself a Sufi, was greatly influenced by Sufism, the mystical or esoteric form of Islam. He was often opposed by orthodox Islamic clergy who did not want

him to have an Islamic burial. Ralph Waldo Emerson said, "Hafiz is a poet for poets." I have included six of his poems at various places in this book because of their beauty, spiritual depth, and display of mystical theology and experience from a religious tradition other than Christianity. In addition, in Ladinsky's renderings, they are simply fun!

30. Hafiz, *I Heard God Laughing*, 27.

Chapter 12: The Three Faces of God

1. *Time* magazine July 10, 2006.

2. John 14:28.

3. See Smith, *Is It Okay to Call God Mother*, 96, for a fuller discussion of this.

4. John 10:30 IV.

5. John 8:12.

6. John 14:6.

7. John 14:8 IV.

8. John 8:58.

9. Here is a compact, and probably dense, description of the three standpoints or faces of God in terms of integral philosophy. It is well worth absorbing until it becomes the beautiful and comprehensive way you understand the world.

   We can look at everything from three points of view. Ken Wilber calls these three perspectives the "Big Three" of I, You/We, and It. His full version is four perspectives or quadrants, but he often simplifies to three. (Wilber's fourth quadrant is plural It, or Its.) These three primary perspectives are embodied in almost all languages as 1st-person (I), 2nd-person (You), and 3rd-person (It) pronouns. We can look at any object or event from how we personally see it (1st-person), how others see it (2nd-person), and from the point of view of the objective facts about it (3rd-person). In linguistic terms, the 1st-person is the person speaking *as* him or her self—the subjective "I" realm. The 2nd-person is the person being spoken *to*—the intersubjective realm of "You" or "We." The 3rd-person is what is being spoken *about*—the objective "It" realm.

Or they can be called the subjective realm (I), the intersubjective realm (You/We), and the objective realm (It). Other descriptions of the Big Three spheres of evolution are the realms of self, culture, and nature, which are expressed by us in art, morals, and science. Classically, Plato called them the Beautiful, the Good, and the True. Beauty flows from our subjective self or "I." Goodness is what can happen between us or in the "We" sphere. Truth is found in the "It" of empirical facts. These are the three basic domains of reality that have been recognized by the world's greatest thinkers. We can observe each of these three foundational perspectives of humankind in action in the world.

Here are the Big Three again using each of these descriptors:

1st-person = I = subjective = self = art = The Beautiful

2nd-person = You = intersubjective = culture = morals = The Good

3rd-person = It = objective = nature = science = The True

We can view every moment, event, person, and object from an inner psychospiritual sensibility (1st-person), from an intersubjective cultural appreciation (2nd-person), and from an objective physical apprehension (3rd-person).

If this seems too complicated, then just remember the nine-word sentence which I previously offered:

Jesus Spoke About God, To God, And As God!

Here is one more illustration of the necessity of all three standpoints:

Let's say that you are going to church. That event can be seen from each of these three perspectives. From 1st-person subjective viewpoint, you are aware of why you are going, how you feel about it, and perhaps memories of previous churchgoing.

From the 2nd-person intersubjective perspective you can be aware of how your going to church affects others who are attending church with you. There is a particular person who likes you a lot. They will be pleased. There is another person who thinks you are wicked and they are unhappy to see you. The treasurer is overjoyed because you always write a big check.

From the 3rd-person objective perspective your body is taking signals from the neural network in your brain to get up, get going, and drive to church. Your old, rundown car gets you there, adding to the city's pollution level. You have to stop and get gas because, objectively speaking, cars will not run without gas. So going to church must be looked at from all three viewpoints to get the real picture, the full picture.

These same three perspectives can be seen in the way Jesus related to God. He spoke *about* God from the 3rd-person standpoint. He spoke *to* God from the 2nd-person viewpoint. And he spoke *as* God from the 1st-person perspective. He spoke *about* the "big" God, *to* the "close" God, and *as* the personification of God from within. These translate into the three primary dimensions of God, which I call the Infinite Face of God, the Intimate Face of God, and the Inner Face of God.

10. Romans 1:19-20.

11. CNN report, July 23, 2003 on study by Australian National University astronomers. http://www.cnn.com/2003/TECH/space/07/22/stars.survey.

12. 2 Chronicles 2:6.

13. Psalms 139.7-10.

14. Jeremiah 23:24.

15. Luke 19.40.

16. John 1.2-4 IV.

17. Gospel of Thomas, Saying 77.

18. Acts 17:28 IV.

19. Colossians 1:17 IV.

20. Colossians 3:11.

21. 1 Corinthians 15:28.

22. Ephesians 1:23 IV.

23. Ephesians 4:6 IV.

24. 1 John. 4:16.

25. Taylor, *The Luminous Web*, 74.

26. Tillich, *Systematic Theology Vol. 2*, 10

27. Andrew Cohen, http://www.andrewcohen.org/quote/?quote=148.

28. D' Espagnat, *On Physics and Philosophy*, 277.

29. http://blog.beliefnet.com/prayerplainandsimple/2009/07/praying-st-patricks-breastplate.html

30. Adopted from Jon Zuck, The Wild Things of God.

31. *EnlightenNext* magazine, March-May, 2009, 22.

32. Hopkins, 49.

33. Buber, *I and Thou.*

34. Luke 17:21, Gospel of Thomas, Saying 2.

35. Hafiz, *I Heard God Laughing*, 40.

36. Luke 9:24-25.

37. John 14:9, 28 IV.

38. DiPerna, *The Infinite Ladder*, 123.

39. John 10:34.

40. Hafiz, *The Gift*, 304.

41. Ralph Marcus, "Divine Names," 43-120.

42. In Jesus' day Abba included "mother" as father was the "corporate personality" of the Jewish household. See my book, *Is It Okay to Call God Mother?* for more on this.

43. Genesis 1:2.

44. Joel 2:28.

45. Acts 2:16.

46. The priesthood was a reversion to an earlier and lower stage of development and has been a constant source of distortion of the message of Jesus, which was that we do not need anyone to mediate between

God and us. The earliest message of the New Testament was that we were all priests. But given time, that was discarded and the false division of lay people and priests came into being. The laity (*laos* in Greek) originally meant all the people of God. Now it came to mean the ordinary people of God minus the "special" people of God called "priests" (or "ministers" if you are Protestant).

47. Paraphrasing Ken Wilber, *A Sociable God*, 80.

48. From the currently unpublished Penguin book, *A Year with Hafiz, Daily Contemplations*. Copyright 2010 by Daniel Ladinsky. Used by permission.

49. This last sentence is from Wilber, *A Brief History of Everything*, 201.

50. Acts 17:28.

51. Matthew 28:20.

52. Matthew 5:14.

53. Wittgenstein, *Philosophical Investigations*, 184.

Chapter 13: Owning Our Divinity

1. Josephus, *Against Apion*.

2. Mark 11:17.

3. Paul Tillich, *The New Being*, 55.

4. Isaiah 7:14, 8:8, Matthew 1:23.

5. Colossians 1:27.

6. Wilber, *Sex Ecology, Spirituality*, 371.

7. Marion, *The Death of the Mythic God*, 29.

8. Genesis 1:26. Scholars consider the "let us" a literary device called the "plural of majesty," as when Queen Elizabeth might say, "We are presiding from the throne now."

9. Genesis 3:5.

10. Genesis 3:22.

11. Matthew 5:14.

12. John 9:5.

13. See Appendix E for a detailed look at this passage.

14. John 14:12.

15. Matthew 25:40.

16. Hebrews 2:17.

17. John 17:20, 22 IV.

18. Pagels, *The Gnostic Gospels*, 68.

19. Marion, *Putting on the Mind of Christ*, 8-9, 13.

20. My understanding differs from the Orthodox view in two important ways. The Orthodox view makes a clear distinction between what they call God's "energies" and God's "essence" in order, they believe, to maintain a distance between their view and pantheism. Furthermore, the Orthodox view is placed entirely in the future and is not an already present reality that simply needs to be realized and manifested. I find no biblical basis for either distinction.

21. Here is a fuller explanation of the Greek Orthodox idea of theosis from Bishop Kallistos Ware:

> The aim of the Christian life, which Seraphim described as the acquisition of the Holy Spirit of God, can equally well be defined in terms of deification. Basil described man as a creature who has received the order to become a god; and Athanasius, as we know, said that God became man that man might become god. "In my kingdom, said Christ, I shall be God with you as gods" (Canon for Matins of Holy Thursday, Ode 4, Troparion 3). Such, according to the teaching of the Orthodox Church, is the final goal at which every Christian must aim: to become god, to attain *theosis*, "deification" or "divinization." For Orthodoxy man's salvation and redemption mean his deification.
>
> Behind the doctrine of deification there lies the idea of man made according to the image and likeness of God the Holy Trinity. "May they all be one," Christ prayed at the Last Supper; "As Thou, Father, art in me and I in Thee, so also may they be in

us" (John 17:21). Just as the three persons of the Trinity "dwell" in one another in an unceasing movement of love, so man, made in the image of the Trinity, is called to "dwell" in the Trinitarian God. Christ prays that we may share in the life of the Trinity, in the movement of love which passes between the divine persons; He prays that we may be taken up into the Godhead. The saints, as Maximus the Confessor put it, are those who express the Holy Trinity in themselves. This idea of a personal and organic union between God and man — God dwelling in us, and we in Him—is a constant theme in Saint John's Gospel; it is also a constant theme in the Epistles of Saint Paul, who sees the Christian life above all else as a life 'in Christ.' The same idea recurs in the famous text: "Through these promises you may become partakers of the divine nature" (2 Peter 1:4). It is important to keep this New Testament background in mind. The Orthodox doctrine of deification, so far from being unscriptural (as is sometimes thought), has a solid Biblical basis, not only in 2 Peter, but in Paul and the Fourth Gospel.

The idea of deification must always be understood in the light of the distinction between God's essence and His energies. Union with God means union with the divine energies, not the divine essence: the Orthodox Church, while speaking of deification and union, rejects all forms of pantheism.

—Excerpts from the Orthodox Church by Bishop Kallistos Ware. Part II: Faith and Worship http://www.synaxis.org/OrthodoxChurchWorship.htm

22. Athanasius, *On the Incarnation*, 39.

23. Maximus, *The Philokalia*, 178.

24. Aquinas, *Summa Theologica*, 1.15.2.

25. Fox, *Cosmic Christ*, 75.

26. John 10:30 IV.

27. John 10:34-36 IV.

28. Psalms 82:6. John Dominic Crossan considers Psalm 82 to be "the single most important text in the entire Christian Bible." He says the

instructions "give justice to the weak and the orphan: maintain the right of the lowly and the destitute; rescue the weak and the needy; deliver them from the hand of the wicked" is God's job description. These wicked gods will be dethroned because they were unjust and did not act like God. (*The Birth of Christianity* [New York: HarperOne, 1998] 575.) I think this may well be the most important verse in the Bible for one more reason: Jesus, perhaps the Spirit of Jesus through the early church prophets, quoted these words, applying them to himself and to the corrupt religious leaders.

The theme of "you are all gods" does not seem to be a prominent one in the Bible because it was beyond the capacity of its writers, redactors, interpreters, and collectors to grasp. However, it is amazing that it "leaked" through as often as it did as seen in the pointed and profound biblical passages reviewed in this chapter.

29. Exodus 7:1. The word "like" is in the NRSV translation but not in the Hebrew.

30. Whatever "divinity" means, the point is that Jesus is saying we are exactly like him. If he is divine, then we are divine. Jesus replies in the metaphor of father and son—"I am God's son." If you have a "low Christology," meaning Jesus is less than divine, then you may see Jesus as saying, "Since I am God's representative or God's son, then so are you." If you have a "high Christology" as I do, then it is about divinity, not representation or family resemblance. In high Christology, sonship is about offspring being, in essence, the same as the parent. The word "divinity" is still only a metaphor for God, and who can really define God. We are always left only with arrows that point to reality, not the reality itself, since God's reality does not lend itself to mere words.

31. Lewis, *Mere Christianity,* 174-175.

32. Wilber, *Simple Feeling,* 105.

33. 1 John 3:2.

34. Galatians 2:20.

35. 2 Peter 1:4. "To share in the very being of God." NEB. This beautiful statement from the New Testament about participating in the divine

nature is encased in the Roman Catholic Mass, which is repeated thousands of times every day to the faithful throughout the world: "O God who so wonderfully didst give dignity to human nature, and didst more wonderfully restore it, grant through the mysteries of this water and wine we may partake of His Divinity Who partook of our humanity, Jesus Christ, Thy Son." (Offertory Prayer, Roman Catholic Mass). Ordinary of the Holy Sacrifice of the Mass—The Offertory Prayer, http://www.dailycatholic.org/holymas3.htm.

36.   John 14:9,14:28, and 10:34.

37.   2 Corinthians 3:18, italics mine.

38.   Colossians 1:15 IV

39.   Romans 8:17.

40.   Gospel of Thomas, Saying 108.

41.   Christensen, *Partakers of the Divine Nature*, 23.

42.   Irenaeus, *Against Heresies*, 1:525.

43.   St. Athanasius, De inc. 54,3: *Patrologia Graeca* 25, 192B.

44.   Yannaras, *The Elements of Faith*, 17.

45.   Hafiz, *The Gift*, 217.

Chapter 14: Religion on the Escalator

1.   McIntosh, *Integral Consciousness*, 92.

2.   See *Spiritual, But Not Religious*, Fuller.

3.   Wilber, *Integral Spirituality*, 195.

4.   Ibid., 192.

5.   McIntosh, *Integral Consciousness*, 117.

6.   Quoted in *National Catholic Reporter*, November 25, 2005.

7.   Ken Wilber, *One Taste*, 27.

8.   John 16:12-13 IV.

Chapter 15: Integral Church

1. Pagels, *Beyond Belief,* 173-4.

2. See Jenkins, *Jesus Wars.*

3. See Borg, *The First Paul.*

4. See Laszlo, *Science and the Akashic Field.*

5. Marcus J. Borg, Portrait of Jesus, 4 March 2008. http://www.aportraitofjesus.org/gospels.shtml.

6. There are a number of extra biblical accounts of Jesus' life which appear to be channeled works such as *Edgar Cayce's Story of Jesus.* *Urantia* is another such book that includes an account of Jesus' life in Part IV, the last 700 pages. This section claims to be a year-by-year detailed account of Jesus' childhood, youth, and adulthood. Published in 1955 and 2,100 pages long, it appears to be compiled from various sources. It should be read in a discerning way, as should any book making claims about the spiritual life, including the Bible. Its sometimes strange language and dense metaphors are best understood in their archetypal context. Part IV appears to be perhaps, in some ways, similar at times to recent scholarship and the integral viewpoint of this book. It is available free online at The Urantia Book Online along with reader comments.

7. Barbara Brown Taylor, *Leaving Church: A Memoir of Faith* (New York: HarperCollins, 2006), 38.

8. Clayton, *In Whom We Live and Move and Have Our Being,* an in-depth theological discussion of varieties of panentheism.

9. From personal conversation, 2007.

10. From Colossians 1:15–20, using the Inclusive Version which uses the word "Christ" instead of the pronoun "he," emphasizing "the supremacy of Christ," which is also the title of this section in the NRSV.

11. Davies, *Jesus the Healer,* 151.

12. John 14:6 IV

13. Colossians 1:17 IV.

14. Ten imagoes by Alex Grey—*Cosmic Christ, Sophia, Transfiguration, Holy Fire, Praying, Spiritual Energy Body, Psychic Energy Body, Theologue, Void,* and *Oversoul*—are among the 240 images of Jesus from around the world in Broadway Church's Faces of Jesus gallery. Grey's images can be accessed at http://www.alexgrey.com/posters. html.

15. McIntosh, *Integral Consciousness,* 74.

16. Colossians 1:27.

17. James Dunn's conclusion in his book, *Did the First Christians Worship Jesus?,* is a qualified "no" because God and Jesus were not considered identical. He says that worship of God is enabled by Jesus even though at times it appears that Jesus is worshipped as God. This leaves us with a rather unsatisfactory reservation to our own worship of Jesus which does echo early Christian practice. An understanding of the Infinite, Intimate, and Inner faces of God is an elegant and biblically-informed solution to the question he raises. The worship of (intimate) Jesus is different than the worship of (infinite) God because they are two different perspectives, even as both are worship of God.

18. Cavarnos, "The Functions of Icons" http://www.orthodoxinfo.com/ general/icon_function.aspx.

19. 2 Corinthians 3:18.

20. Lewis, *The Weight of Glory,* 14-15.

21. Fox, *One River.*

22. Seventy-nine percent of Catholics, 57 percent of evangelicals, and 83 percent of mainline Christians believe that there are other paths to God. http://pewforum.org/.

23. See "The Apostle Paul and the Introspective Conscience of the West" in Stendahl's *Paul Among Jews and Gentiles,* 78f.

24. Linn, *Simple Ways to Pray,* 26.

25. For these passages and a fuller explanation, see my booklet, *Hell? No! A Bible study on why no one will be left behind,* available from www. broadwaychurch-kc.org.

26. Luke 17:21.

27. Gospel of Thomas, Saying 3.

28. The enlightenment work of Andrew Cohen is a welcomed exception to the non-communal approach.

29. Luke 4:18-19 IV.

30. From John Cobb, *The Progressive Christian,* Vol 182, Issue 5, 12-14.

31. See his *A New Kind of Christianity.*

32. Fuller, *Spiritual but not Religious,* 4.

33. Wilber, *Boomeritis,* 334-335.

34. Wilber, *One Taste,* 92.

35. Marion, *The Death of the Mythic God,* 146-147.

Chapter 16: "The Shadow Knows"

1. Luke 6:41–42.

2. Matthew 6:34.

3. Wilber, *One Taste,*138-9.

4. Williamson, *A Return to Love,* 59.

5. Lamott, *Bird by Bird,* 22.

Chapter 17: Taking Care of Your Self

1. Kegan, *Immunity to Change,* 1. These researchers go on to outline an effective, although not simple, system for individual and organization change.

2. Mark 12:30. The Integral Institute Life Practice materials are very helpful and include body, mind, shadow, and spirit. www.intregralin-stitue.org.

3. Whitman, *Leaves of Grass,* 109.

4. Wilber, *The Integral Vision,* 179.

5. Pierre Teilhard de Chardin's original statement was, "We are not

human beings having a spiritual experience; we are spiritual beings having a human experience."

6. John 8:58.

7. John 13:3.

8. Pew survey.

9. Grof, *The Ultimate Journey*, 2006.

10. Hafiz, *The Gift*, 73.

11. Matthew 6:6 IV.

12. Keating, *Open Mind, Open Heart*, 34.

13. Bourgeault, *Centering Prayer*, 9.

14. Jesus said, "Those who seek should not stop seeking until they find. When they find, they will be disturbed. When they are disturbed, they will be amazed, and reign over all." Gospel of Thomas, Saying 2.

15. 1 Corinthians 14:30-31. While the context here is the gathering of the community in worship, it also applies to our personal prayer life.

16. Ensley, *Visions*, 13, 14, 41.

17. 1 Corinthians 14:15.

18. Hafiz, *The Gift*, 32.

19. Luke 6:6 IV.

20. Matthew 4:4

21. There are several versions available such as Holosync and Hemisync.

22. Available from AlexGrey.com.

23. Emily Yoffe, Wednesday, December 3, 2008, http://www.slate.com/id/2205150/pagenum/all/#p2.

24. Hebrews 12:1. I am aware there are other, 3rd-person, perspectives in understanding the phenomena of guides. Once we open up the possibility of the non-physical spiritual universe, all sorts of things may be possible. Some believe these guides are higher parts of ourselves. Others see them as personifications of archetypes or energy field information that has accumulated over the centuries. More

recently, some consider quantum theories about parallel universes to be a potential explanation of guide phenomena. Those are all legitimate 3rd-person standpoint ("upper right quadrant" in integral speak) inquiries. I report from my 1st-person subjective viewpoint that I have quite specific auditory, imaginal, and kinesthetic experiences which I interpret as spiritual guides on the basis of Jesus' Transfiguration and the extensive experience of both mystics and common folk today and down through the centuries. Everything can and should be viewed from all three (1st-, 2nd-, and 3rd-person) standpoints to see the whole picture. All three standpoints are true and partial.

25.   Psalm 46:10.

26.   Gospel of Thomas, Saying 3.

27.   2 Peter 1:4.

28.   Doidge, *The Brain That Changes Itself.*

29.   Romans 12:2.

30.   Marion, *The Death of the Mythic God,* 166-167.

31.   Gospel of Thomas, Saying 6.

Chapter 18: The Worshipping Community

1.   Shortly after I finished seminary I received a letter from my much admired theology professor Morris Ashcraft. He was on sabbatical in England studying Charles Williams, a British poet, novelist, theologian, literary critic, and Christian mystic of the early twentieth century. Knowing my interest in small groups and the charismatic movement, Morris recommended Williams to me and said that Williams considered Paul a "mystic with a community." I loved the phrase and since then it has characterized the Christian life for me. The inspiration for our faith, Jesus, was a mystic with an intentional community of those who were also learning to be mystics in the company of the committed.

2.   Andrew Cohen, Quote of the Week, April 10, 2008. http://www.

andrewcohen.org/quote/?quote=287.

3. "The Guru & the Pandit" *EnlightenNext* magazine, Issue 42. Dec. 2008-Feb. 2009.

4. Borg, *The Heart of Christianity*, 160.

5. Thirty years ago I stopped calling my time in the worship service a "sermon." The phrases "dull as a sermon" and "Don't preach at me," are familiar because that's what people think of when they hear the word "sermon." Instead, at Broadway, we call it "the teaching." This also puts on me the responsibility of seeing that I am actually teaching something important to the congregation, and not just giving a "nice, little talk." They see it as looking forward to learning something they haven't heard before.

6. Davies, *Jesus the Healer*, 124.

7. Used by permission. Mark is a well-known Christian composer, Dove Award winner, and former member of Broadway Church. His music is available on his website, www.markhayes.com.

8. Public domain.

9. Words © 2010 Paul R. Smith. May be used without permission as long as accompanied by Words by Paul R. Smith.

10. Words © 2010 Jann Aldredge-Clanton. Used by permission. Sung to the tune of any 8.8.8.8. hymn such as "O Bless the Gifts" in the Methodist Celebration Hymnal. Author may be contacted at www.jannaldredgeclanton.com.

11. Luke 4:18 KJV.

12. Hunt, *Infinite Mind*, 310.

13. www.markhayes.com.

Chapter 19: Jesus' Most Astonishing Statement

1. Matthew 5:14.

2. Matthew 5:1-2.

3. Luke 6:17-20.

4. Luke 10:1, Acts 1:15, 1 Corinthians 15:6.

5. Acts 11:26.

6. John 9:5.

7. Hafiz, *I Heard God Laughing*, 1.

8. Matthew 5:15-16, IV.

Bibliography

* Highly Recommended

Anderson, Allan. *An Introduction to Pentecostalism: Global Charismatic Christianity*. Cambridge: Cambridge University Press, 2004.

Aquinas, St. Thomas, *Summa Theologica*. trans. from Josef Pieper, *The Silence of Saint Thomas*: Chicago: Henry Regnery, 1966.

Ardagh, Arjuna. *The Translucent Revolution: How People Just like You Are Waking Up and Changing the World*. Novato: New World Library, 2005.

Armstrong, Karen. *The Case for God*. New York: Alfred A. Knopf, 2009.

Athanasius. *On the Incarnation*. Scotts Valley: CreateSpace, 2007.

Augustine of Hippo. *The City of God*. Trans. Henry Bettenson. New York: Penguin Classics, 2003.

Barna Group. "Is American Christianity Turning Charismatic?" http://www.barna.org/FlexPage.aspx?Page=BarnaUpdateNarrowPreview&BarnaUpdateID=287.

Barclay, William. *Spiritual Autobiography*. Grand Rapids, MI: Eerdmans, 1975.

Barrett, David. *The Encyclopedia of Christianity*. New York: Oxford University Press, 2002. World Evangelization Research Center, June 6, 2008 < http://www.gem-werc.org/.

Baylor Religion Survey. 2006, http://www.baylor.edu/content/services/document.php/33304.pdf.

Beck, Don, and Christopher Cowen. *Spiral Dynamics: Mastering Values, Leadership and Change*. Hoboken, NJ: Wiley-Blackwell, 2005.

Blacker, Hal. "A Spirituality that Transforms," *Ken Wilber Online*. http://wilber.shambhala.com/html/misc/spthtr.cfm/.

Borg, Marcus J. *A Portrait of Jesus,* http://www.aportraitofjesus.org/borg.shtml.*

_____. "Me & Jesus: The Journey Home: An Odyssey." *The Fourth R* Volume 6:4, http://westarinstitute.org/Periodicals/4R_Articles/borg_bio.html.*

_____. *Meeting Jesus Again for the First Time.* San Francisco, CA: HarperSanFrancisco. 1994.*

_____. *Reading the Bible Again for the First Time.* San Francisco, CA: HarperSanFrancisco, 2001.*

_____. *The God We Never Knew.* San Francisco, CA: HarperSanFrancisco, 1997.*

_____. *The Heart of Christianity.* San Francisco, CA: HarperSanFrancisco, 2003.*

Borg, Marcus J. and John Dominic Crossan. *The First Paul: Reclaiming the Radical Visionary Behind the Church's Conservative Icon.* New York: HarperOne, 2009.*

Boring, Eugene M. *The Continuing Voice of Jesus: Christian Prophecy and the Gospel Tradition.* Louisville, KY: Westminster/John Knox, 1991.

Bourgeault, Cynthia. *Centering Prayer and Inner Awakening.* Lanham, MD: Crowley Publications, 2004.*

Bradley, Sculley, ed. *The American Tradition in Literature.* New York: Grossett & Dunlap, 1974.

Brock, Rita Nakashima and Rebecca Ann Parker. *Saving Paradise: How Christianity Traded Love of this World for Crucifixion and Empire.* Boston: Beacon, 2008.*

Buber, Marin. trans, Walter Kaufman. *I and Thou.* New York: Simon & Schuster, 1996.

Caird, G.B. *New Testament Theology.* Oxford: Oxford University Press, 1995.

_____. *A Commentary on the Revelation of St. John The Divine.* London: A & C Black, 1984.

Campolo, Tony, and Mary Albert Darling. *Connecting Like Jesus: Practices for Healing, Teaching, and Preaching.* San Francisco: Jossey-Bass, 2010.

Christensen, Michael J. and Jeffery A. Wittung, eds. *Partakers of the Divine Nature: The History and Development of Deification in the Christian Traditions.* Grand Rapids, MI: Baker Academic, 2007.

Clayton, Philip and Arthur Peacocke, eds. *In Whom We Live and Move and Have Our Being: Panentheistic Reflections on God's Presence in a Scientific World.* Grand Rapids, MI: Eerdmans, 2004.

Collinge, William. *Subtle Energy: Awakening to the unseen forces in our lives.* New York: Warner Books, 1998

Combs, Allan. *Consciousness Explained Better: Towards an Integral Understanding of the Multifaceted Nature of Consciousness.* St. Paul, MN: Paragon House, 2009.

Csikszentmihaly, Mihaly. *Finding Flow: The Psychology of Engagement with Everyday Life.* New York: Basic Books, 1997.

_____. *Flow: The Psychology of Optimal Experience.* New York: Harper Perennial. 1990.

Davies, Stevan L. *Jesus the Healer: Possession, Trance and the Origins of Christianity.* New York: Continuum, 1995.*

d'Espagnat, Bernard. *On Physics and Philosophy.* Princeton: Princeton University Press, 2006

DiPerna, Dustin and Kate Wilson, *The Infinite Ladder: An Introduction to Integral Religious Studies,* 2007, http://www.infiniteladder.com/drpi/books_files/drpi_preview.pdf*

Doidge, Norman. *The Brain That Changes Itself: Stories of Personal Triumph from the Frontiers of Brain Science.* New York: Penguin Group, 2007.

Dowd, Michael. *Thank God for Evolution.* New York: Viking 2007.

Dunn, James D. G. *Jesus and the Spirit: A Study of the Religious and Charismatic Experience of Jesus and the First Christians as Reflected in the New Testament.* London: SCM Press, 1975.

_____. *Did the First Christians Worship Jesus? The New Testament Evidence.* Louisville, KY: Westminster John Knox Press, 2010.

Dyckman, Katherine Marie and L. Patrick Carroll. *Inviting the Mystic, Supporting the Prophet: An Introduction to Spiritual Direction.* New

York: Paulist Press. 1981.

Ehrman, Bart D. *Lost Christianities: The Battle for Scripture and the Faith We Never Knew*. New York: Oxford Press, 2003.*

Ensley, Eddie. *Visions: The Soul's Path to the Sacred*. Chicago: Loyola Press, 2000.*

Finlan, Stephan and Vladimir Kharlamove, eds. *Theosis: Deification in Christian Theology*. Eugene: Pickwick, 2006.

Fox, Matthew. *A New Reformation*. Rochester, NY: Inner Traditions, 2006.

_____. *Creation Spirituality*. San Francisco: HarperSanFrancisco, 1991.

_____. *One River, Many Wells*. New York: Penguin, 2000.

_____. *The Coming of the Cosmic Christ*. New York: HarperCollins, 1988.*

Fuller, Robert C. *Spiritual, But Not Religious* New York: Oxford University Press, 2001.

Funk, Robert W., Roy W. Hoover, and The Jesus Seminar, *The Five Gospels: What Did Jesus Really Say?* San Francisco: HarperSanFrancisco, 1993.

Gold, Victor, Thomas Hoyt, Sharon Ringe, Susan Thistlethwaite, Burton Throckmorton, and Barbara Withers, eds., *The New Testament and Psalms: An Inclusive Version*. New York: Oxford University Press, 1995.

Grey, Alex. *Art Psalms*. New York: CoSm Press, 2008.

_____. *Sacred Mirrors: The Visionary Art of Alex Grey*. Rochester, NY: Inner Traditions, 1990.

Grof, Stanislav. *The Ultimate Journey: Consciousness and the Mystery of Death*. Ben Lomond: MAPS, 2006.

Hafiz. *I Heard God Laughing*, trans. Daniel Ladinsky. New York: Penguin Compass, 2006.*

_____. *Love Poems from God, Twelve Sacred Voices from the East and West*, trans. Daniel Ladinsky. New York: Penguin Compass, 2002.

_____. *The Gift*, trans. Daniel Ladinsky. New York: Penguin Compass, 1999.*

Harrison, Everett, ed. *Dictionary of Theology*. Grand Rapids, MI: Baker, 1960.

Harmless, William. *Mystics.* Oxford: Oxford University Press, 2008.

Harvey, Andrew. *The Direct Path: Creating a Journey to the Divine Using the World's Mystical Traditions.* New York: Broadway Books, 2000.

_____. *The Son of Man: The Mystical Path to Christ.* New York: Tarcher/ Putnam, 1999.*

Helminiak, Daniel A. *The Transcended Christian: Spiritual Lessons for the Twenty-first Century.* New York: Alyson Books, 2007.

Henson, John. *Good As New: A Radical Retelling of Scriptures.* Hampshire, U.K.: O-Books, 2004.

Herzog, William R. *Parables as Subversive Speech: Jesus as Pedagogue of the Oppressed.* Louisville, KY: Westminster, 1994.

Hopkins, Gerard Manley and Catherine Phillips. *The Major Works.* New York: Oxford University Press, 2002.

Hunt, Valerie V. *Infinite Mind: Science of the Human Vibrations of Consciousness.* Malibu, CA: Malibu Publishing, 1996.*

Integral Institute. http://www.integralinstitute.org/.

Irenaeus, *Against Heresies* 5, pref: in *Anti-Nicene Fathers*, 10 vols. A. Roberts and J. Donaldson, Buffalo: Christian Literature 1885-96, reprinted, Peabody: Hendrickson, 1994

Isbouts, Jean-Pierre. *Young Jesus: Restoring the "Lost Years" of a Social Activist and Religious Dissident.* New York: Sterling, 2008.

James, William. *The Varieties of Religious Experience.* BiblioBazaar, 1902.

Jaoudi, Maria. *Christian Mysticism, East and West.* New York: Paulist Press, 1998.

Jenkins, Philip. *Jesus Wars: How Four Patriarchs, Three Queens, and Two Emperors Decided What Christians Would Believe for the Next 1,500 Years.* New York: HarperOne, 2010.

Johnston, William. *The Mirror Mind: Zen-Christian Dialogue.* Bronx: Fordham University Press, 1990.

Johnston, William. trans. *The Cloud of Unknowing: And The Book of Privy Counseling.* New York: Image Doubleday 1996.

Josephus. *The Life. Against Apion.* London: Cambridge, 1966.

Kärkkäimen, Veli-Matti. *One With God.* Collegeville, PA: Liturgical Press, 2004.

Keating, Daniel A. *Deification and Grace.* Naples, FL:Sapientia Press, 2007.

Keating, Thomas. *Open Mind, Open Heart.* New York: Continuum, 2006.

Kegan, Robert and Lisa Laskow Lahey. *Immunity to Change: How to Overcome It and Unlock the Potential in Yourself and Your Organization.* Boston: Harvard Business Press, 2009.

Kittel, Gerhard, and Gerhard Friedrich, eds., Geoffrey W. Bromiley, trans. *Theological Dictionary of the New Testament.* Grand Rapids, MI: Eerdmans, 1964

LaChance, Albert. *The Modern Christian Mystic: Finding the Unitive Presence of God.* Berkeley: North Atlantic Books, 2007.

Lamott, Ann. *Bird by Bird.* New York: Pantheon Books, 1994.

Laszlo, Ervin. *Science and the Akashic Field: An Integral Theory of Everything.* Rochester, NY: Inner Traditions, 2007.

Lewis, C. S. *Mere Christianity.* New York: Macmillan Company, 1952.

_____. *The Weight of Glory.* New York: Macmillan Company, 1949.

Linn, Matthew, Sheila, and Dennis. *Good Goats: Healing our Image of God.* New York: Paulist Press, 1994.*

_____. *Simple Ways to Pray for Healing.* New York: Paulist Press, 1998.*

_____. *Understanding Difficult Scriptures in a Healing Way.* New York: Paulist Press, 2001.*

Marcus, Ralph. "Divine Names and Attributes in Hellenistic Jewish Literature," *Proceedings of the American Academy for Jewish Research.* 1931-32.

Marion, Jim. *Putting on the Mind of Christ: The Inner Work of Christian Spirituality.* Charlottesville, VA: Hampton Roads, 2000.*

_____. *The Death of the Mythic God.* Charlottesville, VA: Hampton Roads, 2004.*

Maslow, Abraham H. *Religions, Values, and Peak-Experiences*. New York: Penguin Compass, 1976.

Maximus the Confessor, *The Philokalia: A Second Volume of Selected Writing*, Belmont: Institute for Byzantine and Modern Greek Studies, 2008.

McLaren, Brian D. *A New Kind of Christianity*. New York: HarperOne, 2010.

McIntosh, Steve. *Integral Consciousness and the Future of Evolution*. St. Paul, MN: Paragon House, 2007.

Merton, Thomas. *New Seeds of Contemplation*. New York: New Directions, 1962.

Merzel, Dennis Genpo. *Big Mind—Big Heart: Finding Your Way*. Salt Lake City, UT: Big Mind Publishing, 2007.

Minister Commissioner Report on the 215th PC(USA) General Assembly to the Presbytery of East Tennessee. June 17, 2003 Rev. David Garnett, http://www.witherspoonsociety.org/03-may/mystics.

Movement of Spiritual Inner Awareness, http://www.msiacanada.org/devotionmsia.html.

Nadeau, Robert and Menas Kafatos. *The Non-local Universe: The New Physics and Matter of the Mind*. New York: Oxford University Press, 1999.

Nelson-Pallmeyer, Jack. *Is Religion Killing Us? Violence in the Bible and the Quran*. Harrisburg, PA: Trinity Press International, 2003.

_____. *Jesus Against Christianity: Reclaiming the Missing Jesus*. Harrisburg, PA: Trinity Press International, 2001.*

Pagels, Elaine. *Beyond Belief: The Secret Gospel of Thomas*. New York: Random House, 2005.*

_____. *The Gnostic Gospels*. New York: Random House, 1979.

Pew Survey. Religion in America, http://pewforum.org/.

Sahajananda, John Martin. *You Are the Light*. New York: O Books, 2003.*

Sanguin, Bruce. *The Emerging Church: A Model for Change and a Map for Renewal*. Kelowna, BC, Canada: CopperHouse, 2008.

Schaef, Anne Wilson. *Living in Process: Basic Truths for Living the Path of the Soul.* New York: Ballantine Wellspring, 1999.

Schlitz, Marilyn Mandala, Tina Amorok, Cassandra Vieten, and Robert A.F. Thurman. *Living Deeply: The Art & Science of Transformation in Everyday Life.* Oakland: New Harbinger Publications, 2008.

Schmidt, Frederick W. ed. *The Changing Face of God.* Harrisburg: Morehouse, 2000.

Schwartzentruber, Michael. ed., *The Emerging Christian Way.* Kelowna, BC, Canada: CopperHouse, 2006.

Smith, Paul R. *Is It Okay to Call God Mother? Considering the Feminine Face of God.* Peabody, MA: Hendrickson, 1993.*

_____. *Hell? No! A Bible study on why no one will be left behind.* Kansas City: Broadway Church, 2006. Booklet may be ordered from www.broadwaychurch-kc.org.*

Smoley, Richard. *Inner Christianity.* Boston: Shambhala, 2002.

Spiral Dynamics. http://www.spiraldynamics.org/Graves/colors.htm.

Spong, John Shelby. *Why Christianity Must Change or Die.* San Francisco: HarperSanFrancisco, 1998.

Stark, Rodney. *The Rise of Christianity.* San Francisco: HarperSanFrancisco, 1996.

Stendahl, Krister. *Paul Among Jews and Gentiles.* Philadelphia: Fortress, 1976.

_____. *Energy for Life: Reflections on a Theme: "Come, Holy Spirit—Renew the Whole Creation."* Brewster, MA: Paraclete Press. 1999.

Talbot, Michael. *The Holographic Universe.* New York: HarperCollins, 1991.

Taussig, Hal. *A New Spiritual Home: Progressive Christianity at the Grass Roots.* Santa Rosa, CA: Polebridge, 2006.

Taylor, Barbara Brown. *The Luminous Web: Essay on Science and Religion.,* Cambridge, MA: Cowley Publications, 2000.

Tertullian. *Against Marcion,* bk 1, www.newadvent.org/fathers/o312.htm.

Thayer, Joseph. *Greek-English Lexicon of the New Testament.* New York: Harper & Brothers, 1889.

Tillich, Paul. *The New Being*. New York: Charles Scribner's Sons, 1955.

_____. *Systematic Theology, Vol. 2*. Chicago: University of Chicago Press, 1975.

Tolle, Eckhart. *A New Earth: Awakening to Your Life's Purpose*. New York: Penguin Group, 2006.

Vaughan, Curtis. *Ephesians*. Grand Rapids, MI: Zondervan, 1972.

Visser, Frank. *Ken Wilber: Thought as Passion*. Albany, NY: State University of New York Press, 2003.

Ware, Bishop Kallistos. The Orthodox Church, http://www.synaxis.org/OrthodoxChurchWorship.htm.

Watts, Isaac. *Watt's Works*. New York: AMS Press, 1971.

Weil, Andrew. *The Natural Mind*. Boston: Houghton Mifflin, 1972.

Whitman, Walt. *Leaves of Grass*. New York: Pocket Books, 2006.

Wilber, Ken. http://kenwilber.com/home/landing/index.html.

_____. *A Brief History of Everything*. Boston: Shambhala, 1996

_____. *A Sociable God*. Boston & London: Shambhala, 2005.

_____. *Boomeritis: A Novel That Will Set You Free*. Boston: Shambhala, 2002.

_____. *Grace and Grit: Spirituality and Healing in the Life of Treya Killam Wilber*. Boston: Shambhala, 1991.*

_____. *Integral Life Practice: A 21st-Century Blueprint for Physical Health, Emotional Balance, Mental Clarity, and Spiritual Awakening* with Terry Patten, Adam Leonard, and Marco Morelli. Boston: Shambhala, 2008.

_____. *Integral Spirituality: A Startling New Role for Religion in the Modern and Postmodern World*. Boston: Shambhala, 2006.

_____. *No Boundary: Eastern and Western Approaches to Personal Growth*. Boston: Shambhala, 1979.

_____. *One Taste: Daily Reflections on Integral Spirituality*. Boston: Shambhala, 2000.*

_____. *Sex, Ecology, Spirituality: The Spirit of Evolution*. Boston: Shambhala, 2nd rev. ed. 2000.

_____. *The Eye of Spirit*. Boston: Shambhala, 1998.

_____. *The Integral Vision: A Very Short Introduction to the Revolutionary Integral Approach to Life, God, the Universe, and Everything*. Boston: Shambhala, 2007.*

_____. *The Marriage of Sense and Soul: Integrating Science and Religion*. New York: Random House. 1999.

_____. *The Simple Feeling of Being: Visionary, Spiritual, and Poetic Writings*. Boston: Shambhala, 2004.*

Williamson, Marianne. *A Return to Love: Reflections on the Principles of "A Course in Miracles."* New York: HarperCollins, 1992.

Wittgenstein, Ludwig. *Philosophical Investigations*. Saddle River, NJ: Prentice Hall, 1973.

Wombacher, Michael. *11 Days at the Edge*. Findhorn, Scotland: Findhorn Press, 2008.

Wright, N.T. http//www.ntwrightpage.com/Wright_Five Gospels.pdf.

Yannaras, C. *The Elements of Faith*. Edinburgh: T & T Clark, 1994.

Yoffe, Emily. December 3, 2008, http://www.slate.com/id/2205150/pagenum/all/#p2.

Young, Janet A. and Michelle D. Pain. The Zone: Evidence of a Universal Phenomenon for Athletes Across Sports. *Athletic Insight: The Online Journal of Sport Psychology*, http://www.athleticinsight.com/Vol1Iss3/Empirical_Zone.htm.

Zahl, Paul F. M. *The First Christians: Universal Truth in the Teachings of Jesus*. Grand Rapids, MI: Eerdmans, 2003.

Zuck, Jon. *The Wild Things of God*, http://frimmin.com/faith/godinall.php/.

Index